Dream It!
Do It!

My Half-Century Creating
Disney's Magic Kingdoms

Dedication

For Dad and Mom
Leon and Lilyn Sklar
and all those they taught ethics and a love of learning

Professor Robert Sklar and Adrienne Harris

Howard Sklar
Katriina Koski Sklar
Gabriel and Hannah Sklar
and
Leslie Sklar
Rachel and Jacob Dahan

For
Helen and Bob Aaron
and *Harry Gerber*

and of course my one and only love
Leah Gerber Sklar
who made my career and life a dream come true

Dream It! Do It!

My Half-Century Creating Disney's Magic Kingdoms

By **Marty Sklar**

Disney Legend and Imagineering Ambassador

Introductions by Ray Bradbury and Richard M. Sherman

EDITIONS

New York • Los Angeles

Pages ix-xi: Excerpt from THE HIPBONE OF ABRAHAM L. by Ray Bradbury is published with the permission of Don Congdon Associates, Inc. as agents for the Ray Bradbury Living Trust ©1988, 1991 by Ray Bradbury.
Pages 59-61, 141, 189: From the book DESIGNING DISNEY by John Hench with Peggy Van Pelt. Copyright © 2004 by Disney Enterprises, Inc. Reprinted by permission of Disney Editions. All rights reserved.
Pages 79-80, 82-86, 236-337: From the book IN SERVICE TO THE MOUSE by Jack Lindquist. Copyright © 2010 Neverland Media. Reprinted by permission. All rights reserved.
Pages 126-127: From The Miami Herald, May 27, 1965 © 1965 McClatchy. All rights reserved. Used by permission and protected by the Copyright Laws of the United States. The printing, copying, redistribution, or retransmission of this Content without express written permission is prohibited.
Pages 142-143: From The New York Times, October 22, 1972 © 1972 The New York Times. All rights reserved. Used by permission and protected by the Copyright Laws of the United States. The printing, copying, redistribution, or retransmission of this Content without express written permission is prohibited.
Pages 171-173: From the book WORK IN PROGRESS by Michael Eisner. Copyright © 1998, 1999 by The Eisner Foundation, Inc. Reprinted by permission of Hyperion. All rights reserved.
Pages 240-241: From EVERYTHING BY DESIGN © 2007 by Alan Lapidus. Reprinted by permission of St. Martin's Press. All rights reserved.
Pages 186-188: From BUILDING TALL: MY LIFE AND THE INVENTION OF CONSTRUCTION MANAGEMENT by John L. Tishman and Tom Shachtman Copyright © 2011 John L. Tishman. Reprinted by permission of The University of Michigan Press. All rights reserved.
Pages 241-243: From the book WORKING TOGETHER by Michael Eisner. Copyright © 2010 by The Eisner Foundation, Inc. Reprinted by permission of HarperBusiness. All rights reserved.

For information address Disney Editions, 1101 Flower Street; Glendale, California 91201

Library of Congress Cataloging-in-Publication Data
Sklar, Marty.
Dream it! do it! : my half-century creating Disney's magic kingdoms ; the people, the places, the projects / by Marty Sklar, Disney Legend and Imagineering Ambassador ; introductions by Ray Bradbury and Richard M. Sherman.
p. cm.
Includes bibliographical references and index.
ISBN 978-1-4231-7406-6 (alk. paper)
1. Disneyland (Calif.)—History. 2. Walt Disney World (Fla.)—History. I. Title.
GV1853.3.C22D5782 2013
791.06'8794--dc23

ISBN 978-1-4231-7406-6
G475-5664-5-13186
Printed in the United States
First Edition
10 9 8 7 6 5 4 3 2 1

Acknowledgements

When I retired from The Walt Disney Company on July 17, 2009, I announced that a primary goal would be writing this book. In the four years since, hardly a day has gone by when someone—Imagineering colleague, Disney fan, theme park industry associate—has not asked me: "How's the book coming?" "When will your book be available?" I thank all of you who made it clear that what I have to say is something you wanted to read. And I thank some extraordinary people who helped make this book possible.

For their introductions to this book, I am greatly indebted to two world-renowned talents who became friends through our Disney relationship. The stories and prose of the late, inimitable Ray Bradbury inspired me long before we met, and continue to, to this day. With brother Robert, Richard Sherman's storytelling through songs and music brought new magic to Disney films and television, and to our Disney park attractions.

Richard Curtis, president of Richard Curtis Associates, my literary agent, gave me early lessons In Publishing 101. I appreciated his honesty. This is good, Richard said, as a Disney park history, *and* as a business book. And then he dropped the other shoe: "But it still needs a good editor, and lots of work." He was correct.

When we contracted with Disney Editions, a key reason was the promise that Wendy Lefkon, editorial director at the Disney Global Book Group, would be my editor. Wendy and I had worked together on many successful books about the Disney parks—I often wrote introductions, setting the tone or the historical context—including two wonderful hardcover books about Walt Disney Imagineering, *Walt Disney Imagineering: A Behind the Dreams Look at Making the Magic Real*; and a reprise of the same title, adding *Making*

MORE Magic Real. Together, they have sold over 150,000 copies.

As I anticipated, Wendy was the editor I needed: honest and direct, smart and clear, knowledgeable and supportive. Her structural flow, title, and content ideas were always reasoned, and usually reasonable. If you enjoy this manuscript, don't forget to thank Wendy, too!

My daughter, Leslie Ann Sklar, and my wife, Leah Regina Sklar, were big supporters—and very active critics. (Nothing new there!) Leslie took my handwritten copy—I wrote the whole manuscript longhand—and did lots of editing and suggesting as she computerized the manuscript. Leah, Leslie, and my son, Howard, have been "cleaning up my act" for many years (Leah and I were married in 1957); in this context, "my act" was my writing. I never wanted for input from "the two Ls"—always direct, considerate, and fun to argue with. (Yes, we differed on a number of issues; they even won a few!) Howard, an excellent wordsmith, lives with his family and teaches in Helsinki, Finland, and was not available to defend me—or join the critique.

Finally, I owe a great big debt to so many mentors, teachers, and colleagues who helped shape my fifty-four-year Disney career. You will meet them throughout this book. Walt's best writers and songwriters could never have scripted the scenario of talented associates Disney wrote for my career. As I have written, "they were my mentors, my friends, and in their golden years, my staff," as I grew up from staff writer to vice chairman and principal creative executive (my favorite title) at Imagineering.

I owe them all a great debt. I only hope that I passed on their amazing standards to a new generation, and left the Imagineers at least as respected and admired as the organization they helped Walt Disney create. Walt created Imagineering, but the Imagineers made it sing and dance.

Marty Sklar

TABLE OF CONTENTS

INTRODUCTION
BY RAY BRADBURY

Disney Imagineering artists thrive and pomegranate-seed explode inside a nondescript Glendale, California, building that looks as if it might house a thousand endless noon board meetings. There is no sign out front to indicate that at Christmas and Easter, here hides a madhouse of costumes and ambulatory self-wrapped gifts.

No hint that, at Halloween, Imagineering becomes a ghost manufactory, a giant Ouija board that summons up ghouls, skeletons, a mirror with a grotesque mask frozen in it that runs about telling folks they "are not the fairest of them all," while Maleficent the Dragon inflates herself to tower above the outside parking lot.

Who are the maniacs in charge of this madhouse? John Hench, sent by Disney to study at the Sorbonne in 1939, and the nearest thing to Walt himself. Beyond eighty, John, as he chats with the inhabitants of this millrace, scribble-sketches blueprints and critters with a fine-artist's hand.

Marty Sklar, the quietest of maniacs, keeps Imagineering off the rails but on the tracks. Hired at age twenty-one, while editor of the UCLA *Daily Bruin*, Marty remembers that Disney gave him—a raw, untrained reporter—a chance to edit a Disneyland newspaper the month before Disneyland opened, thirty-six years ago. On Walt's behalf, he gives other young people a chance to jump off cliffs and build their wings on the way down, at Imagineering.

Between these two, Disney Imagineering has hired some fairly improbable, as I mentioned before, gentlemen golfers, to tee off mind-grenades instead of golf balls.

> **Item:** Tony Baxter, whose career was popping popcorn at Disneyland in his spare time, built a working model of a gravity-fall train. This 3-D calling card gained him the Imagineering job of creating the Big Thunder Mountain Railroad that roars down mountain tracks at Disney theme parks. Its twin will soon be built at Euro Disney, and the chief designer for this new Magic Kingdom will be . . . Tony Baxter.

> **Item:** Harper Goff, lover and collector of miniature model railroads. Walt Disney and Goff met in a London railroad-model toy store and saw the glazed stare of an amateur locomotive fiend in each other's faces. Goff wound up helping art sketch-design the Adventureland Jungle Cruise and making sure Disneyland's locomotives ran on time.

> **Future item:** Tom Scherman. The young man was so enamored of Jules Verne that he secretly converted his

Hollywood apartment into a clone of Captain Nemo's *20,000 Leagues Under the Sea* submarine with portholes, periscope, and seashell telephones. His landlady, unaware of the transformation, blundered into the apartment one day and, stunned, threw Scherman out and dismantled the submarine. Scherman wound up with Disney Imagineering, building *Nautilus* submersibles and dreaming up the Jules Verne Discover World.

And so it went and so it goes.

Sklar and Hench, then, are curators of a vast and vital storage hall of history, a living museum, a World's Fair unto itself.

In sum, the Renaissance did not die, it just hid out at Imagineering Inc. You need but ask for Sleeping Beauty's castle, the turrets of Pierrefonds, Mad Ludwig's towers, or touches of Vaux le Vicomte. So summoned, they will sprout in a Glendale back lot to be truck-transited down freeways to Anaheim, Orlando, or across the ocean airs to Japan.

Ray Bradbury
Glendale, California
1991

INTRODUCTION
BY RICHARD M. SHERMAN

It's hard to believe, but half a century has passed since my late brother, Bob, and I first met and worked with a warm, affable, and brilliant young man named Marty Sklar. At that time, Marty was the literary right-hand man of our mutual boss, Walt Disney. As Walt's staff songwriters, Bob and I had just finished a song for the Carousel of Progress Pavilion at the 1964–65 World's Fair. Our song, "There's a Great Big Beautiful Tomorrow," was the musical connecting link in this groundbreaking attraction. Marty, who was cocreator of the project, had written a script for General Electric (the corporate sponsor) in which Walt would present our song and then display how the pavilion worked. Marty provided one of the greatest thrills of our career, as we got to perform and sing on camera with Walt himself.

Over the years, Marty continued to inspire all those

around him, lending his taste and talent to countless Imagineering projects. Bob and I had the privilege of writing songs for many of these, including: "it's a small world," "The Enchanted Tiki Room," and for the Imagination pavilion at Epcot, "One Little Spark" and "Magic Journeys."

As you will learn in this beautifully written and enlightening book, Marty Sklar, the man who rose to become vice chairman and principal creative executive of Walt Disney Imagineering, devoted his entire career to creating, enhancing, and expanding Walt's magical empire. Upon his retirement in 2009, I had the pleasure of singing a special lyric I had written for an unforgettable party thrown by Disney Imagineers, honoring Marty's half century of imagination and inspiration. I'd like to share it with you:

(To the tune of "Supercalifragilisticexpialidocious")

TRIBUTE TO MARTY

Verse I
Before the doors of Disneyland
Were opened to the world
Young Marty Sklar was asked
To have his writing skills unfurled
The Disneyland newspaper
Was first product of his skill
Then PR and Publicity
Young Marty filled the bill . . . He's

Chorus
Never fearing, Imagineering

Mar-ty-sklar-e-docious
For years he's led Imagineers
With passion so ferocious
Through stress and strains
He's held the reins
With leadership precocious
Never fearing Imagineering
Mar-ty-sklar-e-docious. . . .

Verse II
For Walt he wrote his speeches
And his annual reports
Then moved to WED to help create
Attractions and resorts
From Small World to Space Mountain
To eleven Disney parks
Our Marty steered Imagineers
With their creative sparks . . . (and his)

Repeat chorus

Verse III
He's first to give out credit
To the great creative teams
His one persisting goal
Was to perpetuate Walt's dreams
Succeed he did, and so we stand
As one to give three cheers
To Marty Sklar, the champion
Of all Imagineers. . . . He's . . .

Last Chorus

Never fearing, Imagineering
Mar-ty-sklar-e-docious
For years he's led Imagineers
With passion so ferocious
Through stress and strains
He's held the reins
With leadership precocious
Never fearing Imagineering
Mar-ty-sklar-e-docious. . . .

Richard M. Sherman
songwriter
October 2011

THE BLANK SHEET
OF PAPER

It may seem strange to begin a story about my Disney career with a flashback to 1974, but let me explain. That year was a scary year for the theme park and resort business. The worldwide energy crisis drove major gasoline price increases—regular gasoline skyrocketed from 38 cents per gallon to 54 cents—causing the enactment of extreme measures across the country. The national speed limit was lowered to fifty-five miles per hour, and daylight savings time began four months early. *Newsweek* magazine reported, "The one bad spot is Florida, where long lines—especially near the tourist centers of Disney World and Miami—have caused some counties to adopt odd-even programs" (dates for purchasing gas).

Walt Disney World, in its third year and well on its way to being the country's favorite family vacation destination, was strongly affected; attendance dropped by almost eight hundred thousand. So it was a surprise to me to receive a call from Disney CEO E. Cardon Walker about a signature project that had remained dormant since it was first unveiled a few months after Walt Disney's death in December 1966. Walt had been planning the creation of what he called EPCOT— an Experimental Prototype Community of Tomorrow. "What," Card Walker now asked, "are we going to do about EPCOT?"

I had just been promoted to creative leader of Walt Disney Imagineering—the beginning of thirty years in that role for me. From day one, the challenge of that responsibility for what would become eleven Disney parks on three continents was daunting, even as I reminded the Imagineers of our role.

"There are two ways to look at a blank sheet of paper," I told the creative team. "It can be the most frightening thing in the world, because you have to make the first mark on it. Or it can be *the greatest opportunity in the world, because you get to make the first mark*—you can let your imagination fly in any direction, and *create whole new worlds!*"

For the next eight years, the Imagineers, in partnership with the Operations staff at Walt Disney World, would test that axiom. As Epcot prepared to welcome its thirtieth anniversary on October 1, 2012, it celebrated being the sixth most-visited park in the world, trailing only Magic Kingdom Park, Disneyland Park, Tokyo Disneyland Park, Tokyo DisneySea Park, and Disneyland Paris in attendance.

It took a healthy belief in the future of Disney Parks and

Resorts for Card Walker and the Disney board of directors to make that call in the face of all the negatives we faced as a country and as a company in 1974. But we began.

Walt Disney's concept for an Epcot community was a grand vision that drove the planning for all of Walt Disney World from the beginning. Transportation and energy systems; experiments in construction methods, such as the off-site building of completely furnished hotel rooms for Disney's Contemporary Resort and Disney's Polynesian Resort; the care and responsibility for maintaining the Florida environment and ecosystems—all had been thought through following Walt's often stated desire: to "meet the needs of people" and set an example for planning and building for others to learn from and emulate.

Walt Disney did not go to Florida just to build another "theme park" or even a destination resort; he had something far more important in mind. This is what he said about EPCOT in 1966:

> I don't believe there's a challenge anywhere in the world that's more important to people everywhere than finding solutions to the problems of our cities. But where do we begin . . . how do we start answering this great challenge?
>
> Well, we're convinced we must start with the public need. And the need is not just for curing the old ills of old cities. We think the need is for starting from scratch on virgin land, and building a special kind of new community.

Today I believe that the creative insight that led Walt Disney to propose EPCOT is as valid as it ever was, and is needed even more than ever before.

What's missing is the Walt Disney for our times and our

challenges—the risk taker who loved to begin again and again with a new blank sheet of paper. Perhaps he was reaching for a "Waltopia"—a utopian world of Walt's own creation. But in the words I wrote for Walt in the company's 1966 Annual Report to shareholders and employees, he expressed his creative philosophy: "I have to move on to new things—there are many new worlds to conquer."

I was so fortunate to board that speeding train at its first stop, in Anaheim, California, in 1955, and to retire fifty-four years later as the only Disney employee to participate in the opening of all eleven Disney parks around the world. This is my story of those parks as I lived their birth and growth, and helped shape them—the projects, the places, and especially the people who made it happen.

Welcome aboard!

1

"WALT'S DEAD.
WRITE SOMETHING."

The paging system at WED was screaming my name. I picked up the nearest telephone. "Call Card Walker immediately," my secretary said. I did and thirty seconds later, I was on my way to Card's office at the Studio. The three-mile drive seemed to take forever.

It was a few minutes after 9:00 A.M. on Thursday, December 15, 1966, and E. Cardon Walker (who would become the chief executive of Walt Disney Productions, and was then head of marketing and publicity) needed to see me immediately. We had a close relationship: Card had hired me part time after my junior year at UCLA, just as I was about to become editor of *The Daily Bruin*, the UCLA student newspaper. I did finish my senior year and graduate from UCLA in 1956, but starting my Disney career at Disneyland the month before the park opened in July 1955 would shape my entire professional life.

"Walt's dead," Card said the moment I entered his office. "Write the statement Roy will sign and we'll distribute it to the press and our employees."

I admit I was rather shocked. It seemed implausible that Roy O. Disney, Card, and Donn Tatum (board of directors member at the time, and later chief executive officer and chairman of the board) were telling me that no one had prepared an official statement about Walt's death. It was no secret Walt was dying.

Card said, "You've got an hour."

And so I wrote:

> The death of Walt Disney is a loss to all the people of the world. In everything he did, Walt had an intuitive way of reaching out and touching the hearts and minds of young and old alike. His entertainment was an international language. For more than forty years people have looked to Walt Disney for the finest quality in family entertainment.
>
> There is no way to replace Walt Disney. He was an extraordinary man. Perhaps there will never be another like him. I know that we who worked at his side for all these years will always cherish the years and the minutes we spent in helping Walt Disney entertain the people of the world. The world will always be a better place because Walt Disney was its master showman.
>
> As President and Chairman of the Board of Walt Disney Productions, I want to assure the public, our stockholders, and each of our more than four thousand employees that we will continue to operate Walt Disney's company in the way that he has established and guided it. Walt Disney spent his entire life and almost every waking hour in the creative planning of motion pictures, Disneyland, television

shows, and all the other diversified activities that have carried his name through the years. Around him Walt Disney gathered the kind of creative people who understood his way of communicating with the public through entertainment. Walt's ways were always unique and he built a unique organization. A team of creative people that he was justifiably proud of.

I think Walt would have wanted me to repeat his words to describe the organization he built over the years. Last October, when he accepted the "Showman of the World" award in New York, Walt said, "The Disney organization now has more than four thousand employees. Many have been with us for over thirty years. They take great pride in the organization, which they helped to build. Only through the talent, labor, and dedication of this staff could any Disney project get off the ground. We all think alike in the ultimate pattern."

Much of Walt Disney's energies had been directed to preparing for this day. It was Walt's wish that when the time came he would have built an organization with the creative talents to carry on as he had established and directed it through the years. Today this organization has been built and we will carry out this wish.

Walt Disney's preparation for the future has a solid, creative foundation. All of the plans for the future that Walt had begun—new motion pictures, the expansion of Disneyland, television production, and our Florida and Mineral King projects—will continue to move ahead. That is the way Walt wanted it to be.

It was signed, of course, by Roy O. Disney, president and chairman of the board of Walt Disney Productions, and distributed to the media and all Disney employees.

As CBS newsman Eric Sevareid would note a day later:

> *He probably did more to heal or at least to soothe troubled human spirits than all the psychiatrists in the world. There can't be many adults in the allegedly civilized parts of the globe who did not inhabit Disney's mind and imagination at least for a few hours and feel better for the visitation.*

It's been nearly fifty years since that day in Card Walker's office, but I can honestly say that I still resent being put in that position. The truth is they were all scared as hell. Disney without Walt Disney, its founder, leader, creative genius, and sole decision maker in the story, design, and invention business. Disney without "Uncle Walt" coming into your home on television every Sunday night to tell you what he was going to show your family that night, or open in a few months in movie theaters or Disneyland. Disney without the man with those thirty-two Academy Awards and more honors around the world than almost anyone.

In spite of my resentment, I know how I got there, and why it was me they called.

I had become the chief ghostwriter at Disney. It was pretty heady stuff for someone just closing in on his thirtieth birthday, and only six or seven years out of college, to be writing Walt's and Roy's messages in the company's annual report; most of the publicity and marketing materials for Disneyland; presentations to the U.S. government (the Mineral King solicitation for a year-round resort in Central California); initiatives to obtain sponsors for new Disneyland developments; and, finally, the twenty-four-minute film I penned expressing Walt's philosophy for the Walt Disney World project and Epcot.

The seven pages of notes I took at my meetings with Walt about Epcot are still among my treasures. When I re-read them occasionally, I realize how easy Walt made it for me to write the script for the film. This was Walt's favorite method of communication with his mid-1960s audience: film not only allowed him to introduce his concepts and plans, but also gave him the last word. He asked me to write two endings. One was aimed directly at audiences in the state of Florida, because the state's legislature was then debating passage of a law that would establish the Reedy Creek Improvement District (RCID)—a key to Walt's plans for Epcot as an experimental community. The law would give the RCID the power to establish building codes and zoning regulations—and Disney would be controlling the RCID. The second ending for the film was aimed at potential corporate sponsors. Having just completed the presentation of four major attractions at the 1964–65 New York World's Fair, Walt was keenly aware that his ability to communicate with family audiences was highly desirable. As Walt said in his ending for the film: "No one company can do this project [Epcot] alone."

Walt's segments were shot on a stage at the Disney Studios on October 27, 1966. It was the very last day he appeared on camera, just a few days before he entered St. Joseph Hospital directly across the street from his studio lot. To look at that film today is to wonder how that man we see selling his ideas could be so ill. Yet seven weeks later, lung cancer claimed the life of this heavy smoker, and I was in Card Walker's office typing that statement.

And then the Disney world we knew imploded.

2

FORGOTTEN BUT NOT GONE.

A few weeks after Walt's death, I inquired about a writer at the Walt Disney Studio; I had not seen or heard of him since that fateful day. "Oh, he's still there," I was told. "He's forgotten—but not gone!"

In the days "after Walt," it was not unusual to lose touch with and sight of Disney Studio personnel. Many of them got their assignments directly from Walt himself, thus leaving a huge void in key staffing assignments . . . and a "Who's in charge?" question in the production of movies, television shows, and animation. Resolution was slow to come, and the decline in Disney films and television through the 1970s and early 1980s could be traced back to that period of indecision. Ultimately, it led to the conflict between the Walt Disney and Roy O. Disney sides of the Disney family, the ousting of Walt's son-in-law Ron Miller as president of the company, and the Roy E. Disney-led charge that saw the installation of Michael Eisner as chairman and chief executive officer and Frank Wells as president.

At the time of Walt's death, the theme park business accounted for 35.58 percent of the company's bottom line. There were huge decisions to be made, but a path was in place. Pirates of the Caribbean was only months from opening at Disneyland and would achieve a new standard in the amusement industry. Ultimately, it would become the most valuable single property ever created in the theme park business. And right behind Pirates in development was The Haunted Mansion, soon to become the signature ghostly property in real estate history: it helped launch the Halloween celebration phenomenon that has challenged the Christmas season as a theme park attendance driver around the world. (There are now four Haunted Mansions in Disney parks, from California to Florida, and Tokyo to Paris.)

The future growth of the Disney theme park business hung on key questions answered by Roy O. Disney as chairman and CEO: would the company develop the 27,400 acres—twice the size of Manhattan Island—it had acquired in Central Florida for approximately $5 million? And what would become of Walt Disney's concept for the Experimental Prototype Community of Tomorrow?

Disney had acquired the Florida property through seven dummy corporations with business addresses in Kansas and Delaware. Disney attorney Robert Foster worked with two major Florida real estate organizations to purchase the land. The key was to keep hidden that Disney was buying. Many of the property owners had never even seen their land. They had purchased, sight unseen, ten- and twenty-acre parcels by mail order through promotional offers. Much of the "land" was actually under deep swamp water. But with nearly 28,000 acres, Disney now had "enough land here to hold all the ideas and plans we can possibly imagine," as Walt had said during that last television appearance.

On November 15, 1965, Governor Haydon Burns announced that Disney was coming to Central Florida.

Asked by a reporter at the press conference, "Will you have a model community . . . ?" Walt gave a hint of the direction of his thinking for what would become Walt Disney World.

> We have done a lot of thinking on a model community, and I would like to be a part of building a model community, a city of tomorrow as you might say, because I don't believe in going out to this extreme blue sky stuff that some of the architects do . . . I've had in mind one community called "Yesterday" and another one, "Tomorrow" . . . They [visitors] might come one time and they stay in "Tomorrow," and their friends will say, "But have you stayed in 'Yesterday'?" And they'll have to come back.

I was chosen to create the presentation Walt would give at the November 1965 press conference at which Governor Burns would announce that Disney was coming to Central Florida.

It almost got me fired.

As part of the twenty-minute show, I had written a short script that Walt would record, accompanied by appropriate visuals. The overall concept was to glorify Walt, his brand of entertainment, and his entire career. Usually, he would have approved the whole script first and then looked at the entire presentation with a small group. For some reason, my boss, Card Walker, decided to skip that step; instead, he invited two hundred people to a soundstage for a preview of the Florida announcement.

WALT—WITH MICKEY AND THE FIRST OSCAR

> WALT: *That first Oscar was a special award for the creation of Mickey Mouse. The other Academy Awards belong to our group, a tribute to our combined effort.*

BEHIND THE SCENES COVERAGE OF THE DISNEY TEAM

Various shots to show actors, writers, musicians, art directors, Imagineers, etc. *at work* on projects at the Studio, at WED, and at Disneyland.

ACTORS—WORKING ON SET WITH DIRECTOR

> WALT: *You know, people are always analyzing our approach to entertainment. Some reporters have called it the "special secret" of Disney entertainment.*

BEHIND THE SCENES—BUILDING OF SPECIAL EFFECTS (such as Giant Squid, or Flying Model T)

> WALT: *Well, we like a little mystery in our films—but there's really no secret about our approach. We keep moving forward—opening up new doors and doing now things—because we're curious . . .*

SCIENTIFIC-TYPE SHOT—RESEARCH

> WALT: *. . . and curiosity keeps leading us down new paths. We're always exploring and experimenting. At WED, we call it "imagineering"—the blending of creative imagination with technical know-how.*

**EARLY CONSTRUCTION SHOT AT DISNEYLAND—
WALT ON SITE WITH ART DIRECTORS**

WALT: *When you're curious, you find lots of interesting things to do. And one thing it takes to accomplish something is courage. Take Disneyland for example. Almost everyone warned us that Disneyland would be a Hollywood spectacular—a spectacular failure.*

**WALT AND ART DIRECTORS INSPECTING
DISNEYLAND—TODAY**

WALT: *But they were thinking about an amusement park, and we believed in our idea—a family park where parents and children could have fun—together.*

DICK VAN DYKE—WORKING ON SET

WALT: *We have never lost our faith in family entertainment—stories that make people laugh, stories about warm and human things, stories about historic characters and events, stories about animals.*

LAUGHING SCENE FROM *MARY POPPINS*

WALT: *We're not out to make a fast dollar with gimmicks. We're interested in doing things that are fun—in bringing pleasure and especially laughter to people.*

WALT—LAUGHING WITH A GROUP OF ACTORS

WALT: *And probably most important of all, when we consider a new project we really study it—not just the surface idea but everything about it. And when we go into that new project, we believe in it all the way. We have confidence in our ability to do it right. And we work hard to do the best possible job.*

WALT—WITH ROY AND OTHER MANAGEMENT

WALT: *My role? Well, you know I was stumped one day when a little boy asked, "Do you draw Mickey Mouse?" I had to admit I do not draw anymore. "Then you think up all the jokes and ideas?"*

WALT—WITH SONGWRITERS—AT PIANO

WALT: *"No," I said, "I don't do that." Finally, he looked at me and said, "Mr. Disney, just what do you do?" "Well," I said, "sometimes I think of myself as a little bee."*

WALT—ACTING OUT POINT IN STORYBOARD MEETING

WALT: *"I go from one area of the Studio to another and gather pollen and sort of stimulate everybody."* I guess that's the job I do.

In retrospect, I know I succeeded in our objective to glorify Walt. When it was over, Walt sought me out to give me his review: "I didn't know anyone was writing my obituary!" he said.

As it turned out, the presentation I created helped successfully launch Disney in Florida.

3

VEGAS CALLING— "CARD" IS ON THE PHONE

The telephone message was waiting for me when I returned to the Zeta Beta Tau (ZBT) fraternity house at UCLA, after class in mid-May 1955. At first I thought it was a joke played on me by one of my ZBT fraternity brothers; after all, Lennie Kolod's father was one of the executives at the original Desert Inn in Las Vegas . . . and who would have a name like "Card" except a Las Vegas dealer?

So I did not return "the card dealer's call." But fortunately for me, E. Cardon Walker called again. Card Walker was the head of marketing and publicity for The Walt Disney Company. I had just been elected editor in chief of the UCLA student newspaper, *The Daily Bruin*. Johnny Jackson, the erstwhile executive alumni secretary of the UCLA Alumni Association, who had recently left his UCLA leadership position to join Disney, had recommended me. I had known

Johnny Jackson since 1952, when I received one of the prized UCLA Alumni Scholarships. It covered full tuition—a staggering $100 per year! (By 2011, California resident students were paying more than $14,000!)

At the Walt Disney Studio, I met with Card Walker and Jimmy Johnson. Johnson was soon to become the head of Disneyland Records, which was formed in 1956 to create albums of Disney standards by well-known artists, and to develop new material for popular Mouseketeer Annette Funicello (including songs that first brought Richard M. and Robert B. Sherman to the Disney Studio). The good news for me was that both Card and Jimmy Johnson were Bruins. Card began his forty-five-year Disney career in the mail room in 1938, and retired in 1983 as CEO of the company. When World War II began, he enlisted in the Air Force and served on an aircraft carrier in the Pacific. His experiences when the carrier was attacked by Japanese kamikaze pilots would later color all of Disney's early relationships for Tokyo Disneyland, almost killing the deal that became Disney's first international theme park—an amazing business and cultural success.

My interview in Card Walker's office in the old Publicity Department building at the Disney Studio lasted only twenty minutes or so—an eternity by Card's standards, as I would learn during the next thirty years. When the meeting ended, I had my first real job: editor of the *Disneyland News*, which I would soon name, write, and edit. Then I'd lay out the twenty-eight pages and supervise its printing.

My Disney career, which lasted almost fifty-four years, had begun. A month before Disneyland opened its gates, I had become among the first one hundred "cast members" on the Magic Kingdom's payroll.

* * * * * * * * *

I was twelve years old in June 1946 when my parents moved our family from Highland Park, New Jersey, to Long Beach, California. My father, Leon George Sklar, was a highly respected teacher with fifteen years' experience at New Brunswick High School in New Jersey. It was not easy professionally for my dad to move; California schools gave him teaching credit for only three of those fifteen years. Despite having spent nearly thirty-five years in classroom and administrative positions as teacher, vice principal, and principal in the Los Angeles schools, he retired in 1964 with only twenty-three years of tenure.

My mother, Lilyn Fuchs Sklar, had worked at Johnson & Johnson in New Brunswick until I was born on February 6, 1934. She became a stay-at-home mom thereafter. They welcomed my brother, Bob, on December 3, 1936. (More about Bob later. He became a highly respected teaching historian as professor of Cinema Studies at New York University.) In Long Beach, my parents rented and later purchased one of those little houses "à la Lakewood," built just after the Second World War to attract the hordes of veterans who had passed through the Golden State while in military service. I still remember the sight of the first palms I ever saw, as my aunt and uncle, Frances and Bernie Dolin, drove us along Beverly Boulevard from Union Station to their Hollywood apartment, a block or two from the corner of Beverly and La Brea Avenue. (The Hollywood Freeway, from downtown Los Angeles to Hollywood and the San Fernando Valley, wouldn't be built for another four years.)

My father didn't have a job when we arrived in California. He was soon offered a position in the Long Beach school system, and it nearly dissolved our family. The job was on Catalina Island, and my mother refused to live there. Finally, just before school began in September, the Long Beach schools relented, and my dad began his California education career at Long Beach Jordan High School.

He inherited a pretty wild bunch of students at Jordan High, and by the end of our first year in California, he moved to Phineas Banning High School in Wilmington, an urban sprawl community outside Los Angeles. My father became one of the most respected members of the community, and his career in education flourished, earning him a promotion to principal at the school from which he eventually retired— Madison Junior High in North Hollywood, at the edge of the San Fernando Valley.

Years later, after my dad had passed away from a heart attack soon after retiring, my mom told Bob and me some of the stories about the school environment in the 1940s and 1950s at Banning High and Wilmington Junior High. Reluctantly, Dad would tell Mom about the guns and knives he took away from students, and the clothes—even under-wear—he bought for kids whose parents could not afford them. In fact, my dad was so committed to serving that com-munity of immigrants that he returned to Banning at night to teach English to Hispanics and Asians striving to become American citizens. Although I have little personal memory of this, I'm sure it established the example that informed my own commitment to community service when I became a parent and, among other community positions, was elected president of the school board in Anaheim, president of the

Orange County School Boards Association, and served on Anaheim's parks and recreation and cultural arts commissions. For me, that tradition continues to this very day: my wife, Leah, and I are cofounders of Ryman Arts, a program for talented young high school artists that has served more than four thousand students in Southern California during the twenty-two years since it was created.

One day in the late 1980s, when Disney was negotiating with the city of Long Beach to build a park in the harbor area, I was approached following a meeting by Jim Hankla, then city manager of Long Beach. "The reason I'm here today in this position," Jim said, "is because of Leon Sklar. I was not a good kid at Banning High . . . in with the wrong crowd, not a good student. But somehow I got into your father's speech and debate class, and it changed my life—motivated me to go on to college and do something positive with my life. I'll always thank your father; I wouldn't be here without his encouragement."

My father's high school experience also rubbed off on my brother and me. In the fall of 1951, Dad became advisor to the Banning High student newspaper. At the same time, Bob—a ninth grader—became editor of his junior high newspaper, and I was named editor of the Long Beach Poly *High Life*. It was a portent of things to come; two years after I was elected editor of the UCLA *Daily Bruin*, Bob was chosen chairman of the board of the *Daily Princetonian* at Princeton University.

But it was my mother who really and truly propelled the family's writing careers. In 1946, I had entered a college football pool and somehow picked nine out of ten games correctly. I won a cash prize, which became the Sklar family's first television set. I think my mom decided then and there that if a twelve-year-old could do it, imagine what she and my dad could do in the contest world! In those days, contesting was actually skill-based, versus today's blind drawings. Most contests required you to write twenty-five words or less about something. My mom and dad became so proficient at the contest game that we learned never to be surprised when the U.S. mail delivered another prize. And these were not just trinkets: Mom and Dad won a car, cash, vacation trips, furniture, household appliances, and television sets.

Meanwhile, Bob and I were beginning to build on the foundations in education, values, and ethics our parents had created. I headed off to UCLA on that $100 Alumni Scholarship in 1952. Two years later, my brother received full tuition scholarship offers to Harvard, Yale, and Princeton valued at $1,300 each in 1954. Suffice it to say that on a teacher's salary in 1954, Dad and Mom could only have dreamed of sending Bob to Princeton without that scholarship.

As it was, I had to earn a good part of my UCLA education. The summer after high school graduation, I was fortunate to be hired at Douglas Aircraft in Long Beach, bucking rivets being installed on (and inside) the wings of C-124 military transports. (Riveting was a manual operation in 1952.) Another summer I scooped ice cream at a 19-cent hamburger drive-in; one evening between 5.00 and 7:00 P.M. I made seven hundred malts! During the Christmas season, I caught on as a seasonal temp delivering packages for the U.S. Postal Service, only because Dad let me use the family car (you had to have your own wheels to get the job). And during my last year at UCLA, I worked for a West

Coast version of *Advertising Age*, a successful weekly called *Media Agencies Clients* (MAC Publications) in Los Angeles. I became assistant editor before resigning to rejoin the Disneyland staff in September 1956.

Today scholarships are still based on a variety of elements—academics, extracurricular activities, community service, athletics, need, and a live competition with other nominees. I'm not sure, after observing the UCLA Alumni Scholarship selection process as an Alumni Association board member, how my credentials of 1952 would hold up. Editing the school newspaper and captaining the high school tennis team, as I did, would certainly help. But as a loyal Bruin, when I was asked in May 2010 to speak at the luncheon where the UCLA Alumni Scholarships were announced, I couldn't help but poke fun at our crosstown rivals by reciting the questions "purported to be asked" on the "Application for Admission" to the University of Southern California:

- "Have you read a book this year? If yes, why?"
- "Name five of the United States (for instance, California, New York, Texas, etc.)"
- "Are you a football player? If yes, skip to the last line of this application."

To all my Trojan friends, "Just kidding!" (At least, that's what I told the Bruin Alumni Scholarship recipients.)

4

"FAILURE TO PREPARE IS PREPARING TO FAIL." —COACH JOHN WOODEN

In my first year at UCLA, I joined my Zeta Beta Tau fraternity brothers in a Bruin tradition, the annual Spring Sing competition. We performed pretty well singing George Gershwin's "'S Wonderful," but it was one of Tom Lehrer's unmistakable songs that brought out the best in our male chorus. The Harvard math professor turned lyricist and nightclub performer created such satirical tunes as "The Old Dope Peddler," "I Wanna Go Back to Dixie," and "The Wiener Schnitzel Waltz." In the Spring Sing we performed "Be Prepared," the Boy Scouts marching song.

We didn't win any prizes at that Spring Sing, but it was part of my introduction to university life. At UCLA, we freshman were often in classes with veterans who had just returned from the Korean War. And graduate schools, like the UCLA Law School, were often populated by those who had fought in World War II; their undergraduate years, aided by the GI Bill, began in 1946 or 1947.

For me, a key reason to join a fraternity in 1952 was to have a place to live within walking distance of the campus. There were no, zero, men's dormitories at UCLA at the time (the first was opened in 1959), and only one women's dorm, Mira Hershey Hall. UCLA in the 1950s was definitely a commuter campus.

I wanted to be a sportswriter. When I entered Kerckhoff Hall in hopes of becoming a staffer at *The Daily Bruin*, I brought with me some high school newspaper credentials. I was editor of the paper at Long Beach Poly High School and also wrote a sports column called "Sklargazing."

You have to pay your dues as the kid reporter; my first assignments were covering swimming and water polo. But I soon graduated to track and field, and, in 1954, to football in the fall, followed by basketball for the 1954–55 season. What an amazing opportunity.

The 1954 UCLA football team, coached by Henry "Red" Sanders, was conational champion with a 9–0 record. They were "co" because sportswriters for the Associated Press and United Press International split the vote between Ohio State and UCLA. I traveled with the team to Lawrence, Kansas; Corvallis, Oregon; Seattle, Washington; and Berkeley, California, to report on Bruin victories that season by scores of 61–0, 67–0, and 72–0. And 34–0 over our crosstown rival, the Trojans of USC at the Los Angeles Memorial Coliseum.

But it was the opportunity to cover basketball and get to know Coach John Wooden that became the touchstone of my UCLA years. I learned about being a leader from the very best. Yes, the Bruin hoopsters were good; in the 1954–55 season, Coach Wooden's team had a 21–5 record, 11–1 in the Pacific Coast Conference—and split two games with the eventual NCAA champion, the University of San Francisco, with their two dominating stars, Bill Russell and K. C. Jones.

Coach Wooden's remarkable record of ten national championships in twelve years would not begin until ten years later, in 1964, but what I learned by observing Coach as a *teacher* (his preferred term) has lasted a lifetime. At practice, the organization was obvious; Coach Wooden planned out every minute each day, and after each drill—no matter how long or short—an assistant blew a whistle and the team moved on to the next planned teachable moment. *Failure to prepare is preparing to fail* is one of Coach Wooden's best-known lessons, but there were so many more contained in the myriad of popular books Coach wrote before he passed away in 2010 at age ninety-nine. Many of these gems were contained in *The Wisdom of Wooden*, written with Steve Jamison and published by McGraw-Hill after Wooden's passing: *Be quick, but don't hurry . . . Don't let making a living prevent you from making a life . . . Be true to yourself . . . and, of course, Make each day your masterpiece.*

I had two favorite experiences with Coach Wooden—neither of which were on the basketball court. The first occurred in 1954, when a quirk in the NCAA rules allowed an incoming student from San Pedro, California, eligibility to play either varsity or freshman ball, frosh teams were the first step in an athlete's college career at that time. This student was no ordinary athlete; he was the player of the year in the Los Angeles high schools. One day I received a call at *The Daily Bruin* from Coach Wooden, asking me to come to his office. His message was clear; he had decided that Willie Naulls, the player in question, would play immediately for the varsity. To paraphrase Coach's message: *Marty, I would never tell you how to write your story for the student newspaper. But please remember there are four newspapers in Los Angeles and all the sportswriters will write about what an impact Willie will have on our team. He's going to have tremendous pressure from every one of those newspaper reporters.* (In 1954, Los Angeles sports coverage appeared in the *Times*, *Mirror News*, *Examiner*, and *Herald-Express*. Today, only the *Times* survives.)

Coach didn't have to tell me how he was hoping I would handle *The Daily Bruin* story. It was emblematic of how his first concern was always for his players.

Small wonder that all those All-Americans and pro all-stars who came along later—Kareem Abdul-Jabbar, Bill Walton, et al—continued to come to him for advice even thirty and forty years after their playing days ended. (And Willie Naulls did become a star: all-American, first-round NBA draft choice, three-time pro all-star, three-time NBA champion with the Boston Celtics.)

The second event was a talk Coach Wooden gave as part of a wonderful series called "My Last Lecture" at the University Religious Conference in October 1955. By then, I was editor in chief of *The Daily Bruin*, and wrote this editorial urging my classmates to attend his lecture:

All articles appearing on this page are the opinion of the writer and do not represent the opinion of the UCLA Daily Bruin, the Associated Students or the University Administration.

EDITORIALS

Wooden's 'Last Lecture'

There are many facets of university life, both in and out of class room activities. They need not be expounded here. But among the most interesting to this writer is hearing a good talk by a man who really knows his stuff.

It was my contention in an editorial earlier this semester that student government, or any group on campus, should stimulate and sponsor interesting discussions and lectures at UCLA. But right under our collective noses, a program of this sort is already underway. (However, the existence of this program is no reason why other types of lecture-discussions should not become part of the UCLA educational picture.)

Tomorrow at 3:15 p.m. at 900 Hilgard Ave., the Conference Associates of the University Religious Conference will present the second of six lectures given by various members of the faculty.

Entitled "My Last Lecture," the series began last week with a talk by Joseph Spencer of the geography dept. It will continue tomorrow and on forthcoming Thursdays with talks by Basketball Coach John Wooden, James Coleman of the political science dept., Miss Mary Holmes of the art dept., Kenneth Trueblood of the Chemistry dept. and Abraham Kaplan of the philosophy dept.

The question posed to these people is: "What would you tell your audience if you had but one lecture to give? Your last lecture on this earth?"

The latitude of the answers is great; the comments should be most interesting.

Tomorrow, one of my favorite "professors" will be featured. He is a man who, along with Football Coach Red Sanders, has been most responsible for putting UCLA on the athletic map across the nation. His notions and representatives, the team he coaches, have won friends for UCLA wherever he has gone. It would indeed be a formidable blow to UCLA if tomorrow's lecture were to be John Wooden's last at UCLA, but fortunately, it is with all sincerity that I say I hope it will be but one of many, many more in numerous years to come.

Admittedly, I am quite prejudiced when it comes to talking about Coach Wooden. I simply feel he is at the top among gentlemen, friends and coaches.

I wouldn't miss his talk for anything.

You'll enjoy it, too, and the remainder of the series as well.

                                                      Marty Sklar
                                                      Editor

Fifty-five years later, I was a member of the board of directors of the UCLA Alumni Association. Ravi Doshi, the president of the Alumni Scholars Club, approached me with some questions about the "My Last Lecture" series. He had seen my 1955 editorial, and was intrigued by the following idea: "What would the great teachers at UCLA in 2010 tell their students if they had but one lecture to give—their final lecture on this earth?" he asked me. A fellow Alumni Scholar, Max Belasco, had heard online a speech by that title delivered by a professor at Carnegie Mellon University who was dying of pancreatic cancer. I had yet another connection: that professor, Randy Pausch, had worked as a consultant at Walt Disney Imagineering.

Ravi and the Alumni Scholars put their own twist on the idea: they conducted a popular vote in which two thousand students selected the professor they most wanted to hear deliver a "last lecture." In April 2010, Dr. Asim Dasgusta, professor and vice chairman of the Department of Microbiology, Immunology, and Molecular Genetics, launched a new Bruin tradition based on a fifty-year-old idea, when a sold-out lecture hall of students heard him talk. "I just wanted to tell students what I've learned through the years of my life as a scientist for thirty years," Dr. Dasgusta said.

* * * * * * * * * *

UCLA in the early 1950s was sometimes referred to as "the little red schoolhouse." It was the time of McCarthyism, and the UCLA administration shared many of the senator's views. One day Dean Milton Hahn called me to his office. He was standing at the window when I arrived, and his first words amazed me: "Anytime you look over campus," he said, "there are five hundred homosexuals wandering around." Some things you just don't forget. The administrator was paranoid about active political protests.

What worried the administrators was the fear that the student newspaper might be taken over by left-leaning campus reporters and editors. Freedom of the press was not in their vocabulary when they made sure my friend and fellow *Daily Bruin* associate Irv Drasnin became editor in chief in the spring of 1955. When student elections took place before the school term ended, Irv was elected student body president—and I was "elected" editor of *The Daily Bruin*. An election by the student body may have seemed like freedom of choice. I had served my apprenticeship—two terms as sports editor and one as city editor—so I had all the requisite credentials for the top job at *The Daily Bruin*. But it should never have been a popularity contest for a position that the student body at large was truly not knowledgeable enough to fill.

My education at UCLA, by the way, also happened in classrooms and lecture halls. I remember well professors like George Mowry in history and Currin Shields in political science. And I will never forget the opportunity to know the brilliant philosophy teacher Abraham Kaplan, or listen in on a lecture by the demonstrative education professor Frederick Woellner. ("Text," he almost shouted, "from context is *pretext!*")

And beyond all else, I met my wife to be, Leah Gerber, at UCLA. We were married May 12, 1957.

* * * * * * * * * *

My biggest disappointment at UCLA was trying out for, and becoming the last candidate eliminated from more than one hundred competitors, for a special project run jointly by the University Religious Conference and the Ford Foundation to combat the negative image of America in India. It was called, simply, "Project India." Beginning in 1952, Project India sent twelve students of diverse ethnic, cultural, and religious backgrounds for nine summer weeks to India, meeting college students, living with their hosts in villages and cities, and hopefully making friends for America. It was a kind of precursor to the Peace Corps, which began in the early 1960s.

In 1955 I truly felt that I had earned the right to be the second Jewish student selected—to join my friend Sandy Ragins, who later became a rabbi. But I was not chosen, and I wished the ambassadors well as they prepared to depart for India.

Less than a week later, I received a call at the ZBT fraternity house. It was that "Las Vegas dealer," Card Walker, asking if I could come to the Walt Disney Studio for the interview that would change my life. Surely that trip to India would never have had such a lifelong effect.

5

"I'M NOT WALT DISNEY ANYMORE!"

At the end of 1965, Walt celebrated his sixty-fourth birthday, and Roy O. Disney, age seventy-two, began to plan for his own retirement. The presumptive future CEO, Card Walker, called me and the Studio's graphics leader, Bob Moore, to his office. "We have to let the media, our fans, and the entertainment industry know that as great a talent as Walt is, he's not the *only* creative person at Disney," Card told us. "Let's use the annual report to start the dialogue."

Bob Moore and I were good soldiers. With Card's direction, we identified the company's top creative talent, and developed a plan to photograph them at work on their current projects. Some of the pictures would be with Walt, some without. There was Bill Walsh, Don DaGradi, and Bob Stevenson—the *Mary Poppins* team—in live-action films; Dick and Bob Sherman, the Academy Award–winning songwriters; the "Nine Old Men" in Disney animation—all were still working, although Marc Davis had moved to Imagineering; and John Hench, Claude Coats, and Davis at Imagineering. The photographs told the story, and soon, with Bob Moore's page layouts and my captions identifying the talent, we accompanied Card to review the concept with Walt. He listened patiently—and said, "No."

"Look," Walt told us, "I don't want people to say 'that's a Bill Walsh production for Disney,' or 'that's a John Hench design for Disneyland.' I've spent my whole life building the image of entertainment and product by Walt Disney. Now Walt Disney is a thing, an image, an expectation by our fans. It's *all* Walt Disney—we all think alike in the ultimate pattern. *I'm not Walt Disney anymore.*"

In the end, the pictures still told the story in the annual report. Walt okayed the images and caption copy identifying the Disney project only. No names were used; no individuals were identified or credited in the photos. We all got the message.

In thinking about this portion of the book, I realized that few people in the entertainment world have been written about as frequently as Walt Disney. I asked Richard Benefield, then executive director of the extraordinary Walt Disney Family Museum in San Francisco, and Becky Cline, director of the Walt Disney Archives at The Walt Disney Company, to provide the number of biographies they believe have been written about Walt. Despite his death more than forty years ago, the number seemingly expands like the Flubber in his 1961 film *The Absent-Minded Professor*; they estimate the biographies at fifty-two, ranging from the 1950s, 1960s, and 1970s (Diane Disney Miller's *The Story of Walt Disney* and

Bob Thomas's *Walt Disney: An American Original*) to the twenty-first century (Harrison Price's 2003 *Walt's Revolution! By the Numbers* and Neal Gabler's 2006 *Walt Disney—the Triumph of the American Imagination*, the latter a "triumph" in 851 pages that was *not* well received by the Walt Disney family).

While everything worth knowing about Walt Disney hasn't been written, I'm going to tell only personal stories—that is, those experienced directly by me or my peers. Most of these stories have never appeared in print. But I can't help starting with several of my favorite Walt stories told to me by those who were there, illustrating his multidimensional character:

- One of the first Disney traveling art exhibits, "The Art of Animation," was about to open in Denver, Colorado. Walt attended the opening, but arrived in Denver the night before for a final check of the exhibit. At breakfast the next morning, he joined the installation team, which had already ordered their food. Walt made his choice; before the waitress could leave the table, all four of the installation team, one by one, changed his order with a "that sounds good, I'll have that too!" comment. Now there were five identical breakfast orders. "So," Walt said, "it's going to be *one of those days*!" And he was gone.
- A Disney Studio television producer was unhappy because Walt did not consider him to be "creative." Determined to change Walt's view, and recalling Walt's own handiwork on his backyard trains and miniatures built in the workshop barn at his Holmby Hills home, the producer spent weeks making a model to show Walt. He arrived early one morning and set up his work in Walt's outer office, insisting that Walt view his

efforts before starting his day. Enthused over the product of weeks of work, the producer waited for Walt's reaction; however, none was forthcoming. "Well," the producer lamented, "at least you can give me 'E for Effort.'" Reacting at last, Walt replied: "I'll give you 'S for Shit.'"

- As Walt emerged from the Disney Studio Animation Building and attempted to light his cigarette, his lighter malfunctioned. Into the breach stepped one of the Studio's great story and character development talents, Ken Anderson. His lighter worked, so well in fact that he set fire to Walt's signature mustache in front of a large crowd of his fellow animators no less. Ken did not sleep well that night, and when he was summoned to Walt's office the next day just before noon, he expected the worst—that his days at Disney were numbered. Walt was waiting for him—with instructions. "Come on, Ken—let's go to lunch." And they did, in the Disney commissary, where everyone could see them eating and talking together.

Years later, I was reminded of these stories during a recording session for the Ford Motor Company attraction at the 1964–65 New York World's Fair. I had written the narration for the Magic Skyway ride that Walt and the Imagineers had created for the Ford Pavilion. In the second year of the World's Fair, Ford asked Walt to serve as narrator.

We recorded early one morning at the beginning of 1965. Walt's voice was even more raspy than usual. As he mangled line after line, the number of expletives mounted. At first they were directed at me as Walt tripped over the length of some sentences I had written and the pronunciation of the dinosaurs featured in the ride. Here is the flavor of the recording session:

"Thanks to some old-fashioned magic, this Ford Motor Company car will be your time machine for our story—so if your imagination is ready, here we go! We'll be traveling backwards in time—many millions of years—back to a time when giant creatures thundered over the land, and soared like gliders over the sky. You're probably familiar with some of the names: allosaurus, brontosaurus, triceratops, tyrannosaurus . . .

Boy what a mouthful—that's a big long one there—I got a dang frog in my throat . . . Is that any better, Marty? Lousy? Oh, shit—I don't want anyone to hear me cussing, Marty—before you send it to Ford, you'll edit it first, right Marty?"

Yes indeed, Walt!

Walt was *not* a boss who wanted a "yes" at all costs. He just didn't like "no."

In 1953, Walt sent Dick Irvine, Bill Cottrell (president of WED; he was married to Lillian Disney's sister, Hazel), and Harrison "Buzz" Price to Chicago to review his concept for Disneyland with the major amusement park operators of the time, who were all attending a convention of their peers. The WED team reported the reaction of the amusement park "experts": "Bottom line, Mr. Disney's park idea is too expensive to build and too expensive to operate. 'Tell your boss,' they said, 'to save his money. Tell him to stick to what he knows and leave the amusement business to people who know it.'"

The articulate master at "getting to yes" with Walt was his favorite consultant, the self-described "numbers man," the author of *Walt's Revolution! By the Numbers*, Buzz Price. From the very beginning of Disneyland, Buzz focused on Walt's objectives.

"Walt said that his park was to be a work in progress," Buzz wrote later. "Unlike existing enterprises of this kind, it was never to be finished. This idea of constant reinvestment was a new concept. Walt recognized the fickleness of audiences and the challenge of always providing something new. For me, this great entrepreneurial adventure was an exposure to 'yes if' consulting as a more useful format than 'no because' . . . 'Yes if' was the language of an enabler, pointing to what needed to be done to make the possible plausible. Walt liked this language. 'No because' is the language of a deal killer. 'Yes if' is the approach of a deal maker. Creative people thrive on 'yes if.'"

For many of us, Walt was the supreme casting director. He knew the talents of his staff better than anyone, and was constantly seeking ways to expand their skills—as if to ready us for an assignment on a future project still only in his head.

Not long after moving to Imagineering after twenty-seven years as an animator, X. (for Xavier) Atencio was called to Walt's office. "I want you to write the script for Pirates of the Caribbean," Walt explained.

"But Walt," X. replied, "I've never written a script." X. not only became the author of lines later spoken by Johnny Depp in the Pirates of the Caribbean motion pictures—he also became a songwriter when Walt liked his idea for a tune the buccaneers would sing: *"Yo ho, yo ho, a pirate's life for me!"* And when a full-size mock-up of the key auction scene in the Pirates attraction indicated to X. that he had overwritten the dialogue, Walt would not allow X. to cut any lines. "Think of it this way," Walt explained. "It's like a cocktail party: you hear bits and pieces of conversation, and you get the idea of what's going on. Our boat ride is even better; if you want to hear the rest of the conversation, come back for another ride!"

Herb Ryman used to say that Walt was "the conductor of one of the world's great orchestras—and I was proud to be one of the musicians." But John Hench thought of Walt's cast of talents as "dogs on a leash." The "dogs" most trusted, John said, "could wander far to the east and far to the west, trying new tricks." But others were kept on a tight leash; they had to stay close to home and "mind the store." The key for everyone, John explained, was this: "Once Walt decided what direction he was going, no one wandered off. If he decided to go north, *everyone* went north; no one went south."

In the late 1950s, one of my jobs was to write the copy for the *The Story of Disneyland* souvenir guide. As the costs of printing and production grew to 24 cents for a product that sold in the park for 25 cents, the merchandise staff wanted to double the price, to 50 cents. In those days, Walt was the judge and jury for even decisions as mundane as this. I accompanied the merchandise staff to a meeting with Walt, and watched them strike out. "No" was the answer.

Walt's reasons were clear and direct. "Look," he said, "we don't have to make a profit on *every* line of merchandise. Our guests take those souvenir books home, put them on their coffee tables, and their friends see them and think, 'That place looks like fun!' And when they come, they buy tickets to the park, and food, and merchandise inside. *That's* when we'll make our profit. Keep the price at 25 cents; I want as many souvenir books as you can sell in homes across the country—around the world."

Marc Davis, one of the Disney greats in animation since

the 1930s, had a similar experience when he moved from the Studio to Imagineering in the early 1960s. Although he had made dozens of presentations to Walt in the course of creating some of the best known characters in Disney animation—from Tinker Bell in *Peter Pan* to Cruella De Vil in *One Hundred and One Dalmatians* and Maleficent in *Sleeping Beauty*—Marc was still nervous when he pitched his first storyboard sketches for a Disney park show to Walt.

When Walt, deep in thought, did not respond immediately, Marc stepped into the void. "Walt, I've got another idea for this, and it's a lot cheaper." Now Walt responded quickly. Putting a hand on Marc's shoulder, he set the tone for how Imagineers were to create for the Disney parks. "Marc," Walt said, "I have a whole floor of finance people and accountants upstairs who are going to tell me what the cheapest way to do something is. What I pay you for is *to tell me the best way!*"

I experienced an embarrassing situation when I was twenty-five or twenty-six. My lesson became a cardinal rule I shared with Imagineering's creative staff for the next half-century. In a meeting, Walt asked an informational question, and I gave him the answer. Unfortunately, when I got back to my office, I discovered my information was incorrect. Then I made the *real* mistake—instead of calling or sending a note to Walt to correct the error, I did nothing.

About a year later, a similar subject came up in a meeting, and this time I had the right answer. I enthusiastically offered my information. Walt's look of disdain would have withered the Wicked Witch of the West. "The last time we discussed this, you said . . ."

I didn't need Walt's autograph on a memo to explain this

"youthful mistake" to me. Here's the rule: no one is expected to have all the answers. If you are asked a question, and do not know the answer, just say, "I don't know, but I'll find out." And when you do, never fail to pass along the correct information. You can never tell who the elephant in the room may be—because elephants just don't forget.

* * * * * * * * * *

The Disney company aircraft—an early Grumman Gulfstream purchased in 1963—was a favorite of Walt and Mrs. Disney's. When it was finally retired to permanent display on the back lot at Disney's Hollywood Studios in Florida in 1992, it had established both longevity and mileage records for corporate service: twenty-nine years and 12,300 hours in the air as it logged 4.3 million miles!

One of the reasons the Disneys loved that fifteen-passenger Gulfstream in the early 1960s was the cross-country trip it handled between Burbank and New York. Early on, the pilots discovered what became Walt's favorite refueling stop: Grand Island, Nebraska. The family that ran the tiny airstrip and refueling station would roll out a red carpet so passengers could stretch their legs and, of course, make telephone calls—it was the days long before cell phones. But the clincher was the cake the lady of the station baked for visiting executives. It was pure 1960s Midwest America—straight from the heart and the heartland—just like Walt's own product.

On one trip, however, we refueled in Lincoln, the capital of Nebraska. I immediately went inside the terminal and looked up the telephone number for my friend and former UCLA classmate, Sandy Ragins—by then the rabbi of the one Jewish congregation in Lincoln. Imagine my amazement when the Central Lincoln telephone operator answered my call, to inform me, "Rabbi Ragins is on vacation this week."

I'm sure that flying over those endless Nebraska cornfields was one of the inspirations for Jack Lindquist's brilliant idea for "Cornfield Mickey." To celebrate Mickey Mouse's sixtieth birthday, Jack—the marketing manager extraordinaire and later the first president of Disneyland—conceived a portrait of Mickey's head that would be visible to airplane passengers crossing the United States. As Jack related in his autobiography, *In Service to the Mouse*: "The profile of Mickey contained six point five million corn plants and three hundred acres of oats. Mickey's head turned out to have a three-point-five-mile circumference." It was planted outside Sheffield, Iowa—a town of 1,224 residents. When fifteen thousand people showed up to celebrate Mickey's sixtieth and it became an attraction for cross-country air passengers, Cornfield Mickey was showcased on the *Today* show, *Good Morning America*, and CNN. It was just one of Jack Lindquist's incredible marketing coups.

If only that aircraft could talk—what stories it could tell. My favorite was one that Buzz Price told on himself. Preparing for the 1964 New York World's Fair, its organizer, New York City Parks Commissioner Robert Moses, hitched a ride with Walt Disney on the Disney company's private aircraft. While Walt Disney and Robert Moses argued over the location of the designated amusement area for the Fair, Buzz served as bartender—refilling the combatants' glasses with Scotch "more than once," Buzz recalled. Suddenly, Walt changed the subject—to Buzz. "You're too fat to fly on my airplane!" Walt stated quite emphatically.

Buzz took the boss's words seriously. In the next six weeks, Buzz lost thirty pounds. Always the numbers man, he counted every mile run, every weight lifted, and every calorie consumed.

One of Walt's strengths in his relationship with talent was that he made it clear he cared about us. So many of us had worked overtime hours without end for months to create and install the four Disney shows at that New York World's Fair—especially "it's a small world," which was actually created from first sketch in Glendale to opening in New York in eleven months. But the rewards came quickly: Walt put that Gulfstream on a weekly flight path carrying many of us—with our spouses—between Burbank and LaGuardia to spend four days at the Fair.

My wife, Leah, and I had the good fortune—along with the team that created the *Disneyland Goes to the World's Fair* TV show, Ham Luske and Mac Stewart (and their spouses)—to fly to New York with Walt and Lilly Disney. The Disneys occupied the back of the aircraft, just the two of them in a space that could hold eight or nine. The six of us were very comfortable in the forward compartment. But before we even took off, Walt appeared at the entrance to the rear compartment and (with his back to Mrs. Disney) made it clear that the rear bathroom was not exclusive to "Madame Queen"!

Another memorable flight for me was the aftermath of a failed pitch to Henry Ford II to continue his company's relationship with Disney after the Fair, as a sponsor in Disneyland. We had pulled out all the stops in our presentation in Dearborn, Michigan. Claude Coats and X. Atencio made the creative presentation, using a fabulous model we had shipped to Detroit. I had worked with photographer Carl Frith to illustrate a one-of-a-kind commercial song Walt had asked Bob and Dick Sherman to write; it was called "Get the Feel of the Wheel of a Ford"—Dick had even recorded a version in his best faux Maurice Chevalier voice. And Walt made the final pitch, describing what Disney could do for Ford with Disneyland, and the Disney team, as a West Coast base.

Henry Ford II was not only unresponsive, he was seemingly dismissive of the value of all that Disney talent potentially available to endorse his company's product. I know that was what set Walt off once we were on board the Gulfstream. Despite the impact of the Disney-designed Ford Pavilion at the World's Fair (it was second only to GM in the number of guests visiting among the 150 exhibitors participating in the entire Fair), and the fact Walt had agreed to apply his personal one-million-dollar fee for the use of his name during the Fair toward Ford's sponsorship fee in Disneyland, Mr. Ford hardly seemed to be paying attention. Walt spared little in his reaction as we took off from the Detroit airport. "That," he said, "is the stupidest man I ever met!"

In my experience, Walt Disney made clear his reaction to some of the major executives we interfaced with in developing sponsored shows for Disneyland or the World's Fair. General Electric vice president J. Stanford Smith (later the CEO of International Paper Company) came to the WED offices in Glendale to review the Carousel of Progress show being developed for GE's pavilion at the New York World's Fair. The show was a progression dramatizing how family life had changed and improved with the evolution of products for the home; it carried the audience from the days of pre-electricity to "today." Smith complained that the show displayed GE products that the company no longer made. Walt patiently explained his approach, stressing that he often "used nostalgia for a fondly remembered time" to establish a rapport with an audience. "I love the nostalgia myself," he often told us.

Mr. Smith was having none of it—all he could see was old washers and dryers of the 1920s and TV sets of the 1940s that GE no longer manufactured. Finally, Walt lost patience and left the meeting. Later we learned that he had gone directly to the office of WED's attorney with this message: "Get me out of this contract!"

Fortunately, by coincidence, Walt had a prearranged visitor to his office at the Disney Studio the following Monday: Gerald Philippi, GE's CEO. Tommie Wilck, by then Walt's number-one secretary and a good friend, later told me that Walt's first words once Mr. Philippi was seated in his office were: "I'm having trouble with one of your vice presidents!" Mr. Philippi understood the show business term "the show must go on" . . . because that was the last we heard of Mr. Smith's concern. And the Carousel of Progress was not only a huge hit at the Fair, it went on to entertain audiences in Disneyland for six years after the Fair, then moved to the Magic Kingdom in Walt Disney World in 1975, where a version of the original show is still playing, nearly fifty years after its debut in New York.

* * * * * * * * * *

Walt Disney was not prone to lavish praise, even when he truly liked your work.

For a long time, I wondered how Walt—so inarticulate in

personally voicing his appreciation for a job well done—could be rewarded by such enthusiasm from the incredible talent I worked alongside in the 1950s and 1960s, during Walt's lifetime. I have often heard one of the most articulate creators of Disney magic, Academy Award–winning songwriter Richard Sherman, describe Walt's reaction to songs such as "A Spoonful of Sugar" or "Supercalifragilisticexpialidocious" from *Mary Poppins*: "That'll work," was typical, Dick remembers almost fifty years later—"and Bob and I knew that was all the praise we would get," he added.

I believe Walt Disney felt *the praise was in the product*, meaning that the public's positive reaction to a Disney film or television show or Disneyland attraction was all the praise we needed. To sit in a theater and hear the laughter at penguins dancing with Dick Van Dyke or shed a tear with Dumbo as his mother is led away or ride through a Magic Kingdom of all the world's children in "it's a small world," is perhaps to understand why Walt did not believe he needed to voice his own praise. The public spoke for him clearly and enthusiastically.

Yet we did know where we stood in Walt Disney's lexicon of talent. We heard it from our leaders and managers. And we knew it because of the next assignment we received.

One thing I did know from personal experience: nothing in my relationship with Walt Disney or his brother was influenced either positively or negatively because I'm Jewish. In fact, Tommie Wilck told me that Walt had called one day when I was attending services at our synagogue during the Jewish High Holy Days, Rosh Hashanah and Yom Kippur. When Tommie told Walt where I was, she let me know his reaction: "That's where he should be, with his family." I'm sure some of the company's key talent and executives—songwriters Dick and Bob Sherman; Irving Ludwig, the head of Buena Vista Distribution, marketers of Disney films; Armand Bigle, who ran Disney's European operation from Paris—never had a "Jewish issue" or question with Walt or Roy. My belief is that this frequent rumor stemmed from several factors in the Disney brothers' history: first, growing up in the Midwest, where Jews were not your typical neighbors; second, seeming to be outsiders in a Hollywood environment where almost all the studios were established or run by Jews with European roots—the Goldwyns, Mayers, Thalbergs, Steins, Wassermans; and third, the fact that it was Charles Mintz, a distributor and (by the way) a Jew, who pirated away Walt's first successful character, Oswald the Rabbit, and signed contracts with the key animators who created it in the mid-1920s. The good news is this "theft" led directly to Walt's creation of Mickey Mouse, but at the time it was almost a deathblow to the fledgling Disney Brothers Studio.

Perhaps it was Walt and Roy who were the victims of discrimination by whoever it was that started those anti-Semitic rumors. The talent I know and worked with inside Disney, who happened to be Jewish, never experienced that "discrimination". . . except on those occasions when Walt didn't like our work!

* * * * * * * * * *

I never knew which of my assignments placed me on Walt's "favorites" list. Some of my earlier tasks certainly brought me to his attention, because they communicated several of his cherished projects to potential sponsors. They were twenty-four or twenty-eight-page booklets promoting Liberty Street and Edison Square, and the first booklet promoting Disneyland USA itself to potential sponsors of attractions existing or planned. I had also written Walt's copy for the newspaper section in the *Los Angeles Times* describing all the new attractions for Disneyland's first big expansion: the 1959 additions of the Submarine Voyage, the Matterhorn Bobsleds ride, and the first daily operating monorail system in the Western Hemisphere.

But I was not prepared for what occurred one morning early in 1960, when Walt joined me and my boss, Disneyland publicity director Eddie Meck, for a cup of coffee at the Hills Brothers Coffee House in a corner of Town Square at Disneyland. Suddenly the conversation turned to me, when Walt asked, "What are you doing these days, Marty?" I told Walt that I was responsible for writing the publicity material for Eddie to plant with the media. Looking directly at my boss, Walt responded: "Well, we will have to give you something more important to do, Marty."

He was a man of his word. Within the next few months, I had been assigned part time to WED Enterprises and directed to accompany designer John Hench, architect Vic Green, and Disneyland executive Jack Sayers in January 1961 to Dearborn, Michigan, to begin work on the Ford Pavilion for the New York World's Fair of 1964–65.

Suddenly, I was beginning to think that my Disney career, in tune with a song later to be featured in the Disney animated film *Hercules*, had an opportunity to go from "Zero to Hero."

Following are some of the key points made by the participants:

Bob Gurr: "Walt had a way to see a little bit beyond what you had done. He would say, 'That's kind of interesting. What if . . . ,' and you would leave the room more inspired than when you came in. That's leadership."

Marty: "Walt was always looking for somebody to take a chance."

Dick Sherman: "Bob [his songwriting partner and brother] and I always said, 'Yes, we can!' . . . and then found out afterward how to do it!"

Bob Gurr (*Walt thought Bob was an engineer—when he actually had no engineering training*): "Walt was not interested in what kind of certification you brought with you to Disney. On paper, I was not qualified to do most of those early Disneyland vehicle designs. We taught ourselves how to do it."

Marty: "Walt's lesson was that you don't pigeonhole anybody. You never know what a talented person can do if you never give them a chance."

Blaine Gibson: "He would often use one employee's work to stimulate another's enthusiasm."

Dick Sherman: "He emphasized the team concept by his own actions. Everyone was equal in a story meeting—Walt just rolled up his sleeves and was one of the group."

Marty: "It didn't matter who you were, or what your assignment was. He just wanted the best idea. Our job was to give him the best we knew how."

Dick Sherman: "Walt was open to everyone's thoughts. He was the referee."

Buzz Price: "Walt had an uncanny way of zeroing in on the solution to a problem."

Bob Gurr: "He built a trust. No challenge ever scared you because of that trust."

Marty: "He was totally focused on the audience—the guest experience in the parks."

Dick Sherman: "In a sense, *he was the audience*. We had to please the boss. His genius was to *plus* an idea."

Buzz Price: "He had an instinct for people he wanted to work with."

Bob Gurr: "But you never expected, or got, an 'attaboy' from Walt Disney. You only found out secondhand that he liked what you did."

He must have liked the work of this group of Disney Legends. Together, their service to Walt Disney's company added up to more than two hundred years.

Charna Sklar (left) and Henrietta Fuchs Baldoff (right),
my grandmothers. Circa August 1960.

Leon G. Sklar, my father. Principal at Madison Junior
High School, North Hollywood, California.

Lilyn and Leon Sklar, my parents. Circa 1960.

Me (right), at ten, and my brother, Bob (then eight), in New Jersey.
Circa 1944.

Wedding day, May 12, 1957.

Wedding day, May 12, 1957: me, Leah, Helen Gerber (Leah's mother), and Marsha Gerber (Leah's sister at nine years old).

Me, cousin Armin Dolin, Leon (my father), Uncle Bernie Dolin, and Bob (my brother). Circa early 1950s in California.

Leah, Leslie (four), and Howard (six) at Disneyland. Circa 1965—1966. Photographed by me.

Counterclockwise: Harry Gerber (Leah's father), Marsha Gerber (Leah's sister), and Helen Gerber (Leah's mother). Circa 1957.

My mother, Lilyn Fuchs' family (left to right): Martin (my namesake), Armin, Henrietta, John, Lilyn, and Frances.

Me, Leah, Bob, and Adrienne Harris (Bob's wife) in the SoHo section of New York City.

Robert A. Sklar (Bob), professor of Cinema Studies, New York University.

Gabriel at three (my grandson), Leonard Sklar (Bob's son), and Howard Sklar. Circa 1994 at a California Angels game at their Anaheim stadium.

Howard, Leah, Lilyn, me, Flicka, and Leslie. Circa 1990 at our Los Angeles home.

Mickey presents: Leslie, Rachel, Leah, Jake, Gabriel, Walt, Hannah, Katriina, Howard, and me (left to right) in 2012 at Disney California Adventure.

Me, with the love of my life, Leah, 2012, in Los Angeles.

6

"JUST DO SOMETHING PEOPLE WILL LIKE!" — WALT DISNEY

As I've said, Walt's singular focus was on the audience. After several weeks of development, Herb Ryman was sure he had come up with a solution to a design challenge Walt had given him. But Walt took one look and rejected the idea—without offering a hint that would give Herb a direction for his redesign. His frustration boiling over, Herb threw a question at Walt's back as he stalked out of Herb's office: "Well, give me a clue what you are looking for!" Walt turned, his eyebrow raised in mock surprise as he answered: "Just do something people will like!"

One day in the early 1950s, deeply immersed in a drawing for *Peter Pan*—the last animation feature he would work on as one of the Disney Studio's key background artists— John Hench was surprised by the figure peering over his shoulder. Walt nodded as John noticed his presence, but left without saying a word . . . until he reached the door. "I want you to work on my Disneyland project," Walt said, assuming John's knowledge of the then-secret development. "And," Walt stated matter-of-factly, "you're going to like it!"

I had the privilege (as my own career grew from staff writer, to vice president of Concepts and Planning, then to president, and later vice chairman and principal creative executive of Imagineering) of working with all of the amazing talents of Walt's original WED Enterprises team, as well as the Imagineers who followed—many of whom I helped grow into stars in their own right. In the beginning, Walt needed storytellers for his new concept in family entertainment. And so they came, from Hollywood motion picture and television studios, from Disney and Twentieth Century-Fox especially: art directors, set designers, special effects wizards, writers, production designers, model makers. They were joined by a new breed of designer such as Bob Gurr, trained to design cars, but more significantly smart enough to know that "no" and "it can't be done" were never answers you gave to Walt Disney's dreams.

The name "Imagineering" was suggested to Walt in an early meeting by Buzz Price, the economist who recommended the sites in Anaheim and Orlando for Disneyland and Walt Disney World, respectively. The term combines "imagination" with "engineering"—thus "Imagineering." Walt liked it immediately. To assure Buzz received proper credit for the name, Walt sent him a letter in the 1960s thanking him for the suggestion.

Walt also liked—and recorded—the line I wrote to describe WED's process: "Imagineering is the blending of creative imagination with technical know-how."

This talented group included my mentors, my friends, and in their golden years, my staff. They were the best of the best. They defined Imagineer and Imagineering. They developed and led the 140 disciplines that form Imagineering today. Their passion for going beyond what they had done the time before was limitless. Their dedication to Walt, and their comprehension of his passion for excellence, knew no bounds. They were true believers, followers, and leaders. Walt created Imagineering, but the Imagineers made it sing and dance.

It might never have happened if Walt Disney's friend and neighbor, Los Angeles architect Welton Becket, had coveted the design job. When Walt approached him about designing Disneyland, and explained the concept brewing in his head, Mr. Becket gave his friend this advice: "You'll use architects and engineers, of course. But Walt—you'll really have to train your own people; they are the only ones who will understand how to accomplish your idea."

My good fortune in the 1960s and 1970s as "the kid" on the WED staff was that Herb Ryman, John Hench, and the other Disney Legends-to-be (the Legends program was established in the mid-1980s) became my mentors. They may not have thought of themselves as teachers, but anyone who worked around them as they transitioned from animation and live-action films to theme park stories and designs was surely enrolled in a master's program in theme park creation. I write about a few of them on these pages, but in the interest of being as inclusive as possible, the following are the Imagineering Legends who most influenced me: Ken Anderson, X. Atencio, Mary Blair, Roger Broggie,

Harriet Burns, Claude Coats, Bill Cottrell, Rolly Crump, Marc Davis, Marvin Davis, Don Edgren, Bill Evans, Blaine Gibson, Harper Goff, Yale Gracey, Bob Gurr, John Hench, Dick Irvine, Fred Joerger, Bill Martin, Sam McKim, Wathel Rogers, and Herb Ryman. I also count three Disney Studio Legends as teachers: advertising and graphic art icon Bob Moore, and songwriters Richard and Robert Sherman. And no Marty list would be complete without mentioning Al Bertino, T. Hee, Vic Green, Bob Jolley, and Bob Sewell of Imagineering; Jim Love and Norm Nocetti of the Disney Studio; and that "Vegas dealer," Card Walker.

It was author Ray Bradbury who perhaps best captured the essence of the Imagineering organization. Ray had once urged Walt Disney to run for mayor of Los Angeles, only to be told, "Why should I run for mayor when I'm already king of Disneyland?" In a talk to an assembly of Imagineers in December 1976, during the development of Epcot, Bradbury spoke of the group as "Renaissance People":

John [Hench] and Marty told me I was supposed to come up here and explain you to yourselves . . . and to tell you what you are and what I am and what I'm doing here. There are a lot of places in the world I could be, but I've been coming through WED and going to Disneyland for many years now, and I like what I see . . . And so, really, what you are is Renaissance People. If ever there was a Renaissance organization, this is it. You haven't peaked yet, but you're peaking, and sometime in the next twenty years, when you peak completely, the whole world's going to be looking at you.

The WED Model Shop, where designs are studied in three dimensions, became the hub of the Legends' classroom tutorials, always disguised as design sessions for submarine voyages and bobsled rides, pirate adventures, and ghostly surprises. Every day was a learning experience, as Walt challenged his most trusted designers and storytellers to imagine new experiences for Disneyland, the New York World's Fair, and, just before his death, Walt Disney World. Those of us fortunate enough to be assigned to their teams—*always* a team effort—were also challenged to grow from undergrad to graduate students, earning our degrees under the wings of these professors: John Hench for design, color, and philosophy; Marc Davis for story, character, and animation; Claude Coats for dramatic staging and continuity; Herb Ryman for overall concept and key story illustrations; Bill Evans for theme setting through landscaping; Rolly Crump for weird and wonderful iconography; Blaine Gibson for turning cartoon sketches into real people; Yale Gracey for the tinkering that created the most simple—and magical effects; Roger Broggie for making anything (and everything) work; and so many more. They (and some of the amazing technical talents at the Studio, notably the film, camera, and projection genius Ub Iwerks) were the leprechauns who helped Walt find the rainbow that led to the pot of gold called Disneyland.

The lessons were taught outside of WED's quarters in Glendale, as well. Without a food facility on the Glendale campus, lunch was always a short walk or drive to a local eatery, where a focused discussion frequently took place about a local theater production, museum exhibition, or travel experience. Often the subject was how to solve that day's creative challenge, and it was a way for the top Imagineers to stay informed about what each was doing. My lunch companions were frequently Coats, Gibson, Joerger, and Sewell, administrator of the Model Shop and a talent in his own right who had helped create the quintessential dioramas in New York's American Museum of Natural History in the late 1930s.

One of the preoccupations at these meals was my companions' observation of other diners and servers. One night in Florida, during the building of Epcot, we were having dinner at a local restaurant. I noticed that Blaine Gibson, our chief sculptor, was totally absorbed in studying the chef, who had come into the seating area to converse with patrons. When I asked, Blaine admitted he was focused on the chef's huge hands. Sure enough, when we all looked, we realized his hands were out of scale to the rest of his body. For Blaine, they were not just curiosities: he was making a mental note of those hands to use later on one of our Audio-Animatronics figures.

I knew that Blaine's love of animals, and understanding of their anatomy and movement, came partly from his years in Disney animation. But even more, they were the result of growing up as a farm boy in Colorado. When it came to the human figures he sculpted for our park attractions, my curiosity got the best of me. One day I asked Blaine where his inspiration for human characters in our shows came from— for example, the incredible buccaneers of Pirates of the Caribbean. Reluctantly, Blaine admitted that his wife, Coral, had mastered the kick under the chair at dinner: when Blaine would stare too long at another diner or server, Coral would let him have it. But she had not found a way to stop him from focusing on the special characteristics and features of fellow churchgoers.

"You mean," I asked cautiously, "that some of our pirates may resemble congregants in your church?" "Yes, it's very possible," Imagineering's chief sculptor admitted. "Walt wanted realism in the pirates, and I found ideas and inspiration in many places!"

Realism in life experiences was critically important to the great illustrator Herbert Dickens Ryman, who drew the first overall concept illustration of Disneyland in 1953. A graduate of the Art Institute of Chicago, Ryman had become one of the most skilled artists in the MGM art department in the 1930s, working under the legendary Cedric Gibbons to illustrate scenes and locations around the world for such classic films as *Mutiny on the Bounty*, *David Copperfield*, *The Good Earth*, *Tarzan*, and *A Tale of Two Cities*. Then one day Ryman realized he had seen nothing of people and places, and he became a world traveler, spending weeks in China, Cambodia, Japan, and Thailand in the 1930s. Eventually, he visited Europe, Africa, and—as a Disney artist—he became part of Walt Disney's goodwill tour of South America in the 1940s. (Herb's sketches played a role in the design of the two films inspired by that trip for the U.S. State Department, *Saludos Amigos* and *Fun and Fancy Free*.)

"I used to think I could research everything out of books; that I could trace or copy a horse, an eagle, an oak tree, or a girl on a beach," Herb said. "I thought it was all in *National Geographic*. By actually touching ruins, feeling the wind on my cheeks as I walked along the Great Wall, and resting in the oasis of the desert, I began to realize this is real, and nature is where you have to go. This is the greatest source of my inspiration."

Shortly after his first odyssey to Asia in the 1930s, Herb was invited by John Ringling North to spend a summer traveling with the Ringling Brothers Circus, in the days of outdoor circus tents. He was given a private suite on the show train in 1949, 1950, and 1951. Ryman's backstage sketches and watercolor renditions were so alive that quintessential circus clown Emmett Kelly said that Herb "put the smell of sawdust into paint."

Walt called Herb one Saturday in 1953 to ask his help in producing the first overall illustration of Disneyland. Herb kept a detailed diary, and in the book *A Brush with Disney: An Artist's Journey, Told Through the Words and Works of Herbert Dickens Ryman*, published in 2002 by Ryman Arts, he described in detail how it came about:

> It was about 10 A.M. on September 26, 1953, when Walt called unexpectedly. When I remarked that he was at the Studio on a Saturday morning, he commented, "Yes, it's my studio and I can be here anytime I want."
>
> I was not working at the Disney Studio at that particular time, because in 1946 I had gone back to 20th Century-Fox. I had deserted Walt, which was a very criminal act (at least he thought it was).
>
> However, I was curious, and flattered, that Walt would pick up the phone and call me. I had no idea what he wanted.
>
> He asked how long it would take me to get there. . . . "I'll be out front waiting for you," he said.
>
> . . . Bill Cottrell, Dick Irvine, and Marvin Davis were there, all friends of mine. Walt said, "Herbie, I'm in the process of

doing an amusement park, we're working on it right now." . . . I asked, "What are you going to call it?" He said, "I'm going to call it Disneyland," and I said, "Well, that's a good name. What is it that you want to see me about?" He said, "Well, my brother Roy is going to New York on Monday morning. He's flying out of here to New York to see the bankers. Herbie, we need $17 million to get us started. . . . You know the bankers, they have no imagination. They can't visualize when you tell them what you're going to do, they have no way of visualizing it. So, I've got to show them what we're going to do before we can have any chance of getting the money." I said, "I would love to see what you're going to do. Where is it?" He pointed at me and said, "You're going to do it!" I said, "No. I'm not. You're not going to call me on Saturday morning at 10 A.M. and expect me to do a masterpiece that Roy could take and get the money. It will embarrass me and it will embarrass you." Walt asked the other guys to leave the room.

We were alone. Walt paced around the room with his arms folded, . . . kind of looked back at me over his left shoulder with a little kind of sheepish smile, like a little boy who really wants something. With his eyes brimming, he asked, "Herbie, will you do it if I stay here with you?" I began to think, well he's very serious about this, and Walt, after all, was my friend, and so I said, "Sure, if you stay here all night tonight and all night Sunday night and help me, I'll stay here. I'll see what I can do."

Our agreement cheered Walt, and he sent out for tuna salad sandwiches and malted milks and we started to work. It was just a carbon pencil drawing with a little color on top of it, but Roy got the money—so I guess it turned out all right.

Few would question that "it turned out all right." But in his personal copy of the book *Disneyland: Inside Story*, published in 1987, Herb wrote this note under a reproduction of the drawing: "First drawing of Disneyland—Sept. 23, 1953. Done under considerable stress and without thought or preparation."

There's no question I learned more from John Hench than anyone but Walt himself. They were so closely connected, in fact, that most of us considered them two sides of the same coin—Walt the intuitive risk-taker and master motivator; John the philosophical thinker and articulate spokesperson for Disney park and resort design concepts.

John loved to tell the story of his complaint to Walt, during John's animation days, that male ballet dancers were more effeminate than athletic. "How do you know?" Walt asked. When John admitted it was his impression, Walt arranged with impresario Sol Hurok for John to spend a week backstage with Hurok's ballet company during its stay in Los Angeles. The experience totally changed John's view; forever after he raved about the strength and athleticism of the ballet dancers—male *and* female.

Assigned by Walt to redesign Disneyland's Victorian-style Plaza Inn in the early 1960s, John complained that he knew nothing about restaurants. "Well, find out!" Walt responded. John enrolled in a course in restaurant management at UCLA, and from then on he was not only the quintessential designer, he was the design staff's authority on back-of-house restaurant organization and requirements.

John Hench holds all The Walt Disney Company records for longevity. He was still working every day when he became ill at age ninety-four, in the sixty-fourth year since he'd joined the company as a sketch artist on *Fantasia* in 1939. His insatiable curiosity and desire to learn led him to work in many of the key departments at the Studio: story, layout, background, effects animation, camera, multiplane camera, special effects. We all considered John a true Renaissance man.

One Friday I decided to find out how John knew so much about so many things, so I asked his assistant, Sandy Huskins, to bring me "all the books and magazines John takes home this weekend." She dutifully complied, and on Monday, thirty-five books and magazines arrived (in shifts) on my desk! They ranged from *Women's Wear Daily* to *Scientific American*. That very day, I determined I would not stray far from John Hench for as long as he would allow me to be near him. We became great friends and collaborators for many of John's sixty-four years at Disney. Our "partnership"—Hench the design guru, Marty the content quarterback and sponsor liaison—was the key to creating the Epcot theme park, and numerous attractions from Anaheim to Tokyo and Paris.

In his seminal book, *Designing Disney: Imagineering and the Art of the Show*, published in 2004 by Disney Editions, John drew on his years as the "color guru" of the Disney parks to communicate the importance that color plays in the guest experience:

> *We pay close attention to color relationships and how they help us to tell our stories. Nothing in a theme park is seen in isolation. Story threads help us to coordinate the relationships of adjacent attractions. We visualize the buildings and their facades next to one another, and also in*

the context of the surrounding pavement, the landscape, the sky with its changing weather, as well as the props and decorative furnishings that might be adjacent to these structures. In one sense, designing a park is all about creating distinct yet related experiences of color from one end to the other. . . . Each attraction has a color scheme that identifies its story clearly for the guest, yet also complements those of attractions nearby.

Color assists guests in making decisions because it establishes the identity of each attraction in a park. The color of an object is an inevitable part of its identity—color is as important as form in helping us to recognize what we see. . . . After a lifetime as a designer, I have become convinced that some kind of ancestral memory, a collective conscious inheritance of sensory impressions, images, and symbols, also plays an important role in our response to what we see.

Even though he contributed to every Disney park around the world, including Hong Kong Disneyland, John never wavered in his view that the original park was the most significant. In his book, he wrote:

When I am asked, "What is our greatest achievement?" I answer, "Disneyland is our greatest achievement. Disneyland was first, and set the pattern for others to follow." Disneyland has been an example for many enterprises in the entertainment industry, and its design principles have been embraced by other industries as well. The concept of "themed" environments—places designed so that every element contributes to telling a story—was developed and popularized by Walt Disney. Its influence has been extraordinarily widespread, and can be seen today in many aspects of our daily experience—in shops and shopping malls, hotels, restaurants, museums, airports, offices, even people's homes.

As much as John enjoyed walk-throughs at Disneyland with Walt to discuss future projects, he was constantly on guard against being mistaken for Walt, as they were about the same size and shared a particular feature: a well-trimmed dark mustache. One day, four or five different guests asked for John's autograph—while Walt stood by, observing in silence. Later, alongside the Frontierland river, the Mark Twain Riverboat sailed past, and a father on board excitedly exclaimed to his son, "Look! There's Walt Disney!" Overhearing, Walt pointed down the riverbank toward John, and responded: "No—that's him over there!"

* * * * * * * * * *

The master planning, creative design, and engineering organization originally called WED Enterprises was incorporated in December 1952 for the express purpose of working with Walt Disney on the creation of Disneyland. The initials were Walt's: Walter Elias Disney. It was a private company 100 percent owned by Walt and his family, and remained that way through the opening and expansion of Disneyland, the early planning for Walt Disney World, and the creation of the four Disney shows at the New York World's Fair 1964–65.

Walt had a handshake agreement with his brother Roy O. Disney that he would bring any project offered to him through WED, his personal company, to Roy on the chance that Walt Disney Productions wanted it for the company's portfolio of work. In the case of the four New York World's Fair attractions, the public Disney company preferred not to take on the General Electric, Ford Motor Company, or State of Illinois pavilions, enabling WED to become the designer of these three hit shows. However, Roy did bring the fourth production into the Walt Disney Productions aegis when UNICEF asked Walt to create a show "about the children of the world." It became "it's a small world," now a fixture in every Magic Kingdom-style Disney park around the world.

The potential concern that shareholders might suspect Walt was feeding projects to his family company, WED Enterprises, and thus depriving Walt Disney Productions of potential income, led Walt Disney Productions to purchase the assets of WED from the Walt Disney family at the conclusion of the New York World's Fair in 1965. Those assets were a few buildings in Glendale, and the staff Walt had assembled and trained, which had designed Disneyland and the World's Fair shows.

With the sale of WED to Walt Disney Productions, the Walt Disney family established Retlaw (Walter spelled backward) Enterprises as a legal and business enterprise to manage its personal assets and investments, including the Disneyland Railroad and the Monorail system. Walt had personally financed the railroad during the original construction of Disneyland, and the Monorail when it was added in 1959. Retlaw was sold to Walt Disney Productions in July 1981, and by virtue of that transaction, the company acquired Retlaw's steam train and Monorail assets.

7

"THE GREATEST PIECE OF URBAN DESIGN IN THE UNITED STATES IS DISNEYLAND."

Of all the accolades written and spoken about Disneyland during his lifetime, I believe Walt Disney's favorite was delivered as the keynote speech for the 1963 Urban Design Conference at Harvard University. The speaker was James W. Rouse, developer of the Faneuil Hall Marketplace in Boston, Harbor Place at Baltimore's Inner Harbor, New York City's South Street Seaport, and—when *Time* magazine honored him with its cover illustration—developer of the new town of Columbia, Maryland.

> *I hold a view, that may be somewhat shocking to an audience as sophisticated as this: that the greatest piece of urban design in the United States today is Disneyland.*
> *If you think about Disneyland and think of its performance in relation to its purpose, its meaning to people—more than that, its meaning to the process of*

development—you will find it the outstanding piece of urban design in the United States.

It took an area of activity—the amusement park—and lifted it to a standard so high in its performance, in its respect for people, in its functioning for people, that it really has become a brand-new thing. It fulfills all the functions it set out to accomplish un-self-consciously, usefully, and profitably to its owners and developers.

I find more to learn in the standards that have been set and in the goals that have been achieved in the development of Disneyland than in any other single piece of physical development in the country.

* * * * * * * * * *

I had the good fortune that first summer at Disneyland, before I returned to UCLA to finish my senior year, to practice, as part of my job, a student's thirst for knowledge about Disney and Disneyland. My favorite piece of writing was from a 1953 background document prepared for Walt. From it, the Disneyland dedication plaque evolved. I believe the longer background was written primarily by the talented Bill Walsh, once a publicist but soon the producer of the original *Mickey Mouse Club* and later coscreenwriter, with Don DaGradi, of *Mary Poppins*. It was called "The Disneyland Story":

The idea of Disneyland is a simple one. It will be a place for people to find happiness and knowledge.

It will be a place for parents and children to share pleasant times in one another's company: a place for teacher and pupils to discover greater ways of understanding and education. Here the older generation can recapture the nostalgia of days gone by, and the younger generation can savor the challenge of the future. Here will be the wonders of Nature and Man for all to see and understand.

Disneyland will be based upon and dedicated to the ideals, the dreams, and hard facts that have created America. And it will be uniquely equipped to dramatize these dreams and facts and send them forth as a source of courage and inspiration to all the world.

Disneyland will be something of a fair, an exhibition, a playground, a community center, a museum of living facts, and a showplace of beauty and magic.

It will be filled with the accomplishments, the joys, and hopes of the world we live in. And it will remind us and show us how to make these wonders part of our own lives.

These words began to come alive as we attended what I'll call "the Walt Disney school of story and placemaking." One day that first summer, I accompanied the Disneyland staff photographer Fritz Musser on an assignment in Frontierland. The heavy photo equipment of the time required Fritz to take a shortcut; in those early days, you could drive a car around the perimeter of Disneyland, and park behind the Plantation House restaurant. The only problem was, the dirt road leading to the parking place was "onstage"— completely visible to guests aboard the Mark Twain stern-wheeler and smaller watercraft navigating the Rivers of America.

On this occasion, as Fritz drove the dirt road, some of the dust the car kicked up fell on the lone man walking along the road in a Western hat and cowboy boots. Fritz had barely stepped out of the parked car when that man was poking his finger into Fritz's chest. "What are you going with *that* car here in 1860?" Walt Disney demanded. We had violated a key story principle with our very visible contradiction. The identity of the time period, the foundation of the story of the old West, had been destroyed for our guests. Walt made sure we understood. For me, it was a great lesson, bringing so much that I had read into a real, three-dimensional realm.

* * * * * * * * * *

When I returned to Disneyland's Public Relations department in September 1956, after graduation, I continued to look for ways to best express Disneyland's magic in publicity and promotion materials. Here are quotes that remain special to me:

Gladwin Hill in *The New York Times* (February 2, 1958):

> *What is the secret of Disneyland's success? Many factors have entered into it. But to pinpoint a single element, it would be imagination—not just imagination on the part of its impresarios, but their evocation of the imagination of the cash customers.*
>
> *Walt Disney and his associates have managed to generate, in the traditionally raucous and oftimes shoddy amusement park field, the same suspension of disbelief which has been the secret of theatrical success down the corridors of time. . . . The visitor indulges eagerly in that most ancient of games: let's pretend."*

The second was a letter to the editor of *Nation* magazine on June 28, 1958, by author Ray Bradbury. Responding to a prior critical letter from a guest cited below (Halevy) by describing a day at Disneyland with actor Charles Laughton, whom he called "one of the great theatrical and creative minds of our time," Bradbury wrote:

> I admit I approached Disneyland with many intellectual reservations, myself, but these have been banished in my seven visits. Disney makes many mistakes; what artist doesn't? But when he flies, he really flies. I shall be indebted to him for a lifetime for his ability to let me fly over midnight London looking down on that fabulous city, in his Peter Pan ride. . . . I have a sneaking suspicion that Mr. Halevy truly loved Disneyland but is not man enough, or child enough, to admit it. I feel sorry for him. He will never travel in space; he will never touch the stars.

The third was a special piece we would call op-ed today. It was written by a Disney Studio publicity writer for that very first issue of the *Disneyland News*. This is what Jack Jungmeyer wrote in his "Under the Gaslight" column:

> Yesterday, on the eve of the Disneyland opening, by a kind of Disneyesque Magic, I rediscovered the small town scene of my youth in a park actually 2,000 miles from the place where I was raised.
> The name of the town doesn't matter. But its lively business section and shady residence avenues fit with remarkable accuracy into Walt Disney's Main Street and its adjacent wonderlands of yesterday, today and tomorrow on the sixty-acre site in this pleasant valley betwixt the mountains and the sea . . .
> I was scarcely inside the entrance, getting my first glimpse down Main Street, before I was swept

away in an avalanche of sentimental recollections.

Maybe it was the whistle of the steam engine at the ornate depot that did it all in a moment. Maybe the sight of the shining white paddle wheeler with its high stacks over yonder behind the levee. Or the clang of the horse-drawn streetcar on a trial run down to the plaza. The strangely familiar buildings. The bandstand on the green. The open-faced stores. The whole blessed scene from which I had run away, like hundreds of neighbor boys after the high school years, thinking ourselves cramped by small town restrictions, eager to tackle the big cities off beyond the grain fields, the cotton and tobacco, down the shiny tracks to Kansas City, Memphis, Denver, Chicago, or San Francisco . . .

I caught sight of a man far down the street. Alone. Quietly regarding the place he had so long envisaged, now complete, ready to bring pleasure and happy satisfactions to the millions who will visit it.

And I was reminded that he, too, was a Main Streeter, never weaned away from the common bond with the great majority of American small town and country folk, their taste and ideals, despite long identification with big cities as an eminent world figure.

The fourth was unsigned, but as I was to learn over the years, the handwriting was unmistakable. It was a clear illustration of just how personal Disneyland was to Walt Disney, and how "hands-on" he was about every detail. These are Walt's notes on the copy for the brass plaques all guests see as they pass through the tunnels under the railroad trellis, and emerge in Disneyland's Town Square—the start of their adventure in the Magic Kingdom:

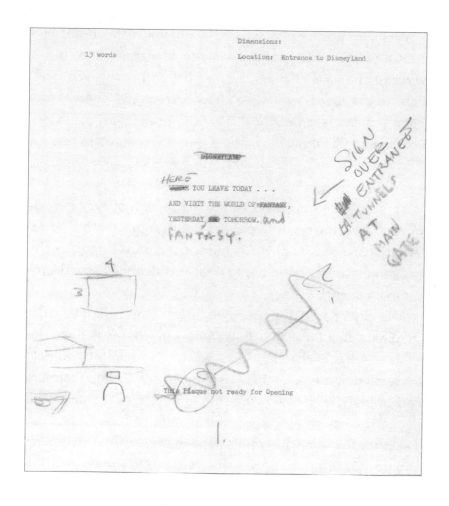

* * * * * * * * * *

The city of Anaheim was a most unlikely bride for a marriage to Walt Disney's "new concept in family entertainment." I learned much of Anaheim's history from my wife, whose family moved to Anaheim in 1948. Leah Gerber graduated from Anaheim High School in 1952, when Anaheim's total population was around 14,000. Today, that attendance number would be seen as a "bad day" at Disneyland Park.

Anaheim was already nationally known in the 1940s and 1950s before Walt selected his site for Disneyland, but it was not the kind of publicity that city fathers rejoice over. Fans of the Jack Benny radio show had long laughed at Mel Blanc's character's famous train station call that most listeners outside California probably thought were fantasy names: *"Train leaving on track number nine for Ana-heim, A-zus-a, and Cu-ca-monga!"*

A list of California cities today will show that Anaheim, as of 2010, was the tenth largest city in the state, with a population of 353,643. Anaheim is the second most populous city in Orange County (after Santa Ana) and also the second largest in land area.

The city's name is a composition of "Ana," derived from the Santa Ana River that flows through what was once the eastern edge of the city, and *"heim,"* German for "home"; thus, when it began in 1857 as a colony of German farmers and vintners, its pioneers thought of it as their "home by the river." The city was incorporated in 1876.

Disney's relationship with Anaheim began soon after Walt and Roy O. Disney engaged the Stanford Research Institute "to determine the economic feasibility of the best location for a new project—Disneyland." Buzz Price was given the assignment.

"I asked Walt if he had a bias about the location for his Magic Kingdom," recalled Buzz many years later. "Absolutely not," Walt responded. "You tell me where the best location is."

Price analyzed potential sites in the Southern California area, ultimately focusing on Orange County after considering population trends, accessibility, and climate factors.

He selected, and recommended to Walt and Roy Disney, 160 acres of orange groves in Anaheim, just off the still-under-construction Santa Ana Freeway at Harbor Boulevard.

"We hit it right on the nose . . . dead center," Buzz enthused to me shortly before his death at age eighty-nine in 2010. "That was the perfect place for it."

Although enough land was available (the noted 160 acres were purchased initially for an average of $4,500 per acre from seventeen property owners; today the Disneyland Resort, including two parks and three hotels, encompasses 456 acres), there were hidden issues never reported in any media. Keith Murdoch, the highly respected city manager of Anaheim from 1950 to 1976, told me about the biggest concern: "You have to remember that we were still less than 15,000 population in 1954. Several of our city council members were worried about what they perceived to be a 'carny' environment; in those days, we only had the old amusement parks like The Pike in Long Beach to go by."

Murdoch and the farsighted Anaheim mayor, Charles Pearson, found the solution for assuring Disney the city's cooperation if they purchased the land: a trip to the Disney Studio in Burbank and a storyboard presentation of the concept for Disneyland by Walt Disney himself. As I have told many people through the years, Walt could sell any-thing, anytime. He was a great salesman because he totally believed in his product. Walt made the sale to the Anaheim councilmen that day, and ground was broken for Disneyland a year before its Grand Opening on July 17, 1955.

That opening day will forever live in infamy in Disney lore. It's known as "Black Sunday," with many events that time has memorialized as urban legends:

- Ladies wearing high heels sank in wet asphalt: true. Fresh ground cover, mostly asphalt, was poured during the previous day; when the temperature soared to a hundred degrees, the asphalt softened and became perfect for entrapping heels. It would be surprising to see today, but 1955 was a time when women did wear dressy shoes to amusement parks—and always to grand openings.
- There were not enough drinking fountains because Walt "forced" thirsty guests to buy Coca-Cola and Pepsi-Cola, both sold in the park at that time: true, and also definitely *false*. There were not enough drinking fountains because an Orange County plumbers' strike had halted all work on water elements. The strike was settled several days before the opening, forcing Walt to make the executive decision to finish the bathrooms and toilets, and "let them drink Coke."
- The official invitations would have brought 10,000 to 15,000 guests to a park whose actual capacity no one knew, but twice as many people showed up: true. Counterfeit tickets were everywhere, and no one respected the various times indicated on their tickets, designed to spread the crowd throughout the day.

The result of all this was huge queues for the attractions, and many pinch points—areas where openings in passageways narrowed, resulting in jams very much like rush hour on the California freeways. One of the worst was the entrance to Fantasyland. Crossing the drawbridge was nearly impossible—there were stories about the choice language some celebrities used in trying to reach the Peter Pan or Dumbo attractions while parked with their children on the castle's drawbridge.

The black-and-white kinescope recording of the Disneyland Grand Opening is quite a sight to see. It was the most ambitious live television show ever attempted at that time, with ABC Television positioning seventeen cameras to catch the action—and the bloopers. Walt had asked television and radio star Art Linkletter to be one of the hosts, and he in turn enticed two of his friends into being cohosts: actors Bob Cummings and Ronald Reagan. Walt was everywhere, dedicating the whole park in Town Square with California governor Goodwin Knight, and introducing each of the various lands at their entrances. The frequent "Am I on?"—and seeming surprise on the hosts' faces when the red light must have signaled "Yes!"—made the show look like amateur hour. But the audience was huge for its day, and by the end of that very first summer, Disneyland had welcomed its one-millionth guest.

I have vivid memories of Black Sunday. As the junior member of the Public Relations team, I had started the workday exactly where I ended the previous one: in the PR office, located in the old homestead that had been purchased with the land, and converted to the park's Administration Building. However, our offices had been totally transformed for the occasion, taken over for a local television segment that took place during the last five minutes of each hour, anchored by Los Angeles television personality Hank Weaver. I was a runner for anything they needed—coffee, water, and, of course, paper and carbon paper for their typewriters.

My assignment for the second half of the day was simple: wander the park and offer support to any reporter or photographer who saw my badge and sought my help. No matter where I roamed, it was a "people zoo," summed up for me when Davy Crockett himself rode up to me on his horse, noted my I.D., and pleaded: "Marty, help me get out of here before this horse kills somebody!" I did manage to help Fess Parker (and his horse) reach a backstage area.

The rest of the day was a blur. By nighttime, I was headed back to Long Beach, where I was still living with my parents. I believe I stopped at every one of the friendly bars along that seventeen-mile stretch!

Media reaction to Black Sunday immediately influenced everything all of us at Disneyland in Anaheim and at WED Enterprises in Glendale did that first summer.

- H. W. Mooring in the *Los Angeles Tidings* (circulation: 59,777): "Walt's Dream is a nightmare—a fiasco the like of which I cannot recall in thirty years of show life."
- *Los Angeles Mirror News* (circulation: 232,176):

"CROWDS GRIPE OVER LONG WAITING LINES EVERYWHERE—DISNEYLAND, ORANGE COUNTY'S NEW $17 MILLION PLAYGROUND, WAS A LAND OF GRIPES AND COMPLAINTS AGAIN TODAY, AS A HUGE, MILLING THRONG OF 48,000 [SIC] PEOPLE HAD THE PLACE BULGING AT THE SEAMS."

- United Press dispatch in Alameda, California's *Times-Star* (circulation: 8,139): "The opening was a confused mess. The first headache was the bumper-to-bumper traffic for seven miles before reaching the park, dubbed 'the worst traffic mess we've ever seen' by police."
- Cora Ulrich in the *Santa Ana Register* (circulation: 32,557): "Many citizens of Anaheim are beginning to regard the

opening of Disneyland with dismay and 'mixed emotions'—the kind the man had when he pushed his mother-in-law over the cliff in his new Cadillac."

- Syndicated columnist Sheila Graham: "To sum up, Disneyland was a disappointment . . . but don't be discouraged, boys and girls—Walt Disney has always been a smart trader, and I'm sure there'll be some changes made."

Sheila Graham was correct. In fact, Walt was focused on fixing the challenges that caused many of these negative media reviews even before he left the park on Black Sunday.

For the PR staff, the plan was simple: get every one of the media outlets to come back to Disneyland without the mobs of people, so they could actually *see* the park—and experience the attractions that were so unique in the amusement world: Adventureland's Jungle Cruise, Tomorrowland's Flight to the Moon, Fantasyland's Peter Pan's Flight, etc. To accomplish this, Public Relations Director Ed Ettinger and Publicity Manager Eddie Meck devised a strategy to invite each news organization to an early dinner at the Red Wagon Inn on Main Street, or the Plantation House restaurant on Frontierland's Rivers of America—followed by a sampling of the park's adventures and entertainment. After working all day, those evenings made for a full summer for all of us. We hosted four Los Angeles newspapers (*Times, Mirror News, Examiner, Herald-Express*); the wire services (Associated Press and United Press); the Hollywood trades (*Variety* and *The Hollywood Reporter*); the local staffs of key national newspapers, like *The New York Times*; and even international media. Radio and television also received attention, although the local influence of television news was not significant in 1955.

The plan started working almost immediately. Witness this column by Dick Williams, entertainment editor of the *Mirror News*:

> *If you're planning a trip to Disneyland, go out in the late afternoon, arriving anytime between 5 and 6 P.M. . . . I paid the amusement park another visit . . . We had dinner at Swift's Red Wagon Inn . . . Lines everywhere moved swiftly, with only brief waits . . . In my opinion, the entire park looks much more captivating by night than day.*

These evenings proved to be a heady experience for a twenty-one-year-old neophyte. It brought me introductions and contacts with the top news media personalities and staffs of the day: editors, city editors, and reporters local and national, including Bob Thomas of the AP and Vernon Scott of UPI. What an on-the-job education!

* * * * * * * * * *

In September, I returned to my formal education as a senior at UCLA. The following year before I graduated and resumed working at the company in September 1956 was a true learning experience for everyone associated with Disneyland. The park was a huge success overall, with 3.6 million in attendance in its first year—but there were many ups and downs. The gates were closed Mondays and Tuesdays (until going to a seven-day operation on February 6, 1985), and weekday attendance was sparse, because the vital national and international tourism that would reach a steady 40 percent of total attendance in future years had not yet materialized.

The guests taught Walt and his staff many key lessons. For instance, the live Mickey Mouse Club Circus, so popular on the television show, was a flop the first Christmas season; visitors came to ride Dumbo the Flying Elephant—but not to see elephants in a live circus.

Walt Disney also was quick to correct the few mistakes he did make. Noting the popularity of Autopia, where young drivers, usually accompanied by a parent, steered real gasoline-powered, scaled-down sports cars along ribbons of highway, Walt added a Midget Autopia in Fantasyland. But it actually violated his own intent that Disneyland would be a place "where parents and children could have fun— together!" Midget Autopia was accessible to only young children, and after a year it was gone.

The failure of the Mickey Mouse Club Circus did not in any way slow Walt and his entertainment and marketing teams from launching a whole array of special events: Date Night at Disneyland on Saturday summer nights; Big Band Nights featuring the great names of the day (Duke Ellington, Benny Goodman, Count Basie, Bob Crosby and the Bobcats, and more); New Year's Eve parties; and themed parades by the bushel, topped in the early years by the 1959 celebration featuring Meredith Willson leading seventy-six trombones— all playing in unison that famous tune from *The Music Man*.

Two of the most popular were Grad Nite and Dixieland at Disneyland. Grad Nite began as a request from local parent groups for a safe and sane way for their high school graduates to spend the most important night in their young lives. The event was launched in 1961, with 8,000 attending from twenty-eight Los Angeles area schools. The rules were very strict: obviously, no alcohol, tobacco, or drugs; no attendee could drive (only group transportation was allowed, in order to prevent attendees from getting behind the wheel of a car after too much celebrating); a strict dress code (no "revealing" clothes or school-related jackets); and one chaperone for every twenty students from each school. The program has been so popular that the number of graduates attending passed the five million mark in 2009. When Grad Nite celebrated its fiftieth anniversary in 2011, there were seven separate nights from May 12 through June 16, with 1,052 schools participating, and an attendance of 133,000 graduates!

That first year, 1961, is etched strongly in my memory not just because it began an important tradition, but because we convinced *Life* magazine to cover it. Ten of their finest photographers, including legends such as Ralph Crane and Lawrence Schiller, were given the assignment. Altogether *Life* shot 10,000 photos that night, and planned a cover and multiple pages inside for a mid-August edition. Then, on August 13, in one night, the Russians began building the Berlin Wall. The wall won; Grad Nite lost. In fact, many years later, long after *Life* ceased to be published weekly, we tried to buy the photographs for Disneyland's historical records. Time, Inc. refused to sell them, even though they had no plans to ever use any of those 10,000 photos.

Another of my favorite events took place on the Rivers of America in Frontierland from 1960 to 1970. Called Dixieland at Disneyland, it featured some of the greatest jazz musicians in the country: trumpet legends Louis "Satchmo" Armstrong, Al Hirt, and Teddy Buckner, plus New Orleans clarinetist Pete Fountain, banjo player Johnny St. Cyr, and The Young Men from New Orleans (who were all in their eighties or nineties), The Firehouse Five Plus Two, and many more. It began with each group of musicians—six bands in all—floating down the river on separate Frontierland rafts, each playing their special brand of jazz. Then for the finale, all the musicians gathered aboard the Mark Twain Riverboat, performing the classic "When the Saints Go Marching In" while dozens of Disneyland cast members waved sparklers and fireworks exploded overhead. It was a spectacle not even New Orleans and the muddy Mississippi have ever equaled.

My good friend and associate Jack Lindquist, longtime marketing head and later president of Disneyland, described the celebration of the 1962 Dixieland at Disneyland in his book, *In Service to the Mouse*:

> We invited the mayor of Anaheim, the city manager, the city council, various department heads, and some prominent business and social leaders to meet the bands and to celebrate [at the Disneyland Hotel].
>
> The party started at about midnight but remained quiet and staid until one in the morning, when a few musicians started jamming. Then a few more joined in and by two in the morning, the joint was jumping. Everybody knew that at two, the bar would have to shut down and the party would end. But Mark Stephenson, the Anaheim chief of police, proclaimed the event a private party and ruled that as such the bar could remain open. With this last-minute reprieve, the party found new vigor. More musicians, including Nellie Lutcher and Sweet Emma, loaned their voices to what I consider one of the greatest jam sessions ever held outside New Orleans.

At about five in the morning, the curtain fell on the event with Louis Armstrong playing a soft, almost religious rendition of "When the Saints Go Marching In" as the sun rose over the park. I don't think anybody who was there ever forgot that night. I know I haven't.

And neither have I. It was a thrill to be there—even though we had to be at work at 9 A.M. sharp.

* * * * * * * * * *

My boss in those early days of Disneyland was a true icon of the publicity business in Hollywood. Eddie Meck had promoted everything from Frank Capra comedies to Clark Gable and Jimmy Stewart films in the 1930s and 1940s. He could tell you about promotions like the one for *You Can't Take It with You*: "We painted dozens of bricks gold, and set them out on the sidewalks along Hollywood Boulevard. When someone picked up a 'gold brick' and turned it over, they read the copy—'You can't take it with you'!"

There's little doubt that Eddie Meck was the most trusted publicity manager around. One day I accompanied him on his rounds to plant a story at the *Los Angeles Times*. We stopped by the office of the newspaper's publisher, Norman Chandler, only to find that he was in a board of directors meeting. His secretary insisted the publisher would want to know that Eddie was there, and she took a note into the meeting. Almost immediately, Mr. Chandler emerged to apologize to Eddie, and send his regards to Gertrude, Eddie's wife. Another day I stopped by Eddie's office to find him joined in song, via telephone, in a terrible rendition of "Wabash Cannonball." When the ordeal ended, I asked Eddie who was at the other end of the line. His reply: "That was Aggie [Agnes Underwood, city editor of the Los Angeles *Herald-Express*]."

Maybe because of slow weekday attendance, our little public relations team had plenty of time in those early days to poke fun at Eddie Meck's sincere and straightforward ways. I think it started the day Eddie welcomed and threw his arms around Jayne Mansfield, only to discover that Miss Mansfield was still inside the car, and he had greeted her secretary. (*We* were not fooled!)

Our group used every means we could think of to push the new park. The bane of Eddie's newspaper world were the newsboy promotions. Basically, Jack Lindquist's team worked with local newspapers to reward their delivery boys for building circulation, all the while publicizing the trips to Disneyland that the carriers could win. The problem was twofold: first, newspaper staffs often neglected to follow the rules, especially the one about *advance* reservations; and, second, because it involved newspapers and publicity, there was a handoff from Jack to Eddie when it came time for the actual visit to the Magic Kingdom.

One day we just had to have our little fun and games, so we arranged for the security team at the Main Gate to call Eddie and inform him that "Shorty Rogers," the editor, and the carrier boys from the "Martian Evening Star" had arrived. Now Shorty Rogers was actually one of my favorite jazz musicians of the era, and the venerable "Martian Evening Star" had yet to publish its first edition (as far as we knew). Neither their publisher's name nor the title of the "newspaper" rang a bell with Eddie—but not because of the fictional names. For him, it was all about the lack of prearrangements—for this very professional man, they had *sinned* by failing to make advance reservations with his office. As Eddie raced out of our offices in Disneyland's City Hall to confront "Shorty Rogers" and his carrier boys at the Main Gate, we realized that we had gone over the line. Eddie didn't speak to us for days afterward. We never again played our cheap tricks on this wonderful pro, revered by the press as if he, himself, were a Disney character. (The great San Francisco columnist Herb Caen once wrote that Eddie Meck was "no relation to Mecky Mouse.")

Jack Lindquist was to become the quintessential marketing guru for creating promotions in the modern amusement industry (I wasn't around when Barnum was doing his thing). Jack and I were often the instigators of these pranks, and it began early on, when our team was assigned to supervise one of the divisions in the annual Halloween parade in the city of Anaheim. This was no small, or small-town, task. The Halloween Festival Parade had begun as a local tradition in 1924. It had become one of the biggest events in Orange County; in the early years of Disneyland, it would draw as many as 150,000 viewers to see the parade move through Anaheim's downtown streets.

Jack gave his version of our PR staff's participation in the 1956 parade in his book *In Service to the Mouse*. He called it "Halloween Mischief":

> When Disneyland opened, the biggest annual event in town was Anaheim's Halloween Festival, so Disneyland became involved right from the start. This included pumpkin-judging contests, kids' costume contests in school, the traditional night of trick-or-treating, and the Halloween

Festival Parade up Anaheim Boulevard, from Lincoln to La Palma Park. The event also included the Anaheim High School Band, plus bands from other Orange County high schools, color guards, horses, and floats representing local groups, such as Rotary, Kiwanis, Boy Scouts, Girls Scouts, the mayor and the city council, as well as a few floats representing local businesses, and finally, the Jaycees to clean up after the horses. [On a personal note, ours was the 20/30 Club of Fullerton. Their consumption of alcohol easily exceeded the amount of horse droppings they retrieved.] There were four divisions in the parade and my boss, Ed Ettinger, was asked to be a division captain.

About a week before the event, Ed called me into his office and told me he was going to be out of town on business and asked if I would take his place. It wasn't actually a question, so of course, I said yes. He said that there wasn't much to do except to make sure the division was lined up correctly and ready to move in position. I could ask our staff to help. And there was one other thing: division captains rode on the back of new Thunderbird convertibles and dressed in top hats and tails.

First, I assembled my team from my Public Relations division compatriots. Dressed as Indian braves (courtesy of Disneyland wardrobe), my mighty war party consisted of Marty, Lee [Cake], Walter Scott, and Milt Albright, our group sales manager and one of the first employees on the Disneyland payroll. I also prevailed upon wardrobe to provide me with the top hat and tails.

On the night of the parade, we were on the job ready and willing after a quick stop at a local bar to fortify ourselves against the brisk fall night. As I met the other division captains, I noticed that I was the only one dressed in top hat and tails.

Score: one for Ed Ettinger!

Later, he insisted he only did it to make me look good, not to stand out. He thought I should represent Disneyland with class. I never bought his line of bull. I felt like Fred Astaire looking for Ginger.

Anyway, back to the parade where everything went well: my Indian escorts, whooping and hollering all the way, thrilled the kids. I rode in the back of a convertible, waving and saying hi to everybody, though nobody had the slightest idea who I was.

When we finally reached the end, the parade disbanded, and that's when my Indian friends turned on me because they were cold and thirsty. They complained that I got to wear a top hat and tails and ride on a convertible while they had to wear loincloths and headdresses and dance barefoot along the whole parade route. I suggested we all go over to the Disneyland Hotel and discuss the matter civilly.

I drove the motley crew to the hotel in my car, but when we settled in the bar, we made a devastating discovery: the Indians' money, keys, and identification remained in their cars at the park. I only had $20 with me; obviously, our charming little victory party wasn't going to get far. Then, Fred Werther, owner of the Little Gourmet Restaurant at the Disneyland Hotel, came over to our table, and after a few rather snide remarks about the inappropriateness of our dress in a fine dining establishment such as his, he lamented that a small convention group dining in a private room upstairs had booked some entertainment, but the entertainment failed to show up.

"Oh, what to do?" Fred sighed.

"This is your lucky day," I told him.

"Maybe we can help," Marty chimed in, before he looked at me and nodded.

"Fred," I said, "tell your group that in just five minutes Jack Lindquist and his authentic Traveling Troop of Indian Dancers will be ready to perform. Rain dances, chants, magic—the works!"

Fred agreed and thanked us.

"We'll appear," I told him, "but we want five steak dinners before we go on."

While Fred went upstairs to tell the client the "good" news, our little group of parade-performers-turned-night-club entertainers enjoyed a delicious T-bone steak dinner. By 11 P.M., the convention people had become unruly, so Fred finally announced us: "Direct from Oklahoma, the Fantastic Lindquist Indian Show!"

After our introduction, we started out with some soothing chants and dances to mild applause. I then introduced our "famous authentic rain dance." Marty, Lee, Scott, [and] Milt performed magnificently. I half expected it to rain! We performed completely fake Native American dances and chants, all recalled from old Gene Autry and John Wayne films. We jumped around with lots of whooping and hollering. Hearty applause followed the closing number.

Marty then unexpectedly announced that now I, as their Great White Chief, would pull that tablecloth off the head table without upsetting any of the dishes, glasses, or silverware on the table. The audience was silent in anticipation.

Lee, Scott, and Milt grabbed one end of the tablecloth while I held the other end. Marty stood in the middle and started the countdown. A drum started beating faster and faster for the crescendo.

One . . . two . . . three.

I pulled as hard as a I could. Dishes, glasses, wine bottles, entrees, rolls, butter flew in every direction. Guests jumped from their chairs to avoid the mess. We ran out the door, down the stairs, through the kitchen, out the backdoor, to my car, and back to Disneyland.

Then we started to breathe again.

After a few minutes, the Indians got in their cars and drove home. I did the same. A few days later, we ran into Fred. He seemed angry and said that the group had told him they would never come back to the hotel again. Fred complained about the china and glasses that had been broken; the linen napkins, carpeting that had been stained with wine and food; and the broken chair. Then, he got a little grin on his face, his eyes lit up, and he said, "That was sure a better show than if that damned accordionist had shown up."

Jack and I love to recall one of our favorite memories of the late 1950s in Anaheim. From a Santa Ana dealer of questionable ethics, he had purchased a 1947 Cadillac with a special habit: it blew head gaskets on a regular basis. But Jack loved that Cadillac, so he (and we) dealt with it. One day on the way to lunch, Jack drove us up West Street and turned onto Ball Road, when the Cadillac's motor suddenly burst into flames. We jumped out of the car, and someone raced to the corner gas station to alert the fire department.

But before they could place the call, less than a minute after we stopped, we saw Fire Chief Ed Stringer's car across the road; thirty seconds later, Chief of Police Mark Stephenson arrived. One more, and we'd have a quorum for a city staff meeting.

I became so excited that I ran into the orange grove at the closest street intersection to the park. My emergency, unlike Jack's, was that I had to relieve myself. That orange grove was destined for extinction, because the location was so strategic. But when the trees suddenly began to die a few weeks later, Jack credited me.

*　*　*　*　*　*　*　*　*　*

I had two great offices in the late 1950s; one on the second floor of the City Hall, and the other in what is now part of the Guided Tour service. If you veer left when you enter Disneyland (as most people do) and walk under the railroad trestle, the first building you encounter is that small office. When the park opened, two light fixtures at each side of the stairs identified the building as the "Police Station." It was not; it was my office.

Two experiences, both of which were to happen on many occasions, influenced much of my future Disney career—and, I believe, had a key role in communicating to the public about Walt Disney's Magic Kingdom. The first resulted from my mistake: one day I neglected to lock my door that led onto Town Square, allowing several guests to enter the "Police Station." Suddenly, I was confronted by questions about the park that were the province of trained hosts in Disneyland's City Hall. As I pondered the half-dozen questions those early guests asked, it occurred to me that this was a prime source of useful information for those of us charged with making the public aware of what Disneyland was all about. Remember, this was the late 1950s; it wasn't until the big expansion of 1959 that the park's yearly attendance exceeded five million. From that open-door day forward, whenever I was in that Police Station office, my front door was never locked.

Just as important were my ventures to the nearby Main Gate to watch and listen to what guests were asking at the ticket windows. That was the biggest surprise of all. Often the questions went like this: "I want to go on the Jungle Cruise, the Rocket to the Moon, and the Mark Twain Riverboat—*but I don't want to go on any rides!*" What did *that* mean?

As we analyzed these comments, we realized that Walt had done such a great job of telling his television audience about Disneyland that the public had separated its offerings from the old amusement parks of the 1930s, 1940s, and 1950s. In their minds, the whips, shoot-the-chutes, whirl-a-gigs, and lose-your-lunch thrills of those amusement parks were *the rides*—which Disneyland did not have.

Years later, columnist Norma Lee Browning, writing about Epcot in the *Chicago Tribune*, recalled asking Walt about his drive to create new concepts. Walt's response was typical and duly noted by Browning:

"Oh, you sound like my wife," he said, with an impatient gesture and a sip of his early morning coffee. "When I started on Disneyland, she used to say, 'But why do you want to build an amusement park? They're so dirty.' I told her that was just the point—mine wouldn't be."

Disneyland grew out of his disenchantment with

amusement parks he visited on weekend excursions with
his daughters. Most of them, he found, were neither
amusing nor clean, and offered nothing for daddy.

He decided to fix all that by building his own amusement
park, one where daddy could be entertained along with the
kids. That's why Disneyland appeals as much to adults as to
children, as do all Disney cartoons and films, from Mickey
Mouse on. ("You're dead if you aim only for kids. Adults are
only kids grown up, anyway.")

Since I was one of the key publicity writers, and the first editor of the new *Vacationland* tourist magazine we created in 1957, it was on my watch that we invented a new language to describe what you would encounter at Disneyland. The key new terms were *adventures, experiences, attractions,* and of course *stories*. Soon, there was action terminology (Submarine Voyage, Matterhorn Bobsleds) and place-setting names (Haunted Mansion, Pirates of the Caribbean, Splash Mountain, Big Thunder Mountain Railway)—all reflecting the absence of "amusement park rides."

For years—in fact, through the opening of Walt Disney World in 1971—I was the last word on these copy issues for publicity and marketing . . . and my red pen eliminated the word "ride" wherever I found it. The Fantasyland attraction Mr. Toad's Wild Ride survived—until it was replaced at Walt Disney World in 1999 by The Many Adventures of Winnie the Pooh. The "Truth Squad" would say that today there are only four attractions in the eleven Disney parks worldwide that use the word "ride" on the marquee: The Great Movie Ride (Disney's Hollywood Studios—Florida); Listen to the Land Boat Ride (Epcot—Florida; now known as Living with the

Land); Monsters, Inc. Ride & Go Seek! (Tokyo Disneyland); and the original Mr. Toad's Wild Ride at Disneyland.

As recently as 2008, as the word *ride* became an easy crutch for publicity and advertising writers, I wrote a memo to my successors, the leaders of Walt Disney Imagineering: Craig Russell and Bruce Vaughn, and their principal creative advisor, the great storyteller John Lasseter of Pixar. Here's what I said in part:

> When we only *describe our attractions as "rides," we
> fall into the category of Six Flags, Knott's, Universal, etc.
> describing their stuff. We should rise above them
> (because our stuff does!) and describe what we do as
> "attractions, adventures, immersive experiences, and of
> course stories"* . . . *When you are creating Disney Magic,
> the words to describe it should support the magical
> experiences!*

I sent a similar memo to Jay Rasulo, then chairman of Disney Parks and Resorts. He supported my view—but I'm afraid it's a losing battle. With all the shortcuts the digital world has wrought, I imagine I'll still be advocating this concept until the day I ride off into the sunset. Besides, the adventures, attractions, and experiences the Imagineers create today for the parks around the world are so "signature Disney" that they need no other description than: "New!"

* * * * * * * * * *

Three projects from the 1950s and 1960s at Disneyland were personal favorites: first was *Vacationland Magazine*. The publication originated as a way to communicate the Disneyland story, new attractions, hours and days of operation (remember, the park was closed for maintenance on Mondays and Tuesdays until 1985), special events, and other information to tourists visiting California. The *Disneyland News*, even as a tabloid reduced in size from a daily newspaper, was too big and cumbersome. We needed a magazine-sized publication. So in the spring of 1957, we created *Disneyland Holiday*. As editor, my job was to produce the stories, photos, and information content. The strategy developed by our PR division director, Ed Ettinger, and advertising manager, Jack Lindquist, was to determine where and how to distribute it. They decided that the prime outlets would be through hotels and motels within a one-day drive of Disneyland. This meant Santa Barbara to the north, Las Vegas and Phoenix to the east, and San Diego to the south. They hired our own distributor, whose job was not just to deliver magazines, but to become a welcomed visitor to the hotel and motel staffs, many of them mom-and-pop operations in the 1950s.

Over time, we were blessed to employ two people who fit the role perfectly: Frank Forsyth and Bill Schwenn. They were more than distributors—they were traveling salesmen who established friendships with owners and managers who saw that our information was prominently displayed for their guests.

From the beginning, *Disneyland Holiday* was a hit. By the third issue in the spring of 1958, it had grown from twenty to thirty-two pages, and contained not just Disneyland stories and photos of VIP guests (actress Shirley Temple Black, Supreme Court chief justice Earl Warren, Vice President Richard Nixon), but was also full of advertising for other attractions: Knott's Berry Farm, Catalina Island, Apple Valley Inn, even Forest Lawn Memorial Park (a cemetery). We had a major hit on our hands. There was only one problem: *Holiday* magazine threatened a lawsuit if we did not "cease and desist using the name *immediately!*"

Thus, in the fall of 1958, *Vacationland Magazine* was born. Same Disneyland stories and operating information; same publication dates; same publisher, editor, and distributor; and same result: a big hit with tourists and the hotel industry. Today, it has even become a collector's item. If you can find one of those early issues on eBay or Amazon, you will pay handsomely.

My next favorite undertaking came in 1959, a watershed year in the growth and popularity of Disneyland. The fulfillment of Walt's opening-day promise that "Disneyland will never be completed, as long as there is imagination left in the world" had begun, with the most important expansion in the park's history. With one fell swoop, Walt added these iconic attractions:

- The Disneyland Monorail—the first daily operating monorail system in the Western Hemisphere.
- The Submarine Voyage, which allowed people to explore "liquid space" aboard "the eighth largest submarine fleet in the world."
- Two new Autopia Freeways, giving even more young drivers their very first opportunity to drive and steer an individually powered vehicle on a freeway scaled to their size, and simulating a real driving experience.
- Two new motorboat cruises—one of which continued to operate until 1993.
- Matterhorn Mountain, with its two bobsled runs—the first roller coaster in the world to employ tubular steel and an

electronic dispatch system, enabling more than one vehicle to be on the track simultaneously. The Disneyland Skyway attraction had opened three years earlier (and closed in 1994), and carried visitors on an aerial journey right through the Matterhorn. When King Baudouin of Belgium visited Disneyland and rode the bobsleds with the queen and Walt, he asked why the mountain "had holes in it" [for passage through by the Skyway vehicles]. "Because," Walt responded, "it's a Swiss mountain!"

For me, this expansion meant that I got to ghostwrite Walt Disney's message for a twenty-four-page section that appeared as a supplement in the *Los Angeles Times*. The copy was pretty simple and straightforward. He reminded readers about his promise that "there will always be something new and different for you and your family to enjoy." He concluded by stating:

> Since our opening four years ago, Disneyland has played host to millions of Southern California families, as well as additional millions of other Americans and foreign visitors from all over the world. All of us at Disneyland appreciate this privilege, and it is my sincere hope that you will find as much pleasure and enjoyment in Disneyland's new adventures this summer as we had in creating them for you.

I also enjoyed producing a 1965 supplement for the *Los Angeles Times*. Even though I had moved to Imagineering, I continued to handle the most important writing assignments for Disneyland—especially if Walt was involved. These stories were some of the best from my Disney writing days: "The Many Worlds of Disneyland," emphasized that the Magic Kingdom was "many different worlds"; "Daytime Fun—Nighttime Magic" had an opening paragraph that I liked very much: "A popular Disneyland story tells of the Texan watching the Fantasy in the Sky fireworks, and boasting, 'Nice, but we have 'em bigger down home.' And the lady nearby quietly asking, 'Every night?'"

In addition, I wrote two "Walt articles." Under a cover photo of Walt in front of Sleeping Beauty Castle, Walt showed his respect for the public—the fifty million visitors who had already experienced his Magic Kingdom. "This Tencennial Souvenir Edition is really a 'birthday card' in reverse—from all of us at Disneyland to all of you, saying 'thanks' for helping make our first decade so wonderful. We've had a lot of fun playing host to you and your family."

The piece titled "Yesterday, Today, and Tomorrow" described the addition of Great Moments with Mr. Lincoln to the Opera House in Town Square. It ended with these words:

> The way I see it, Disneyland will never be finished. It's something we can keep developing and adding to. A motion picture is different. Once it's wrapped up and sent out for processing, we're through with it. If there are things that could be improved, we can't do anything about them anymore. I've always wanted to work on something alive, something that keeps growing. We've got that in Disneyland.

I've always thought that those lines truly expressed Walt Disney's vision, his restless sprit of creativity, and his enormous pride in what he and his team had already achieved in Disneyland's first decade. It was also a repledging to the public that—as Walt told his Disneyland and Imagineering staffs when celebrating those first ten years: "We're just getting started—so don't any of you start resting on your laurels!"

Disneyland was a much simpler place in those early days, especially for its marketing and operating staffs. As Jack Lindquist has said, "We were willing to try anything, because there were no precedents." If it worked, it became a tradition. If it failed, we dropped it and moved on. And we could test out new ideas. I wrote the first script for Disneyland's Guided Tours, which began in 1962. I also got to be the first tour guide for that tour. That way, I could see what worked, and what needed revision or punching up in the script. The second and third tours were led by Dick Nunis, director of park operations, and by Jack Lindquist. I received plenty of suggestions—which was great, because even before we started charging guests ($3 for adults, $2 for children under twelve), I had input from the "how it functioned" and the "how to sell it" sides of the house.

Practically from the beginning, as one newspaper reported, Disneyland became "almost an instrumentality of American foreign policy." There are great photos of Walt touring Disneyland with Prime Minister Nehru of India, the Shah of Iran, and King Mohammed of Morocco. One visit he missed was with President Suharto of Indonesia. Although the park worked closely with State Department security for all of these visits, somehow the "Western bad man" in Frontierland—who performed fast-draw duels daily with the sheriff using pistols that made a loud noise when blanks were fired—did not get the word about the head of state's visit. When "Black Bart" started to go into his act, and reached for the gun in his holster, he realized just in time that there were at least half a dozen weapons pointed at him—and none of them had blanks.

Distinguished visitors included many national leaders, such as former presidents Eisenhower and Truman and Supreme Court chief justice Earl Warren. I loved the reaction of Harry Truman when the media wanted him to take a ride on Dumbo. "Not me," he insisted, refusing to board the elephant—symbol of the Republican Party.

Even though only part of my head is visible, I treasure a 1959 photo taken of presidential candidate Senator John F. Kennedy emerging from Disneyland's City Hall. He had used one of our offices for a meeting with President Sékou Touré of the African nation of Guinea. Indeed, it was a much simpler time.

* * * * * * * * * *

After that 1965 newspaper supplement came eighteen months of writing for Walt . . . in the company's annual reports, as well as the script for "Walt's Epcot Film." Then in 1966 he was gone. A new world was germinating on the other side of the country, in a place even more pristine and sleepy than Anaheim. As Walt would say in the film about our Project X, "It's the most exciting project we have ever tackled at Walt Disney Productions."

But first on deck was the New York World's Fair, a stepping-stone to that new Walt Disney World yet to be Imagineered.

8

"TWENTY-SIX! YOU'RE YOUNGER THAN MY SON!"

Mott Heath, the Ford Motor Company executive assigned to welcome the Imagineering team to Dearborn, Michigan, did not seem happy. The success of the Ford Pavilion at the 1964–65 New York World's Fair would be a feather in the cap of anyone seeking to promote their company. But mediocrity would stunt anyone's career growth. Ford had already lost one opportunity: the potential partnership between Walt Disney and the Imagineers and architect Minoru Yamasaki, whose Federal Science Pavilion had drawn critical raves at the 1962 Seattle Century 21 World's Fair. But after an initial meeting, Yamasaki determined his building design, and Walt Disney's shows and exhibits, would likely compete rather than complement each other. Yamasaki turned down the commission, leaving Walt and the Imagineers to handle all pavilion design. (Yamasaki would later become famous for another New York design: Towers 1 and 2 of the World Trade Center, which vanished from the New York skyline on 9/11/2001.)

Now, with the arrival of the Disney team, Mott Heath's confidence had been shaken by a member of Walt's entourage—me! I was twenty-six years old—younger than Mott's own son. Perhaps Mott did not know the history of The Walt Disney Company. Walt was only twenty-one when he came to California from Kansas City and convinced his brother Roy to create The Disney Brothers Studio. It may explain why Walt never hesitated to interweave age and experience with youth and exuberance—as he did on that Ford project team.

Our arrival in Dearborn in January 1961 was the beginning of my maturation process. I was assigned to be one of the key storytellers in creating the second largest pavilion at the Fair. Only GM's Futurama (a follow-up to their exhibit at the 1939 World's Fair) was larger, handling 70,000 people per day.

The 1964–65 World's Fair was opened by President Lyndon Johnson on April 22, 1964, and celebrated the three hundredth birthday of the city of New York. Built on the same Flushing Meadows site where the iconic Trylon and Perisphere marked the entry to the 1939 World's Fair, it continued the dream of the Fair's president, Robert Moses—inimitable parks commissioner for the city—to create a permanent park in that location.

The Fair's theme, "Peace Through Understanding," attracted fifty-one million people to its sprawling 646 acres during its two six-month schedules. The optimistic attitude that permeated the Fair's fare—someone called it "an

Olympics for Industry"—was perfect for Walt Disney-style entertainment. In many ways, it reflected the "anything is possible" point of view Walt strived for. At the same time, in retrospect, it was almost the last major fortress of an "age of innocence." Ahead lay the the turbulence of the civil rights movement and the Vietnam War, leading to the decision by President Johnson not to run for reelection, which was followed by the violence at the 1968 Chicago Democratic convention. Even as early as 1964, the opening of the World's Fair was punctuated by demonstrations by CORE, the Congress of Racial Equality, whose leader, James Farmer, was at the forefront of civil rights activism.

* * * * * * * * * *

My teammates on the Ford Pavilion trip were Vic Green, an architect best known for designing the Matterhorn; Jack Sayers, vice president of corporate sponsorships; and John Hench, Disney Legend and designer of park iconography— and much later, my "partner" in the creation of Epcot.

Because Ford, in a push to diversify, was soon to acquire the electronics maker Philco and its aerospace subsidiaries, we were soon en route to Philco's headquarters in Philadelphia; Western Development Labs in Palo Alto, California; and Aeroneutronics (later Ford Aerospace), the satellite designer and builder in Newport Beach, California. The Detroit-to-Philadelphia leg of the trip is etched forever in my memory. Not only was it my first and only ride aboard a DC-3 (a Ford company aircraft ready to retire after years of service in South America), but I have never experienced a more tumultuous flight, as the DC-3 pilots bounced their way through a thunderstorm. It was not a great prelude to our dinner that night at the renowned Bookbinder's Restaurant.

As our Ford traveling companion, John Sattler, said in introducing our team at each stop, it was my job to take copious notes. The purpose of all this barnstorming was twofold. First, we were to learn as much as we could in as short a time possible about the Ford Motor Company. The reason was soon obvious: no one at Ford could simply sit us down and tell us. This period was the aftermath of the changes wrought by the ten so-called "Whiz Kids" who joined Ford after World War II, including Robert McNamara, who served as Ford's president before joining President John F. Kennedy's administration as secretary of defense. The Whiz Kids are credited with bringing modern planning, organization, and management control systems to Ford in the postwar period. But even John Sattler, a real PR pro in Ford's New York City office, could not give us a complete picture of the company; he had never been to most of the places we visited, nor had he met the people we encountered in Dearborn, Philadelphia, Palo Alto, and Newport Beach.

The second objective of our travels to Ford's outposts (I admit that occasionally we wished we could "See the USA in your Chevrolet!") was to provide background for the ideas the Imagineering design staff would develop for the Ford Pavilion. In that sense, it was a very productive trip for these reasons:

- We were told that Ford wanted to present an international image. Our solution: all guests entering the pavilion passed through an area where Ford cars were displayed in settings of miniature villages from around the world. It was inspired by the small-scale Pinocchio's Village and other exquisite models, based on Disney films, in the Storybook Land canal boat trip at Disneyland.

- Ford wanted the pavilion to create "a bridge from yesterday to tomorrow." Walt's belief in the use of nostalgia for a once-treasured past, as a way to engage an audience, led us to Henry Ford's Model T, which of course had revolutionized automaking in the early part of the twentieth century. Using the "Pepper's Ghost" technique displayed later for Disneyland's Haunted Mansion ballroom scene, our special effects whiz Yale Gracey depicted an infinity of Model T's as guests were carried past on a moving ramp. You could almost count every Model T that ever came off the assembly line.

- The assembly line—or rather all the parts that come together to form a car—inspired Rolly Crump to design the Ford Parts Orchestra. He used stylized hubcaps, crankshafts, pistons, windshield wipers, and other car parts to create an animated "orchestra" that played music specially arranged by Disney composer George Bruns.

- The true stars of the show were the Ford, Lincoln, and Mercury automobiles. In his continuous quest to move people in our parks more efficiently, Walt had been developing, with the mechanical talents of Roger Broggie and Bob Gurr, a transit system in which there were no moving parts on the vehicles. The so-called WEDWay Transit System propelled its vehicles along a prescribed guideway by using one-half to one-horsepower drive motors set three to four feet apart in the elevated guideway. The rubber wheels ran continuously, and as they rotated, they engaged a flat metal "platen" on the underside of each vehicle, thus propelling the vehicle along the guided surface. This system, introduced as the WEDWay

PeopleMover in Disneyland in 1967, became the power source for moving cars through Ford's eight-minute Magic Skyway. For this ride, moving at an average of 4.5 miles per hour, I recorded Walt's voice describing the cavemen, dinosaurs, and City of Tomorrow that people were viewing.

The WEDWay system accomplished a brilliant marketing one-upsmanship for Ford. While its rival, General Motors, sat its Futurama visitors in a chair-ride, three abreast, Ford's pavilion guests rode in a real automobile. The cars were kept spick-and-span in an area between the embarkation and debarkation areas (in theme park terms, between the "load" and "unload" areas), where each was vacuumed and wiped clean between pass-throughs. Only convertibles were used in order to speed up entry and exit and avoid banging heads on rooftops. During the Fair's two, six-month seasons, almost fifteen million people rode in 178 Ford automobiles, many experiencing a Ford product for the very first time. During the first year alone, Ford estimated the cars had traveled the equivalent of thirty-four times around the world.

But there was an even greater exposure for Ford's cars. John Hench designed a marquee featuring two elevated, glass-enclosed tubes that carried the cars outside in opposite directions, sweeping across the exterior of the pavilion and thus exposing all the Ford automobile styles to a huge area of the fairgrounds. Even if they did not enter the pavilion, World's Fair guests saw Ford cars showcased just by walking by. They watched the convertibles emerge from the pavilion inside two glass tubes above the entrance, glide in opposite directions before reentering the building and disappearing back inside. Fair audiences had been introduced to one of Walt Disney's favorite, and most effective, visual concepts: the wienie.

I learned so much from this experience, especially from the opportunity to travel with, observe, and listen to John Hench. We had some amazing adventures. One day, we were riding with the Ford test track drivers on a banked track in Romeo, Michigan, at 120 miles per hour. Suddenly our driver took his hands off the wheel and turned around to talk to us in the backseat. Scary! At that speed and with the angle of the track, the car held steady and "drove itself." Another interesting moment occurred when we visited Ford's "Advanced Styling" unit. When we found two designers working on reversible seat cushions, John asked them if either one had any inkling if the public was interested in this feature. "No," both designers responded. "Then why," John inquired, "are you doing it?" "Because we like it," they said. "Well," John pursued, "has anyone ever tried this before?" "Oh, yes," the designers answered. "It was on the last Packard ever built!"

Before it was destroyed by fire in 1962, the Ford Rotunda visitor's center in Dearborn was a major tourist attraction the fifth most popular in the United States in the early 1950s. (Niagara Falls was number one, before Disneyland.) The Rotunda was originally designed by famed architect Albert Kahn for the Chicago "Century of Progress" World's Fair in 1933, then disassembled after that Fair and moved to Dearborn, where it was seen by some eighteen million people.

Typically, a visit to the exhibits and demonstrations included a trip through the River Rouge assembly plant. It was located so close to the Rouge River that at one time, iron ore was shipped in by barge, turned into steel in the plant, and ultimately emerged as a finished car. The only problem was that when we observed some of the 1961 action along the assembly line we noticed parts that did not fit and assembly workers using crowbars to force the closure of doors; there were even cars pushed off the line at the end because they would not start. John Hench made a recommendation that chilled our Ford hosts: "Never show another potential customer your River Rouge assembly line." "But we host a million people every year," they protested. "Well," John countered, "I can't imagine they will buy a Ford car when they see how they are built!"

The four pavilions that Walt and the Imagineers helped create—along with GM's Futurama and the Vatican Pavilion, which displayed Michelangelo's *Pietà*—were all in the Top Ten favorites at the 1964–65 New York World's Fair. While I spent most of my time working on the Ford Pavilion, I also had assignments on two of the other Disney projects. Walt was so proud of the work of the Imagineers' creation for UNICEF, "it's a small world," that he asked me to compose a twenty-eight-page booklet saluting their accomplishment. It was called *Walt Disney's "it's a small world"—Complete Souvenir Guide and Behind the Scenes Story*. It turned out so well that it was sold at the Pepsi-Cola–sponsored pavilion. The photo of Walt surrounded by the small world "dolls"—taken by the great *Look* magazine photographer Earl Theisen for its cover—is still one of my all-time favorites.

In writing the souvenir booklet, I developed several key phrases that have identified the show in five international Disney parks: *Join the happiest cruise that ever sailed around the world . . . A Magic Kingdom of all the world's children.* The iconic graphic depicting a boatload of children of many cultures and colors, flying the colorful flags of various nations, was created by graphics designer Paul Hartley to accompany Walt's introductory message in the souvenir guide. Even today, a blowup of this graphic stands at the entry to every version of this uplifting show.

My second major responsibility for the World's Fair resulted in lifelong friendships with several wonderful people from GE spanning the three-decade connection between the companies. One was Dave Burke, a marketing and PR executive who represented GE's corporate staff in relations with Disney. Another was Ned Landon, the spokesman for the GE scientific community, specifically the GE Labs in Schenectady, New York.

My assignments included several shows within a big GE pavilion called Progressland. It featured Walt Disney's Carousel of Progress show that was one of the most popular attractions at the Fair. The pavilion also included Progressland, a whole "community" of experiences for visitors.

The pavilion ended with a bang—literally. It was Ned Landon's assignment to work with GE's scientists to create an actual demonstration of nuclear fusion—diminished, of course, so that it could harm no one—but real, nonetheless. John Hench insisted that every "bang" had to be measured and recorded, on the off-chance that a guest would claim injury from the minuscule radiation. He was right: there were nuisance lawsuits, but the data proved that the demonstration was completely harmless. And Ned Landon celebrated his ninetieth birthday before his passing in 2011.

My job was to work with designer Claude Coats and

special effects expert Yale Gracey to create the setup for the demonstration. It was simply called "The Dome Show" because it was projected on the interior ceiling of the pavilion. We introduced audiences to the power of the sun, as a lead-in to the actual creation of "sun power" in Ned Landon's demonstration.

In retrospect, the other show I wrote (and rewrote, and rewrote) for Progressland epitomized the frustration we often experience in working with corporate sponsors. Progressland was designed like a main street in a community, with storefronts and small interior spaces that offered boutique presentations. My assignment was to tell a story about atomic energy utilizing a talking toucan—brought to life by Disney's patented three-dimensional animation system, Audio-Animatronics. My frustration finally boiled over when I had written eight scripts, all rejected by GE, and was about to launch into number nine. Who is the audience for this show? I demanded of the GE liaison, after he objected to most of what would interest the general fairgoer. His answer stopped me cold. "Four people," he admitted. "My boss, his boss, the VP my boss reports to, and the executive VP who heads our division." Fortunately, not many visitors to Progressland stopped by to sample our "atomic boutique." (I understand the executive VP was very pleased with the exhibit.)

One of the lessons I learned in our creative work for the World's Fair was never to underestimate the talents of my Disney associates. To ensure the success of the four Disney experiences, Walt called on the whole company—not just the Imagineers, but also Studio writers like Larry Clemmons (Carousel of Progress) and James Algar (Great Moments with

Mr. Lincoln); songwriters Bob and Dick Sherman ("it's a small world" and "There's a Great Big Beautiful Tomorrow" for the Carousel of Progress); operations staff from Disneyland under Dick Nunis's direction to run the "it's a small world" Pavilion; and many sound, projection, lighting, and electronics personnel.

One of my early assignments resulted from a call from Walt. I had written and recorded a twenty-minute slide presentation that we used to give Henry Ford II and other Ford executives an idea of the scope of the pavilion, with emphasis on the ride attraction—"the wienie," as Walt called it, the "beckoning finger" that says "come this way!"—a technique the Imagineers use at key junctions throughout the Disney parks. Walt wanted George Bruns to write the music and called to request that I run the presentation for George.

I was thrilled, as George Bruns was a king of Disney music composition. His "Davy Crockett, King of the Wild Frontier," sung of course by "Davy" himself (the aforementioned Fess Parker) had helped fuel the national craze for the TV show and coonskin caps in the mid-1950s. When George arrived at WED, we sat down in a small conference room I explained to George, who was a hefty man, that the narration was recorded, but I had to punch up the slide film visuals. And so we began.

After five minutes, a sound like logs being sawed in half filled the conference room. George was fast asleep, and snoring like a "b'ar"! What to do? There was no sense in continuing to run the presentation; I already knew it by heart. So I woke him up, and asked, "Anything else you need so you can write the score, George?" "Nope," he answered, "I'm all set." And in fact, he was. The piece he composed and conducted for the Magic Skyway ride was easily one of the musical highlights of the whole Fair.

Walt's objectives in devoting his, and his creative staff's, energies to the World's Fair in the early 1960s are, in retrospect, quite clear. First, he wanted to show that the kind of entertainment he had been creating for Disneyland for almost ten years would play anywhere—especially in New York City. Thus, the Fair truly was a stepping-stone from west to east; from Anaheim, California, to Orlando, Florida. Second, he wanted to expand Disneyland, and in one form or another, the four Disney-designed Fair attractions were reincarnated in Anaheim.

In fact, Walt's vision for using a temporary event as a testing ground for permanent attractions proved to be a stroke of genius. Three technologies that would play key roles in the future growth of Disney parks around the world were introduced, or took a giant leap forward, at the New York World's Fair:

- **Audio-Animatronics:** Disney had never created a "human figure" for one of its shows until it presented Great Moments with Mr. Lincoln for the state of Illinois; the families of GE's Carousel of Progress; and the cavemen in Ford's Magic Skyway attraction.
- **Ride Capacity:** The boat ride in "it's a small world" and the Carousel of Progress rotating theater each generated theoretical capacities of over three thousand people per hour—almost double the largest previous capacities for an attraction in a Disneyland.
- **Transportation:** The WEDway PeopleMover technology used to transport Ford cars at its pavilion became an attraction

in Disneyland and, later, the Magic Kingdom at Walt Disney World. As a "real-world" transportation system, it was installed in 1981 at the Houston (now George Bush) Intercontinental Airport, transporting travelers between terminals.

Undoubtedly, the strongest statement about Walt's dedication to growing his theme park relates to the "name fee" that WED Enterprises charged for using Walt Disney's name during the course of the Fair. The fee was set at $1 million, to be paid by GE and Ford. It would be considered a down payment for sponsorship participation in the future. GE chose to continue; Ford declined.

It wasn't a matter of money for Walt Disney—it was a matter of *commitment*. If you were with him, you were "family." If you chose a different course, you could buy your own ticket to get into Disneyland.

* * * * * * * * * *

The New York World's Fair was a watershed in many ways for the Imagineers. When we began work on the pavilions in 1960–61, there were only one hundred Imagineers. Over the years, I have been told many times by creative designers and engineers that their visit to the World's Fair as a kid set the course for their future. That "sensory overload" visitors experienced became the dream that triggered many a career for youngsters like Tom Fitzgerald, now executive vice president, senior creative executive for Imagineering.

Tom's family lived in Briarcliff Manor, a small town about an hour from the Fair in Westchester County, New York. They visited the Fair several times, the first being when Tom was eight years old. "When I saw the Disney shows, it was a huge revelation to me," Tom recalls. "They were so unique . . . The art direction, the sets, the Audio-Animatronics figures, the music, the actors that voiced it all, and the wizardry of moving audiences in cars, on boats, and rotating theaters—who else but Disney could do that to the level that Walt did?

"We saw all four of the Disney shows . . . GE Progressland was pure magic! And I loved *small world*—the color, the animation, the song, the wonderful boat," adds Fitzgerald. "My grandparents had given me a silver dollar, and I used it to buy the 45 record from the show. I played it over and over.

"That Fair," says Fitzgerald, "was what convinced me I wanted to be a part of the Disney team."

Those of us taking the red-eye flights from Los Angeles to New York and back carried such a quantity of construction drawings, props, audiotapes, and so much more that today, we would not be able to pass through security. WED leased apartments in the new LeFrak City alongside the Long Island Expressway. Don Edgren, whose engineering career at Disney had begun as a consultant in the early days of Disneyland, was our resident-in-chief; Don spent three years in New York as the Disney rep, interfacing with the contractors on the Ford and GE pavilions and managing construction of the "it's a small world" building. Many of us would make our appearances at midnight or seven in the morning after a red-eye flight, find the room we had been assigned to, and pass our friends heading out to work at the site as we arrived.

Once I arrived about 1:00 A.M. and tumbled into the sack. I had been told that the silver-headed Vic Green would be my roommate in the second bed. That morning I was up bright and early. Having shaved and showered, I knew that Vic was going to be late if I didn't act, so I shook him awake. "Vic—wake up! We're going to be late!" The gray-domed person in "Vic's bed" rolled over, looked me in the eye, and said: "I'm not Vic Green, and I'm not going to work this morning!"

I also quickly became educated about dealing with the unions in New York in the 1960s. Working with an electrician in the far reaches of the ride area at the Ford Pavilion, where the show's dinosaurs roamed, I was setting sound levels when the electrician announced that he needed some piece of equipment, and would "be back in ten minutes." I became very familiar with the roaring of Tyrannosaurus Rex during the next two hours, while I waited for the electrician to return.

Compounding the issues we faced were short construction time frames, causing the overlap of tasks and trades. For me, the problem came to a head a few weeks before the Fair's opening, concerning the installation of the Ford ride's narration. It was the first year of the Fair; I had written and recorded a narrator with a spiel somewhat similar to the one Walt would record for year two. The challenge had been writing dialogue for the theoretical timing of each scene. What I really needed was the opportunity to ride through the show—not once, but over and over again. I still had time to revise the length of each scene's piece by rerecording based on actual timing.

Unfortunately, running the vehicles through the pavilion was one of the true challenges of the Ford Pavilion. Running the ride meant stopping the work of not only my favorite electrician, but also painters, iron workers, welders, engineers, laborers, and clean-up workers. As much as riding in those

Ford cars was the key to Ford's success and popularity with Fair visitors, the narrative storytelling was the tail wagging the dog.

Finally, there was no more flex time in our schedule: I had to do my tests, or there would be no audio emanating from the car radios. I had been promised "ride time," and arrived in New York Sunday evening for an early start Monday morning. But Monday passed with no ride movement, as did Tuesday and Wednesday. On Thursday, at last the vehicles moved—in fits and starts, but never a complete cycle. Desperate, I appealed to Don Edgren, who promised, and delivered, several complete cycles of the track by early Friday afternoon.

My helper was a talented young member of the Audio-Animatronics installation team. Although only in his early twenties, Jim Verity was a third-generation Disney employee—his father and grandfather had worked at the Studio. As we circled the track, I sat in a car with my tape recorder, playing the narration. Jim's job was to walk rapidly alongside the auto, holding a can of black spray-paint; my signal told him where to spray a mark along the unpainted cement walkway, parallel to the track. At each mark, a mechanism would be installed later, triggering the start of the recording for each scene.

You can imagine the satisfaction I felt at midafternoon that Friday. Now I could catch my 7:00 P.M. flight to Los Angeles, pleased that finally I could record a narration track that would turn on and off precisely where I wanted it to.

I said my good-byes to Don Edgren, and as a last check before departing for the airport, asked Jim Verity to accompany me on a walk around the ride track. It took only moments to discover what the next trade group had accomplished in meeting *their* schedule after we had completed our job: they had painted the entire walkway black! Not one of my markings was visible; my entire week in New York had been painted out.

I missed my flight home that evening. It was a very wet night in New York, and I don't mean rain.

One day Walt came to inspect our progress, and designer Claude Coats, special effects wizard Yale Gracey, and I drove him back to his hotel. The conversation turned to our New York experiences, and Walt asked how our spouses were enjoying the city. No one responded. "Oh, I get it," Walt said. Walt knew that we were all family men and women and that we'd been away from home for some time. The next morning, before we had even left for the fairgrounds, each one of us received a call from WED's finance staff with one question: "When do you want your spouse to arrive?"

For Walt, the most difficult event occurred at the State of Illinois Pavilion, where Great Moments with Mr. Lincoln brought the immortal words of our sixteenth president (and Illinois' favorite son) to audiences a century after they were first spoken. Writer/producer James Algar of the Studio had combined lines from six different Lincoln speeches into one potent short message, and a team led by designer Marc Davis, sculptor Blaine Gibson, mechanical craftsmen Roger Broggie and Bob Gurr, and programmer/animator Wathel Rogers had breathed mechanical life into the amazing figure. The only problem was that on opening day, the president refused to utter a word or move a muscle, disappointing the governor, the state's United States senators, a packed theater audience, the media, and of course Robert Moses, who had sold the concept of an Audio-Animatronics Lincoln to the state of Illinois. It wasn't until several days later that Honest Abe was ready to talk. Walt, unfortunately, was forced to explain why "the winkin' blinkin' Lincoln" could not perform.

For the Imagineers, another depressing event was Walt's review of GE's Carousel of Progress. It was a late morning walk-through—just Walt and the Imagineers—but it was in preparation for an early evening event that same day: a preview Walt was hosting for the GE board of directors. The show lasted only a few moments; *nothing* worked—no Father upset that Cousin Orville had taken over the family bathtub; no dog barking in each of the four main acts; no Sherman brothers' "Great Big Beautiful Tomorrow" song. Walt was clearly irritated; he wanted to see and discuss each act with the key Imagineers, and potentially tweak the show, before his guests arrived five or six hours later. And what if nothing worked *then*?

When the GE directors assembled that evening, Walt gave a lighthearted disclaimer, making clear that the show was still in test mode, and "anything can happen" . . . or not happen. The show began with actor Rex Allen's Western twang words: "Welcome to the General Electric Carousel of Progress. Now most carousels go round and round without getting anyplace, but on this one, at every turn, we'll be making progress." And they did: every animation cue, every line, every lighting nuance—was perfect. It was the carousel's moment to spin and shine, and it did. The board of directors was so pleased that Walt could have been elected the next CEO, right then and there.

For me, the Ford Pavilion created so many special memories. As part of our behind–the-process tour, I had sat in while Ford's advertising agency pitched the launch campaign for the original Mustang to the vice president of the car and truck group, Lee Iacocca. It was all advance preparation for the gala introduction of the Mustang at the Fair, just outside the entrance to the Ford Pavilion. The Mustang was an instant success, and so was its sales and marketing chief. Lee Iacocca was on his way to becoming president of Ford, from 1970 to 1978. (When Henry Ford II fired him in 1978, Iacocca became CEO of Chrysler.)

I like making Top Ten lists, and the New York World's Fair provided grand memories to rate. Aside from the four Disney shows, here's my list:

1. The film in the Johnson's Wax Pavilion. Francis Thompson's *To Be Alive* was an inspiring tour of life and people living it to the fullest around the world.

2. The DuPont Pavilion. You walked into a chemistry laboratory where all the beakers and burners were giant size—wow!—and a live jazz band played during the "experiments." And then the film story unfolded, with live actors handing flowers to celluloid actors—as though they were both right there in front of you. It was pure magic.

3. The Vatican Pavilion. The prime attraction was the *Pietà*, an incredible loan to the Fair from Pope John XXIII. But for this non-Catholic, there were two other special treats: the marvelously designed, religious-themed banners by French-Canadian artist Norman Laliberté; and the miniature dimensional scenes, the Nativity, and much more, created by Los Angeles artist Sister Mary Corita.

4. The IBM pavilion, shaped like a giant egg with it's "People Wall" (a tiered grandstand holding five hundred people that ascended hydraulically into the heart of the sphere to start each show). It was the design inspiration of Charles and Rae Eames and the architectural firm Eero Saarinen Associates.

5. GM's Futurama II. The $38 million (in 1960s dollars!) lavished on this show was extravagant—and made for a beautifully executed show.

6. The Zulu dancers, recruited from Africa to perform their amazing dances.

7. Introduction of the Mustang. The car is still a classic, and to be there when it was unveiled was incredibly exciting.

8. The Unisphere, symbol of the "Peace Through Understanding" world theme. One of its design and construction impresarios was Harper Goff, designer of the original Adventureland Jungle Cruise at Disneyland, and later my good friend, a Disney Legend, and, more than anyone, responsible for the look and layout of Epcot's international area, the World Showcase.

9. The Bell System's "Picturephone," demonstrated throughout the day in calls back and forth from Flushing Meadows to Disneyland!

10. And the Fair's "most popular experience"—eating a Belgian waffle! Originally introduced at Expo '58 in Brussels, it became the mouthwatering favorite of visitors in Flushing Meadows. How could you go wrong with a waffle smothered in whipped cream and strawberries?

9

THEY LEFT ME BEHIND— AND WENT HOME!

In 1967, the year after Walt Disney's death, it often seemed as though the company was literally dead in the water. Unfortunately, the water in the Disney-owned Florida swampland seemed the most stagnant. In fact, there was a serious question about whether Disney would actually move ahead with the development of the big piece of property, "twice the size of Manhattan Island." Walt Disney World, or Project X, was not yet three years old at the time of Walt's death if you counted from the initial land acquisition.

While he was alive, Walt had made it abundantly clear that WED (Walter Elias Disney) Imagineering, despite the fact that it was no longer his personal family company, was still his personal "laughing place." It was where creative development for Project X happened. The executives at the Disney Studio got it, and stayed away to give Walt his space. Although it was only three miles from their offices in Burbank, Roy Disney had visited WED's building at 1401 Flower Street in Glendale *once*; Card Walker and Donn Tatum had *never* been inside Imagineering's headquarters at the time of Walt's death.

To the credit of Dick Irvine, John Hench, and Joe Fowler (vice president and general manager of Disneyland Park, but soon to become chairman of Imagineering), their almost-daily lunches at the Studio with the corporate executives throughout the early months of 1967 paid dividends. In these meetings, they worked their sales magic to get Project X off the ground. Early in the summer, major earth-moving work began leading to a dirt road running east to west across the northern part of the Florida property to a one hundred-acre clearing where the Magic Kingdom would be built; and the first drainage canals began, ultimately to funnel rainwater to the two natural waterways, Reedy Creek and Bonnet Creek, on opposite sides of the site.

Although many of us, not fully understanding what was occurring in those Studio lunchtime discussions, had expressed our frustration to Dick Irvine about the lack of progress, we were all excited about the new attractions opening and in the works for Disneyland. Pirates of the Caribbean and The Haunted Mansion were destined to become the new standards for our industry—and to affect the planning for Walt Disney World as well.

In the film I wrote for Walt that was shown for the first time in Florida early in 1967, we referenced Disneyland's attendance—6.7 million in 1965–66. That number was the basis for Imagineering's early planning of the Magic Kingdom at Walt Disney World. But sparked by the popularity of

Pirates and Haunted Mansion, Disneyland's attendance had increased to over nine million by 1971. The dilemma for the Disney planners and designers was to commit to construction of attractions and facilities with no attendance track record; an infrastructure originally based on that six million attendance figure—the equivalent of Disneyland when our planning began; and expenditures that threatened to break even the Practical Pig's piggy bank—and certainly Disney's.

Another issue complicated the planning questions: Disney had never built or owned a hotel. Walt's friend and neighbor Welton Becket was called on again. Becket's architectural firm had designed such Hollywood landmarks as the Cinerama Dome and the Capitol Records building, and was well under way on the Dorothy Chandler Pavilion in downtown Los Angeles. This time, Becket said "yes" to a Disney project.

Dick Irvine phoned me one day to announce that I was to be included in what would become one of the most important trips concerning the initial development of the Florida property. Boarding the company Gulfstream I in Burbank early in October 1967 were Irvine, chief of design at WED, and three of WED's key designers and master planners—Marvin Davis, Bill Martin, and John Hench. Also on board were Card Walker, Disney corporate vice president, then responsible for marketing and communications; Dick Nunis, who was in charge of Disneyland operations and, soon, both Disneyland and Walt Disney World; Welton Becket and two of his senior architects; and "the two Joes": retired admiral Joseph W. Fowler, chairman of the Disneyland operating committee, and William E. ("Joe") Potter, a retired general hired from Robert Moses's staff at the World's Fair to head Disney's Florida staff. (Once, in New York, watching Fowler and Potter carry presentation boards to a meeting at GE, Walt marveled that an admiral and a general were "privates" following his marching orders.)

Our itinerary was reflective of the planning and design work still to be done. We stopped in Atlanta to see a new John Portman-designed hotel; visited new resorts in Miami and on Grand Bahama Island; and then headed for Orlando. This was the first trip to Florida for this group since Walt's death in December 1966, and my first ever. On the Walt Disney World site, we caught up with Bill Evans, the company's master landscaper. Bill, who had already established the first tree farm north of the Magic Kingdom site, would soon begin teaching us about Florida flora and fauna ("No, Mr. Becket, we can't grow *that* kind of palm around the Polynesian!"). And that was only one of *many* discussions that would change my weekend plans.

The photo of Dick Irvine, Welton Becket, and me standing on a big yellow "X" in the middle of a one hundred-acre clearing still exists. This was the scraped site for the Magic Kingdom, and the yellow "X" marked the location where the castle would be built. We all agreed on that, but there were so many other disagreements that a quick decision was made: I would be left behind with a photographer to map the property from the air and to provide accurate research for the planners of the hotels, campground, parking lots, roads, and other Phase One developments.

So here's my three-day-weekend itinerary for late October 1967: we rented two helicopters—a big, empty military transport, and a three-passenger Bell job. Photographer Carl Frith took movie footage from the big helicopter and stills from the little chopper—often as I held the belt around his waist while he leaned out "for a better shot."

The film and the still photos are an amazing record of the property as it was "before Disney" (there was only one built road, the dirt pathway that became Vista Boulevard). The pictures also became the early planning tool for so much that has become "The Vacation Kingdom of the World," as I defined it for our early marketing materials. Every October, I make a point to look at that photo of the yellow "X" and blink. Forty years later, on a peak day, there are over 300,000 people on the Walt Disney World property—more than the population of the entire Orlando area in 1967!

As I recall that weekend, I have no regrets that I was left behind to oversee filming of the site. And I think that the Magic Kingdom's millions and millions of guests would agree.

* * * * * * * * * *

Although we arrived in Orlando on the Disney Gulfstream and landed our private aircraft at the small Herndon Airport, Carl Frith and I soon learned that commercial flights to McCoy Field—primarily a military operation in 1967—were almost nonexistent. When we departed from McCoy, we discovered the numbers: four airlines serviced Orlando, with seven flights per day. For a presentation I made some forty years later, I received these numbers from the Orlando International Airport for the twelve months beginning April 1, 2011:

- Annual Passengers: 35,500,000
- Daily Passengers: 95,205
- Annual Flights: 309,000
- Daily Flights: 846
- International Passengers (2009): 2,977,920

In her 1966 interview with Walt for the *Chicago Tribune*, Norma Lee Browning asked why he chose Florida, and especially Orlando, for Walt Disney World. "Florida and Southern California are the only two places where you can count on the tourists," Walt replied. "I don't like ocean sites because of the beach crowd, and also the ocean limits the approach. If you'll notice Disneyland at Anaheim is like a hub with freeways converging on it from all sides. I like it better inland. That's why we chose Orlando."

The search had actually begun in the early 1960s. In his book, *Walt's Revolution*, Buzz Price wrote:

> In 1961, after rejecting some other alternatives, Walt asked us to look at the rest of Florida and figure out where the park should be. Late in 1963, we studied in depth a location in Central Florida. The key conclusion was that Central Florida (not Miami as most people expected it would be) was the main point of maximum interception of Florida tourism, and that Orlando, centrally located, was the point of maximum access to the southerly flow of Florida tourism from both the east and west shores of the state.

There were many challenges that had to be overcome long before the first guest was welcomed on October 1, 1971. Central Florida in the early 1960s was still the "Deep South." As our various staffs began traveling to the area early in 1964 (negotiations for the property began in April), they found many vestiges of the old ways. You didn't drive far from the Walt Disney World site before you found WHITE ONLY entrances to a restaurant, or separate restrooms and drinking fountains for African Americans and Caucasians. In my view, helping to make Central Florida "color blind," and create employment opportunities for African Americans and Latinos, especially, is one of the most significant contributions Walt Disney World has made as a good citizen of the state of Florida. (In addition, the company's financial support and cast members' volunteerism undoubtedly has no equal in the Orlando area and the entire state.)

That first trip to Central Florida was chock-full of new experiences for me. Arrangements had been made to take us by boat into the deepest, darkest part of the Reedy Creek swamp, about ten miles from the site of the Magic Kingdom. Watching all the gators sunning themselves on the shore, and diving into the waters as the boat's noise stirred them awake, was a chill as well as a thrill.

From a rickety wooden dock near the site of today's Contemporary Resort, we were taken by speedboat to Riles Island in the middle of Bay Lake, where we saw our first armadillos. We also came across a shack used by illegal poachers during hunting expeditions for deer, wild boar, and wild turkey.

Of course the land was often very wet. To me, this could be quite spectacular, especially as I looked down from the helicopters on the cypress trees standing offshore in Bay Lake, entirely surrounded by water. Yet the engineers, with their soil borings, were finding all the challenges of building in wetlands. Near that yellow "X" in the middle of the Magic Kingdom-to-be, John Hench dug a hole about one foot deep. When we returned the next morning, the hole was filled with water—a visual demonstration that impressed all of us desert-dwelling Californians.

Almost immediately, the WED designers began to wield their influence:

- The Corps of Engineers had dug fifty yards or so of the first wide drainage canal, following the basic premise that a straight line is the most direct path—perhaps related to retired Major General Potter's six years as governor general of the Panama Canal Zone. John Hench reacted immediately, calling for the visual look of a natural river. He drew an overlay on the plans, creating a curving channel that looked on paper like a slithering snake.

- Bill Martin, who was to become the overall art director for the Magic Kingdom, suggested the key idea for dealing with the wetlands between the Transportation and Ticket Center and the Magic Kingdom: create a "lake," later named the Seven Seas Lagoon, and use the earthen material removed as fill to raise the level of the Magic Kingdom by fourteen feet. Creating higher ground for the park not only made the Magic Kingdom an iconic visual destination, it also enabled one of Walt's Epcot ideas: the creation of "Utilidors" under the Magic Kingdom. These twelve-foot-wide, ten-foot-high corridors became the location for underground utilities, and the opportunity for an amazing backstage staging area, housing a plethora of cast member services and facilities: costuming, cafeterias, maintenance, and audiovisual and other electronics.

- Bill Evans, one of the most respected landscape authorities in the country after his pioneering accomplishments at Disneyland, had already established a tree farm when we arrived that October. He was experimenting with a variety of tree and plant materials not native to Florida, including California redwoods (which did not thrive) and several varieties of eucalyptus. "There are over five hundred varieties of eucalyptus in Australia," Bill lectured us. "We should be

124

able to find some that do well here." And he did, for use as windbreaks and background screening.

- The "two Joes," Fowler and Potter, responded to a major challenge concerning the water quality of Bay Lake, which was to become the site of the Contemporary Resort. The issue was that all those beautiful cypress tree roots, on and off the Walt Disney World property, stained the water a dark brown. The solution: drain the entire lake and control the water running into it. A bonus that resulted was the discovery, at the bottom of the drained lake, of the sugar-white sand that now lines the beautiful beaches at the Contemporary Resort and around Bay Lake. Like so much of Florida, the ocean had receded from this land eons ago, leaving its hidden treasures.

Even though we were initially dealing with only a fraction of the 27,400 acres Disney originally acquired (for $5.5 million, about $200 per acre), this area alone was almost five times the size of Disneyland. Nearly all of it was flat—after all, the highest point in the whole state of Florida, in Walton County, is only 345 feet above sea level. With nothing on the land, distances were hard to estimate, and the relationships of objects, that is structures, were very difficult to judge.

On two different occasions, to aid the designers, helium-filled balloons were raised at key locations around the Magic Kingdom. They marked the entrance to the park, the castle, the Contemporary and Polynesian resorts, and the Transportation and Ticket Center (TTC). At that spot, where guests would park their cars and board Disney transit systems—monorails, ferryboats, and trams—the designers and Disney executives could be elevated twenty feet in major construction equipment in order to appraise the visual distance between major attractions. Getting this bird's-eye view was extremely informative—and often discouraging, as the distances between locations made it appear impossible to forge connections.

The challenges became obvious. For example, Disneyland's Sleeping Beauty Castle, seventy-seven feet tall, would totally disappear when viewed from one mile away—the distance from the Transportation and Ticket Center to the castle. The solution: design a castle reaching skyward 189 feet, just short of the two-hundred-foot height that requires a red light to warn aircraft of a tall object.

* * * * * * * * * *

As WED began planning for the site, it was interesting to read some of the early speculation about the mystery purchasers of that huge tract of land. Under the page one banner headline, "Giant Land Deal Near Orlando Revealed," the May 27, 1965, issue of the *Miami Herald* covered the rumors in a story by staff writer Clarence Jones:

> *A Miami law firm working with $5 million in cold cash has quietly engineered one of the biggest, most-talked-about Florida land deals in years.*
>
> *Twelve miles southwest of Orlando, the firm has bought 30,000 acres of strategically located land that could become the state's largest industrial complex.*
>
> *Hottest current speculation says the purchasers will offer 3,000 acres to the Atomic Energy Commission for its new national accelerator laboratory, then develop the remaining 27,000 acres for related space age industry.*
>
> *Rumor also says the Ford Motor Co. plans to break into*

missile and space technology at the secret site. Ford officials in Detroit deny it.

The McDonnell Aircraft Corp., builder of the Mercury and Gemini space capsules and a series of supersonic warplanes, is also mentioned as a possible buyer. McDonnell now has headquarters in St. Louis. There were some St. Louis men involved in the land negotiations.

Still another possibility is Disneyland East, the long-planned amusement park that would be bigger and better than the original Disneyland in Anaheim, Calif. Walt Disney was at Cape Kennedy several weeks ago, but denied that he's still considering Florida for his new venture.

Bankers and real estate brokers have been trying for months to find out what's in the works. If any outsiders know, they aren't telling.

It wasn't until three weeks before Disney's November 1965 press conference that Governor Haydon Burns officially solved the mystery. He told the *Orlando Sentinel*, "Walt Disney has extended to your governor the privilege of making the official announcement that Disney Productions [sic] is the mystery industry. They will build the greatest attraction in the history of Florida."

Our work was cut out for us. But as we began planning and design, at least we had Walt's answer to Governor Burns's question, which he posed at the press conference:

GOVERNOR BURNS: Will it be a Disneyland?

WALT: Well . . . I've always said there will never be another Disneyland, Governor, and I think it's going to work out that way. But it will be the equivalent of Disneyland. We know the basic things that have what I call family appeal. . . . But there's many ways that you can use those certain basic things and give them a new décor, a new treatment. In fact, I've been doing that with Disneyland . . . But . . . this concept here will have to be something that is unique . . . so there is a distinction between Disneyland in California and whatever Disney does . . . You notice I didn't say "Disneyland" in Florida [laughter]. . . . What Disney does in Florida . . . we have many ideas. I have a wonderful staff now that has had ten years experience of designing, planning, and operating. . . . You get in, we call them gag sessions . . . we toss ideas around, everybody's been thinking of things that might be done if we were redoing Disneyland . . . and we throw them in and put all the minds together and come up with something and say a little prayer and open it and hope it will go. I'm very excited about it because I've been storing these things up over the years and, certain attractions at Disneyland that have a basic appeal I might move here. Then again, I would like to create new things . . . you hate to repeat yourself . . . I don't like to make sequels to my pictures. I like to take a new thing and develop something . . . a new concept.

WED's design leader, Dick Irvine was concerned about all the new staff that would be needed to design and build Walt Disney World. How would we begin to get everyone on the same page?

I suggested to Dick that we put together a selection of background material and articles—not just for new staff, but to remind all of us about the principles that Walt had used to create Disneyland. I compiled this material in a thick spiral-bound book I called *Walt Disney World—Background and Philosophy*. On September 21, 1967, we distributed this booklet at Imagineering with the following memo from me:

> This assemblage has been prepared as a background and starting point for developing a "philosophy" for the Disneyland-style theme park in Walt Disney World. There is a great deal of other material, particularly articles about Disneyland, that might have been included. However, the intent here is to provide, as a foundation, Walt's thinking and philosophy as it was applied in Disneyland, and additionally Walt's thoughts about Walt Disney World as they apply to what we are now beginning.

The original booklet contained sixteen different articles and historical background material, including the early Disneyland philosophy write-up by Bill Walsh, a transcript of the November 1965 press conference, a selection of Walt's quotes with regards to Disneyland, my notes from a meeting with Walt discussing the Epcot film, and a series of articles from various publications that I believed captured key aspects of the spirit of Disneyland and provided insight into its popularity with the public. For me, and many others, the booklet became a kind of philosophical bible that I have continued to reference through the years.

Later, after the Florida Legislature had created the Reedy Creek Improvement District as the overall governing body for the Walt Disney World property, I wrote the preface to the so-called Epcot Building Code. Although the basic purpose was to state the objectives of safety, health, general welfare, and good practice during construction, points two and three in the preface were directly reflective of Walt Disney's Epcot thinking:

- To provide the flexibility that will encourage American industry, through free enterprise, to introduce, test, and demonstrate new ideas, materials, and systems emerging now and in the future from the creative centers of industry.
- To provide an environment that will stimulate the best thinking of industry and the professions in the creative development of new technologies to meet the needs of people, expressed by the experience of those who live and work and visit here.

"Walt's Epcot Film," as it came to be called, was a philosophical and historic statement, looking backward to the success of Disneyland and forward to the establishment of Walt Disney World. But its larger vision was for the "Experimental Prototype Community of Tomorrow" or Epcot.

Here are a few of the key points from those seven pages of notes I took in one-on-one meetings with Walt, in which he laid out the ideas he wanted to communicate through the film. I turned those ideas into Walt's dialogue:

- "EPCOT will be a showcase to the world of American free enterprise."
- "In EPCOT, we can show what could be done with proper city planning."
- "The philosophy behind EPCOT is the same as Disneyland: people will be king."
- "EPCOT's starting point: the *needs* of people (transportation, education, etc.)."
- "Hit all the problems—tick them off—because if we control, we won't let them get to be problems."
- "EPCOT will be a working community. People who grow up here will have skills in pace with the needs of *today's* world."
- "Disneyland: a few years ago, it was 'far out' . . . a dream . . .

nobody believed (in) it. But it had a philosophy founded in a belief in people, and it answered their needs. We have the experience to do EPCOT based on our practical experience in Disneyland."

Here's the first page of my script, where Walt begins to take the audience on a trip across the country, from California to Florida:

WED ENTERPRISES, INC.
October 20, 1966
Third Draft

WALT'S FLORIDA FILM -

WALT'S NARRATION ONLY

1.   THE SET AT THE STUDIO - ALL THE FLORIDA ATMOSPHERE

Walt is standing before a simplified map of the entire state, showing the location of Disney World, and also indicating the names of Florida's major cities, for location purposes.

WALT

Welcome to a little bit of Florida here in California.

This is where the early planning is taking place for

our so-called Disney World project. The purpose

of this film is to bring you up to date about some of

our plans for Disney World. But before I go into any

of the details, I want to say just a word about the site

of our Florida project.

Walt uses the map to describe the central location.

WALT

As you can see on this map, we have a perfect location

in Florida -- almost in the very center of the state.

In fact, we selected this site because it's so easy for

tourists and Florida residents to get here by automobile.

Walt moves to a slightly larger map, this one showing a close-up of the Orlando-Kissimmee area. The Disney World property is clearly outlined. The major highways (Interstate 4 and the Sunshine State Parkway) are shown criss-crossing the state, intersecting adjacent to Disney World.

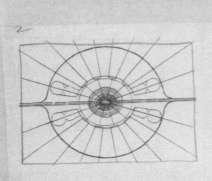

2

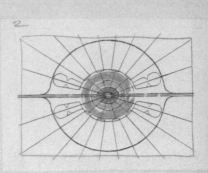

2

... Next the high density apartment housing.

... Then the broad green belt and recreation land

3

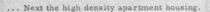

PAN →

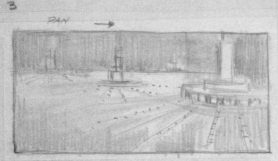

L.A. INSERT

SHOT

EPCOT's dynamic urban center will offer the
excitement and variety of activities found only in
metropolitan cities -- cultural, social, business and
entertainment. Among its major features will be --

Director Ham Luske and Art Director Mac Stewart broke down my script into a visual storyboard, explaining Walt's concept for the EPCOT community. Here's a sample page.

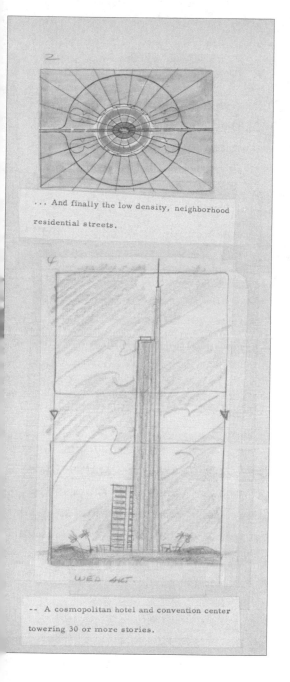

... And finally the low density, neighborhood residential streets.

-- A cosmopolitan hotel and convention center towering 30 or more stories.

Those of us who worked closely with Walt recognized that he had one foot in the past, because he loved the nostalgic, and one foot in the future, because, from his 1937 invention of the multiplane camera (earning his first Academy Award for technical achievement), he was constantly seeking and integrating new technologies that improved what he put on the movie screen. He made it clear that he did not want to repeat himself, and that meant inspiring his artists to continually develop new ways of making magic.

A key source of ideas for Epcot came from Walt's visits to the research and development centers of major companies: IBM, GE, DuPont, RCA's Sarnoff Labs in Princeton, and others. Whenever Walt Disney arrived, those future incubators would trot out the most interesting and far-reaching developments they were working on. Walt was frequently quoted as having asked his hosts, "When can I buy a product that utilizes that technology?" When the answer was often, "We don't know if the public is interested in that," Walt began to see a role that resembled his experience at the New York World's Fair.

At the same time I was developing the public face of the Epcot project through Walt's film, a parallel and, in the larger picture, more important effort was going on behind the scenes. This was the planning and associated legal studies aimed first and foremost to assure that the body of laws the Florida Legislature would ultimately pass included all the bells and whistles Disney needed to accomplish Walt's objectives in Epcot.

On the legal front, early in May 1966, I was assigned to help organize a seminar at the Disney Studios in Burbank, bringing board members and corporate legal staff together with lawyers and other consultants from the state of Florida and Disney legal advisors from a New York City law firm. My assignment was to organize the factual materials gathered by Robert Foster, the Disneyland lawyer who had spent months in Florida working with Sunshine State lawyer Paul Helliwell and real estate advisor Roy Hawkins to acquire the land that would become Walt Disney World. Foster's work through those six corporations in Kansas and Delaware had been so secret that I practically had to threaten him to get him to reveal all the information needed to meet the deadline, two days before the legal seminar would take place. (Forty-five years later, at a Disney D23 Fan Club gathering at Walt Disney World, Foster and I participated in a panel discussion about the resort's background. I was shocked to learn that the "secret" may have been on Bob Foster. He greeted me with this: "You rascal, you—why didn't you tell me what was going to be in your script for Walt's film—I never knew any of the details about Epcot!" I guess Walt and Roy thought the less he knew, the more it would look like a "Florida real estate deal" he was helping to structure. Sorry, Bob!)

Walt set the tone for the meeting, stating it was a key to establishing planning parameters, so that the legal staff could lay out the requests that Disney would make to the Florida Legislature. Walt emphasized the need to control the area, so that what happened around Disneyland—a neon jumble of signs along Harbor Boulevard in Anaheim, fronting the entrance to the park—could not happen again. "By keeping standards high," Walt said, "we can maintain the prestige of the entire area."

Walt outlined four basic developments that had to be

encompassed on the code-named "Project Future" property:

1. The theme park, based on what Disney had learned in nearly eleven years at Disneyland.
2. The resident and guest hospitality areas, including "neighborhoods" and hotels and motels.
3. An industrial complex, providing both a "showcase of industry at work" and an employment base.
4. Other recreational facilities—water sports on Bay Lake, golf courses, campground, etc.

Of these, Walt thought of numbers two and three as the Epcot areas of Project Future.

Day one of the meeting was one of the most tense days I had ever experienced. Both Walt and Roy Disney spent the entire day listening to the presentations, with Walt asking key questions of the New York legal team and Disney vice presidents Donn Tatum, Foster, and Joe Potter, who had become Disney's front man in Florida. Walt had hired him as the company's number one executive in Florida, for his administrative skills and because of his familiarity with the Army Corps of Engineers, which played a key role in creating the drainage canals on the Walt Disney World property.

As Walt stood up to leave at the end of the first day, Joe Potter had the final say. "Walt," he gushed, "I've been in Florida as your representative for three or four months now, and everyone I talk to thinks that you can do *anything* and *everything. They think you can walk on water!*"

Without a word, Walt walked to the door and exited the room. We heard his footsteps, echoing down the hallway. Suddenly, they stopped, and we heard him returning in our direction. The door opened, and Walt Disney stuck his head back inside the room. "I've tried that," he said, before closing the door and leaving all of us to wonder: was he successful?

I doubt anyone in the room thought otherwise.

As the only designated staff writer at WED in those days, I was a jack-of-all-trades, leading a small team in creating the attraction scripts, all the park and resort nomenclature, some of the written marketing materials, and working with our key "Participants" (sponsors) on anything related to the shows, exhibits, and name displays they sponsored. In that connection, Dick Irvine asked me to create a standard for the display and recognition of our valued sponsors. None existed, even at Disneyland; Dick's idea was to make sure everyone—those selling sponsorships, park operators, and our graphic designers—all knew the rules. We recognized the importance of making sure the public, our guests in the parks, knew that the attractions were created by the Imagineers, while providing recognition and an opportunity to associate with a particular attraction for our participants. We developed the form that is still in place today:

TITLE OF ATTRACTION
presented by
Name of Sponsor

For instance, one that exists in Epcot today is:
SPACESHIP EARTH presented by Siemens
Dick Irvine was ahead of his time on this issue. Just turn on your TV set to the New Year's Day football bowl games to see why: Allstate Sugar Bowl, Capital One Bowl, GoDaddy. com Bowl, and, my favorite, the Tostitos Fiesta Bowl. Only

the Rose Bowl in Pasadena has held firm. On a recent New Year's Day it was "presented by Vizio."

A key to maintaining the Disney standard is *consistency* around the world. Thus, guests find these examples: The Broadway Music Theatre, presented by Japan Airlines (Tokyo DisneySea); Hong Kong Disneyland Railroad, presented by UPS (Hong Kong Disneyland); Autopia, presented by Chevron (Disneyland); and Rock 'N' Roller Coaster presenté par Gibson Guitar (Walt Disney Studios—Paris).

As that jack-of-all-trades on the Imagineering staff, I was constantly being given new challenges by Dick Irvine. One day Dick gave me a new assignment: get Herb Ryman to finish the concept design for the Walt Disney World castle.

"Herb is holding up the whole project," Dick explained. "The architects can't do the design and working drawings until they have a concept direction."

"Dick," I asked innocently, "doesn't Herb report to you?"

"Of course," Dick responded.

"Then why don't you talk to him?" I asked.

"Because," Dick replied, "he won't listen to me. So I want you to tell Herb he has to *close his door* and finish the design."

I approached my new assignment cautiously. First, I suggested to Herb that Dick wanted him to keep his door closed: Dick's thinking, of course, was that if Herb had his door closed, he'd stay in his office and focus on finishing the design. Herb complied with part of Dick's request . . . except, with the door closed, it was easy for him to be invisibly *absent* from his office. Herb loved to wander about and help his fellow artists with *their* projects—especially spending time mentoring any young artist who needed a brush-stroke or two to straighten out his or her drawing.

Finally Herb asked me, "Why are you coming to my office every day?" I had to admit that Dick had told me to get him to finish the concept for the castle, which was nowhere to be seen on Herb's easel. With a sigh, Herb told me to come back Thursday, and I would see the first drawing. Upon my arrival a few days later, he proudly unveiled the very first vital concept drawing of the Magic Kingdom's Cinderella Castle: it was an eleven-by-fourteen-inch pencil sketch of *me* as a gargoyle (Ryman called it "Sklargoyle"), clutching my scripts to my breast, and spewing admonishments from the parapets! The original is framed and hanging in my home.

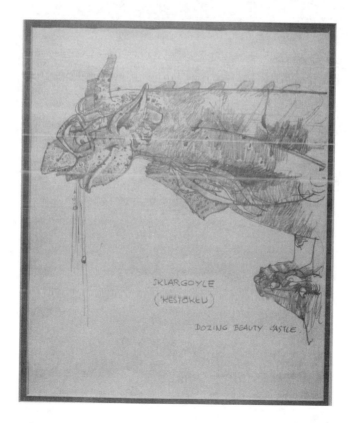

SKLARGOYLE
("RESTORED")

DOZING BEAUTY CASTLE.

Fortunately, Herb understood that this would not satisfy Dick, and he agreed that if I came back the following Tuesday, he would have the sketch. And he did: an exquisite pencil drawing of a Cinderella Castle-to-be. It became the basis for Ted Rich's beautiful architectural design—a perfect fit for the site of that big yellow "X."

Our planning for the Magic Kingdom was not without early mistakes. In Fantasyland, there's still a "pinch point"— a passageway too narrow for the amount of guest traffic—

in the corridor between "it's a small world" and Peter Pan's Flight. And because a new concept by Marc Davis, a "Western River Expedition" featuring Audio-Animatronics cowboys and Indians, was being groomed as a major feature, Pirates of the Caribbean was not included in the original park plans. It was finally added in 1973 as part of the new Caribbean Plaza attached to Adventureland. But the biggest "goof" was the view we held of Florida's audience that resulted in a decision not to build any "thrill rides" for opening day: we figured there would be too many older, retired people. When the audience demographics proved to be almost identical to Disneyland's—*families* with small children and teenagers, as well as young adults looking for a thrill—the call went out for the Imagineers to solve this oversight as quickly as possible.

Two lucky opportunities converged to make a timely response possible. One was the contract with RCA to work with our engineers in designing "the first twenty-first-century information-communications system"—linking computers, telephones, automatic monitoring and control devices, mobile communications, and television. The contract included a significant quid pro quo: RCA agreed to consider sponsorship of a major attraction in the Magic Kingdom Park after its opening, *if* (that was the key word) we Imagineers could develop an attraction that they would be proud to be associated with. Ten million dollars, the equivalent of about $90 million today, was on the line.

Before the Magic Kingdom's opening in 1971, John Hench joined me and artist T. Hee in developing a story and design concept for RCA. It didn't take long; RCA was then in the computer business, and we determined to take Tomorrowland visitors *inside* a computer to tell its story.

Finally, after nine long months working our way up the corporate ladder, we secured an audience with RCA's chairman and CEO, Robert Sarnoff. The night before our big day, we set up our presentation in the RCA board of directors meeting room. We lined one side of the room with nine, four-by-eight-foot storyboards covered with sketches, paintings, and graphic concepts. Everything was positioned so that Mr. Sarnoff, sitting in the center of the boardroom, would see everything directly in front of his chair. As we completed our perfect setup, the meeting organizers played their wild card: Mr. Sarnoff, they said, *always* sits at the head of the table. Sure enough, we made our pitch the next morning with the chairman sitting so far away, he needed binoculars to see our materials. It was impossible to communicate our brilliant concept for the computer story.

For a moment, I thought we might recover, as John Hench, T. Hee, and I joined Mr. Sarnoff and three RCA vice presidents in the seats adjacent to him. But soon Mr. Sarnoff scribbled a note and passed it to the VP next to him, who passed it to the next VP, who passed it to me. When I opened it, I read: *"Who are these people?"*

Reality hit me—hard. The VPs had not even told Sarnoff who we were, or why we were there! Nine months of my life down the drain with four words scribbled on a notepad.

My associates and I returned to California, and I went straight to the office of Card Walker. "Card," I said, "I don't care if you fire me, but I'm not giving another nine months of my creative life to RCA." His response was clear: "Marty, you guys at Imagineering have to figure out a way to get RCA to sponsor an attraction. We need it!"

So we went back to the drawing board. And as good fortune would have it, there was a perfect idea staring us in the face. John recalled the day in 1964 when Walt brought a team of Imagineers together to discuss a "rocket flight into the cosmos" for the new Tomorrowland planned for Disneyland, to open in 1967. "Walt wanted to build a roller-coaster-style ride, but *in the dark*, which no one had ever done before," John wrote in his seminal book, *Designing Disney—Imagineering and the Art of the Show*, published by Disney Editions. "He wanted to have precise control of the lighting and to be able to project moving images on the interior walls."

John's illustration of the now-familiar structure, drawn in 1965, excited the Imagineers—and created a huge stir among Disney fans. But there was one major issue: computer systems were not sophisticated enough to design a ride system to be run safely in the dark. Once again, technology needed to catch up to Walt's vision.

A good idea *may* come back to life in the world of Disney . . . but a great idea *will* find its way into our parks somewhere in the world. Space Mountain was clearly a great idea, so John Hench and I created a way to make it work for RCA. First we had to enlarge the whole structure—at the Magic Kingdom, it's 183 feet high and 300 feet in diameter, versus 200 in later versions at Disneyland, Tokyo Disneyland, and Hong Kong Disneyland. There was a necessary and practical reason for this: we had to create an RCA story before and after the trip through space, so we developed "Spaceports" along the long entry walkway, allowing guests to "view out into space" to see the RCA-developed communications satellites of the 1970s at work. And as a post-show, we created a moving ramp that revealed a "home of the future," filled with RCA products—highlighted by an opportunity to see yourself on color TV as you exited the attraction.

Armed with this complete package—including the thrill ride itself—we had another day in court with Chairman Sarnoff.

This time, as we returned to the scene of our failure, we again set up our presentation of storyboards—and again the RCA people reminded us (after we were already set up) that "Mr. Sarnoff *always* sits at the head of the table." "Fine," I said, "but whoever sits *there*" (pointing to a seat in the center) "is the person I'll be talking to. And if Mr. Sarnoff sits *there*" (pointing to the head seat), "I'll have my back to him for the entire presentation!"

Fortunately, the RCA people stationed an interceptor the next morning, so that when Mr. Sarnoff entered the room (last, of course) the blocker said, "The Disney people would like you to sit *here*"—which he did. (No one, I guess, had ever asked before.) This time, Mr. Sarnoff did not need binoculars.

We made the sale . . . and on January 15, 1975, Colonel James Irwin, pilot of the lunar module on the Apollo 15 mission to the moon, became the first official rider.

To accomplish Walt Disney's goal of a "rocket flight in the dark," ride designer Bill Watkins completed the first all-computer design of a Disney-version roller coaster. Bob Gurr created a brand-new vehicle chassis that shares its basic design with a retrofitted 1974 bobsled for Disneyland's

Matterhorn Mountain. It was also Disney's first *pure* gravity ride, with no boosters or retarders, advancing the state of the ride design art with its own computer-controlled speed and safety zone system.

Blending all the ride and show elements required the Imagineers to create "the most complicated, sophisticated, and accurate model" that had ever been built, Bob Gurr marveled. All the twists, turns, and drops of the ride system are spelled out, as is the location of each and every show light, sound amplifier, the projectors to create asteroids tumbling across the inner surface of the darkened mountain, and dancing, mirror ball-like reflections to depict stars and the endless expanse of space. The result is a sensory experience conveying the convincing illusion of space travel.

But it's the whole look of Space Mountain that stamps it as the definitive theme park statement about space. Here's what designer John Hench wrote in *Designing Disney*:

> Space Mountain begged to be cone shaped. It wanted to echo the expanding spiral of the ride inside. The form housing the ride follows its movement, so that the center of the structure is naturally elevated, like the peak of a mountain being pushed up from the pressure below.
>
> In the construction of the building, the engineers selected precast concrete and steel T-beams for the main roof structure. They wanted the beams facing *inside* the building, but I wanted them facing *outside* to provide a smooth surface in the interior on which we could project images. The distance between the T-beams varies, from narrow at the top to wider at the bottom; on the cone-shaped roof this gives an appropriately dynamic

effect of forced perspective. The resulting exterior design is strong, simple, and visually effective.

Space Mountain has an abstract, contemporary form and tells its story architecturally. The ride is above all an experience of speed, enhanced by the controlled lighting and projected moving images. But it evokes such ideas as the mystery of outer space, the excitement of setting out on a journey, and the thrill of the unknown.

To each of us at Imagineering who played a role in the birth of that first Space Mountain in 1975, we knew we were fulfilling Walt Disney's vision. And it took us only a decade to accomplish! Every time I'm in Tomorrowland, I make sure to watch the faces of our guests exiting from Space Mountain—more than 250 million of whom have enjoyed this original Space Mountain alone. And I never ask, "Who are these people!!?"

* * * * * * * * * *

In a major feature titled "Mickey Mouse Teaches the Architects," published by *The New York Times* magazine on October 22, 1972, (one year after Walt Disney World's original opening), architecture and urban planning writer Paul Goldberger wrote a sidebar entitled "Disney's Secret Ingredient in which he noted the following":

> While $100 million was spent on the new town of
> Columbia, Md., and $85 million for Reston, Va., Disney
> Productions has sunk $400 million into Walt Disney World.
> And it plans to spend another $50 million to $60 million
> in the next few years, expanding the Magic Kingdom and
> moving ahead on Lake Buena Vista, the condominium town

already under way at the eastern edge of the property. And that's all before the EPCOT dream city, for which company officials have not yet begun to prepare financial estimates.

The way all this money was raised would do credit to WED's expertise in creating things out of nowhere; the company has thus far managed to remain entirely free of long-term debt. Through a scheme engineered by Walt's brother Roy Disney, who led the company from Walt's death until he himself died last year, Disney Productions sold convertible debentures which were quickly retired when the price of Disney common stock, stimulated by expected high Disney World profits, moved above the conversion price. The stock—in recent years, one of Wall Street's prizes—has soared from $15 in 1957 to close to $200 this year.

Roy O. Disney hardly looked or acted the part of a financial genius. Yet in the second edition of my Random House *Webster's Unabridged Dictionary*, I find these among the "genius" definitions: "the guardian spirit of an institution"; "a person who strongly influences (for good or ill) the character, conduct, or destiny of a person, place, or thing." Those definitions of genius are remarkable descriptions of Roy O. Disney's impact on Walt Disney Productions.

Even though I had interfaced with Roy closely in the development of four of the company's annual reports beginning in 1964, I never felt a strong bond during Walt's lifetime. But I came to appreciate and respect his love for the company he built with his younger brother, and for the Disney employees who made possible its growth and success. He was a cheerleader, and he made us feel good when he spoke to the media about our team: "The Disney organization brings to this project the most highly creative, experienced, and talented reservoir of personnel ever assembled in the development of an outdoor recreation attraction."

There's no question that, despite the stories of their conflicts about direction and money (mostly true, from what I know), Roy O. Disney was totally dedicated to supporting Walter Elias Disney's brainstorms, new directions, and continuous drive to avoid repeating himself—sometimes at great cost to the corporation. As Walt said in his 1965 Florida press conference: "I would like to create new things . . . you hate to repeat yourself . . . I don't like to make sequels to my pictures. I like to take a new thing and develop something . . . a new concept."

Yet the story of conflicts persisted, from Roy's infamous advice to "stick to shorts" when Walt began to develop the first full-length animated feature, *Snow White and the Seven Dwarfs*, . . . to Roy's reluctance to involve the company in the New York World's Fair shows, leaving production of the first three attractions to Walt's personal company, WED Enterprises, . . . to the time lost in moving ahead on the Walt Disney World project after Walt's death, while Roy and other Disney executives became knowledgeable about (and true believers in) the capabilities of the WED organization.

Diane Disney Miller, one of Walt's daughters, told me this story illustrating Walt and Roy's relationship. In the early 1950s, she accompanied Roy and his wife, Edna, to New York to meet her parents, who were returning by ship from Europe. "Wasn't that nice of Uncle Roy to bring me here!" she enthused to her father. " 'Yeah," Walt replied in a skeptical tone. "He knows I'm mad at him because he took an option on some land in Chatsworth for Disneyland!" (Chatsworth, at one end of the San Fernando Valley, is about sixty miles from the site in Anaheim that became home to Disneyland.)

I write about my experiences with Roy because I became genuinely fond of him in the years between Walt's passing and Roy's death just two months after the opening of Walt Disney World. My respect for him grew as I heard about the conflicts in construction between various Disney company factions and individuals, and outside contractors—and how he resolved these issues. He was the glue that held the whole project together, despite the challenges of building in the Central Florida of the late 1960s, where the infrastructure and ready availability of supplies and construction talents ranged from weak to nonexistent.

* * * * * * * * * *

One of those supply challenges was actually more of a morale challenge. The daily construction grind in the humid, ninety-degree summer heat in Central Florida took its toll on the California staff. That cold beer at the end of the workday was a good idea, except: the Westerners did not like Eastern beers. It took a creative solution by Orlando Ferrante and the PICO (Project Implementation and Coordination Organization) team to resolve the issue, and restore the spirits of the Californians. Ferrante arranged a weekly shipment of Coors to a designated team member's home near the property. Every Friday afternoon, the workday ended with a mass "drive-by" of thirsty Californians, stopping just long enough to pick up their weekly supply of ice-cold Western brew.

* * * * * * * * *

Within weeks after Walt's death, Roy asked me to write a speech for him. It was the most difficult writing assignment I have ever had. The rhythm of Roy's speech pattern, and the emphasis of his words reflecting his role as the chairman and "financial genius" of the company, left little room for soaring thoughts or phrases. But I was truly complimented by his asking for my help, and for the thanks I received following the event.

We became even more conversant on a trip to Japan's "coming out party"—the huge Expo 1970 in Osaka that shouted to the world, and to the Japanese people, that they had fully recovered from the devastation of World War II. Leah, my wife, and I have wonderful memories of that journey, many involving Roy. I think Dick Irvine put the trip together to get everyone thinking about resorts (we stopped in Oahu and the Big Island Hawaii, coming and going) and new kinds of shows; there were several, including big-screen IMAX, new at the Expo in Osaka. The trip included Card Walker, Donn Tatum, Dick Nunis, Joe Fowler, Joe Potter, John Hench, Claude Coats, Roy, Dick, me, and our spouses.

It seemed as though everyone wanted to avoid Roy and Edna, so Leah and I—as the youngest pups—had the duty of accompanying them. It turned out to be interesting and fun, because Roy was so relaxed. In a driving rainstorm, we drove them across Oahu to the Polynesian Cultural Center, and several times in Tokyo and Osaka we breakfasted with the both of them. We heard some great personal stories (which we have never repeated). Roy was a pixie with little comments about Edna when she could not hear him.

Roy was thrust into new responsibilities as the development of Walt Disney World progressed. One involved how to honor the people who created, designed, and built the Magic Kingdom. The tradition had been established at Disneyland by Walt. He personally selected the names that would be placed on the windows of the shops and other facilities that line Main Street—real names, accompanied by fictitious "businesses." For example: PLAZA SCHOOL OF ART—INSTRUCTORS HERBERT RYMAN, JOHN HENCH, PETER ELLENSHAW (the Studio's supreme matte painter, whose work had been a highlight of the early TV show about the park; Peter would later be honored with an Academy Award for his work on *Mary Poppins*). And of course ELIAS DISNEY, CONTRACTOR—EST. 1895—Walt's recognition of his father, who actually *was* a contractor in Chicago when Walt was born in 1901.

Of course, there were many hurt feelings on the Disney staff among those whom Walt chose *not* to honor with their name on a window. So Dick Irvine asked me to write a memo to Roy, suggesting that in the Magic Kingdom we use fictitious names for the proprietors and leaders of those fictitious firms. Roy's response was quick and firm. "No," he handwrote on my memo, "I want to do it exactly as Walt did in Disneyland." And to emphasize the point, as an example, he wrote out a window for me, misspelling my name: MARTY SKALAR.

Today that tradition continues not only at the Magic Kingdom, but in all the Disneyland style parks around the world—Disneyland Paris; Hong Kong Disneyland; and, on a limited basis, Tokyo Disneyland. First, at opening, names of the original designers and builders are included. Then, on retirement, recognition is made of park operators and Imagineering designers who represent only "the highest level of service, respect, and achievement"—determined jointly by individual park management and Imagineering leaders.

On a personal note: my name as an "original creator" appears on windows in the Magic Kingdom, Disneyland Paris, and Hong Kong Disneyland. When I retired on Disneyland's fifth-fourth birthday, July 17, 2009, the park unveiled a window in my honor on the second story of the City Hall building in Town Square. It reads as follows:

ID SOMNIATE—ID FACITE MAIN STREET
COLLEGE OF ARTS & SCIENCES EST. 1852
Martin A. Sklar
• Dean •
Inspiring the Dreamers and Doers of Tomorrow

I'll mention two facts: first, the window selected is part of the office I once occupied in City Hall. And second, my name is spelled correctly.

Another nomenclature issue involved the names of the resort hotels planned for Walt Disney World. The early plans had listed the hotels' styles: Polynesian, Asian, Venetian, Persian, Contemporary. For the latter, John Hench and I recommended a "real name." In an elaborate graphics presentation, reflecting the location on the shores of Bay Lake, we pitched the name "Tempo Bay" to Roy. He listened intently, and let John describe why the name Tempo, together with the graphics we proposed, conveyed the sleek design style of the hotel. When we completed our presentation, Roy spoke for the first time. "What's wrong with Contemporary?" he asked. And four decades later, there's still nothing wrong with the name of this 690-room resort on the shores of Bay Lake.

The creation of the Contemporary also provided two of the most dramatic stories in the development of Walt Disney World. The first occurred when two architects from the Welton Becket firm, who were doing the hotel's working drawings, asked for a meeting with John Hench. They told him they would resign if Disney insisted on running the monorail trains through the center of the hotel. John was shocked; after all, the hotel's distinguishing feature was the monorail system and the service it offered carrying guests to the Magic Kingdom and other Disney hotels. The threat evaporated quickly when Hench wrote "We resign" on a piece of paper and asked the architects to sign it; suddenly they changed their minds.

The second was Roy Disney's decision to buy out the interest of U. S. Steel in the two original hotels, the Contemporary and the Polynesian. The fact is that Walt and Roy Disney did not like having partners in projects. Disney had purchased ABC's interest in Disneyland in the 1950s, and Western Printing's investment in the 1960s. U. S. Steel's foothold in the Disney properties was tied to a unique system it had pioneered for building the rooms in the Florida hotels. They were constructed in an off-site factory, fully equipped with all furnishings, trucked to the construction site, lifted by crane, and "slid" into place like a chest of drawers. While the one-of-a-kind building system worked, the two-of-a-kind decision-making related to issues of operating the hotels proved to be less effective. Not long after opening, Disney became the sole owner of the two resorts.

* * * * * * * * *

There was one other name that Roy insisted on establishing. While the early materials, and even the earliest highway signs, indicated the project's name as Disney World, Roy passionately went to bat for including his brother's full name. Thus, it became *Walt* Disney World.

* * * * * * * * *

One of my favorite stories during the years of secrecy about Project X was told by Donn Tatum. Prior to the 1965 press conference, Walt wanted one more look at the property. He was accompanied by several of the top Disney executives— all of whom were warned to wear hats, and even to paste on some added facial hair, if possible: there were already rumors that Disney was the land buyer. The Disney group spent one night in Orlando, using assumed names at the hotel. At dinner, the waitress kept eyeing Walt, and of course he noticed her penetrating glances. Finally, as the meal was concluding, the waitress approached their table, looked right at Walt, and burst out with, "You look like Walt Disney!" Clearly offended, Walt shot back: "What do you mean I *look* like Walt Disney? I *am* Walt Disney!" And to prove it, he showed the waitress his California driver's license.

So much for disguises and secrecy. Not long after, on October 24, 1965, in a banner headline across its entire front page, the *Orlando Sentinel* trumpeted: "We Say: 'Mystery' Industry Is Disney." And on October 25, the *Orlando Evening*

Star, in front page capital letters one and one-half inches high, screamed, "DISNEY IS HERE!"

With support from writer Randy Bright, who would later play a key role in developing the original pavilions for Epcot, and my favorite film and narration editor at the Studio, Jim Love, we created the most important film presentation communicating the Disney vision for the property. It accompanied a wonderful, detailed model of the resort area— the Magic Kingdom and the five hotel designs located on the master plan. It was created by the storied Model Shop at WED, and was forty feet across and 625 square feet in size. It was a signature piece of work, and (as I will explain shortly) it was to enjoy a long and important life.

On April 30, 1969, Disney demonstrated for the first time in Florida the versatility, experience, and talent of its various divisions:

- The Disneyland Operations staff, which handled all the complex logistics, including renting the Parkwood Cinema in Orlando for the film and press conference featuring Roy Disney and Florida governor Claude Kirk; erecting a tent to display the Phase One model; buying out the entire Ramada Inn in nearby Ocoee for a week to house and feed the media, and serve as the starting point for bus tours of the construction site four miles to the west; and providing the Disneyland staff, including tour guides/hostesses to narrate the site tours.

- The construction team, which created the passable dirt roads providing access for the progression of buses filled with eager-eyed media; Florida state, county, and city officials; industry guests; and VIPs.

- The corporate leaders of Walt Disney Productions, presenters, and media stars for the day: Roy Disney, Card Walker, Donn Tatum, Joe Fowler, and Joe Potter. Dick Irvine represented WED, and Dick Nunis led the Operating staff.
- WED. The Imagineers created all the materials for the presentation: the film; the heroic 625-square-foot model that became the star of photo opportunities with all the Disney and Florida officials; reproductions of all the key artwork depicting the overall project, key attractions in the Magic Kingdom, the Monorail system, and the hotel concepts.

On a recent visit to the Walt Disney Archives at the Walt Disney Studios in Burbank, I was amused to read the estimated numbers of newsmen and dignitaries attending the announcement events of April 30. One report indicated two hundred, another six hundred, and one local Florida daily called it 1,977. In fact, the last may have been the total for the week; there were various levels of invitations, notably for "officials, dignitaries, and VIPs."

But the superlatives from the media drew my attention most. Ormund Powers reported in the *Orlando Star*, "Every major newspaper, wire service, television network, and magazine in the United States, as well as many foreign publications, were at today's Disney presentation on Phase One—a presentation in its way as colorful in detail as the unbelievable plans for Walt Disney World."

The *Titusville Star Advocate* wrote: "The greatest tourist attraction in the country and possibly the world, that has [the] promise of making Central Florida a 'pleasure mecca,' was unveiled today by Walt Disney officials. Larry Vickers in the *Lakeland Ledger* quoted a "sage observer" enthusing:

"This is what God would have done if he'd had the money!"

But perhaps it was left for Governor Kirk, "visibly impressed," according to the *Tampa Tribune*, to put the event in perspective. John Frasca, *Tribune* staff writer, included this statement in his story: "Kirk said he 'didn't take' the U.S. vice presidency because he wanted to be in Florida 'for this great day.'"

* * * * * * * * * *

All the materials created for the April 30, 1969, press event had a huge residual value. On January 10, 1970, we opened the Walt Disney World Preview Center in Lake Buena Vista, just off Interstate 4 and State Road 535. The centerpiece of the preview was the model and the film I had written. In the twenty-one months that it operated before closing on September 30, 1971, the Preview Center attracted 1,332,927 visitors—demonstrating the extraordinary interest in the project. Out-of-state tourists represented 59 percent of the visitors, with Michigan, New York, Ohio, and Illinois residents leading the way.

* * * * * * * * * *

Less than twenty-four hours after the closing of the Preview Center, on October 1, 1971, the most important visitor in the history of the state of Florida (notwithstanding the arrival of Ponce de Leon in 1515, in search of the Fountain of Youth) walked through the turnstiles to enter the Magic Kingdom. Mr. and Mrs. William Windsor, Jr., and their two sons, ages three and one, of Lakeland, Florida, were the very first guests. Unlike the Spanish explorer (who was not expected), the Windsors were part of a shockingly small attendance of only 10,422 visitors on that day. The numbers were a far cry from the planning and predictions of the Orange County, Florida, government.

Earlier that year, in January, the *Orlando Sentinel* quoted Ralph Poe, vice chairman of the county's traffic commission: "Sure, we're going to have a tourist problem, a traffic problem, law enforcement problem . . . But I'll tell you this— we know what to expect . . . Sure, when how many people turn up for the opening—half a million, a million?—we can expect traffic jams and delays."

It seemed as though everyone from Jacksonville to Miami was watching the reported trickle of cars on Interstate 4— everyone but the Disney team. "We're not disappointed by the turnout," the *Atlanta Constitution* quoted Donn Tatum, president of Walt Disney Productions, remarking. "It's just what we want."

"There's a reason we open a new park in October— the kids are back in school, and it's the slowest month of the year," explained Jack Lindquist. "It's a great time to train our staff—we call it a 'soft opening.'" We saved the 'Grand Opening' for the end of the month, for maximum marketing impact—including the ninety-minute television special that aired on NBC on October 29, and starred Julie Andrews, Bob Hope, Glen Campbell, Jonathan Winters, and Buddy Hackett.

On October 25, with the third Florida governor in six years, Reubin Askew, looking on, Roy Disney read the dedication plaque I had written to mimic Walt's Disneyland dedication:

Walt Disney World is a tribute to the philosophy and life of Walter Elias Disney . . . and to the talents, the dedication, and the loyalty of the entire Disney organization that made Walt Disney's dream come true. May Walt Disney World bring Joy and Inspiration and New Knowledge to all who come to this happy place . . . A Magic Kingdom where the young at heart of all ages can laugh and play and learn— together.

By November, on the day after Thanksgiving, traffic on Interstate 4 was bumper-to-bumper for twelve miles, from the city of Orlando to Walt Disney World. By the end of year one, through September 30, 1972, 10.7 million visitors had made the Magic Kingdom the most visited theme park in the world.

One of the earliest national media recognitions of Walt Disney World's success was reported by David Brinkley, then the anchor of NBC's *Nightly News* (and later, the news dean of ABC News). Reporting on the "new town" Disney had created in Central Florida, Brinkley called it "the most imaginative and effective urban planning in America"— totally outside what he called "the Mickey Mouse amusement park." He concluded his report with this comment: "After Disney's people take over the big cities, we'll talk about bringing them to Washington!"

10

"TELL IBM TO GO TO HELL!"

Jack Lindquist and I were in Armonk, New York, for yet another meeting with IBM. We—Jack the marketing guru, me pitching the show—had pulled out all the stops. Meeting with executives in New York and California, we tried to convince "Big Blue" to sponsor Spaceship Earth, the key communications theme pavilion at the entrance to Epcot Center, already in construction as the 1970s came to a close. We had worked all the angles: CEO to CEO, because IBM's Frank Cary and Disney's Card Walker had been classmates at UCLA; and a special reading of the story concept by author Ray Bradbury, whose lyrical prose—written more as a descriptive short story than narrative for a ride-through experience—seemed to fascinate the IBMers.

On this day at IBM's corporate headquarters in upstate New York, our contacts at IBM gave us the word. We can't "officially" tell you, but on Monday, Mr. Cary will send Mr. Walker a letter declining to become an Epcot sponsor.

It was a late Friday morning. As we rode toward New York City, Jack had an inspiration. "Let's call Ed Block at AT&T and see if we can meet with him this afternoon." In the days before cell phones, we stopped at a local watering hole. Jack called, and when Ed Block said, "Come on up," we were on our way.

In our sales effort, we had been playing both ends against the middle, attempting to pit IBM against AT&T all along. Now, armed with our new unofficial knowledge about IBM, we entered the office of AT&T's executive vice president of marketing. Jack went straight to the point. "Ed, IBM just told us they will give us the word on their sponsorship on Monday. This is your last chance to beat them to the punch!"

"Tell IBM to go to hell," Ed responded. "We're in!"

Without corporate sponsors, there would be no Epcot at Walt Disney World. Fortunately, our timing was excellent. Walt Disney World was a big success: attendance passed thirteen million in the Magic Kingdom by 1980, indicating the potential for "spreading the audience" with a second park. As well, the World's Fair identification concept was still alive in corporate America—albeit on its last legs. There was a great deal of media coverage in the early days of Epcot referring to a "permanent World's Fair." Our experience in working with major companies at the New York World's Fair in the 1960s had paid big dividends.

Card Walker's 1974 telephone call and challenging question, "What are we going to do about Epcot?" was the beginning of a long and winding journey to create only the third Disney park anywhere in the world. More importantly, it would be the first non-Magic Kingdom park. We were certainly aware of the objective to complement and not compete with the Magic Kingdom. That was the key to extending guests' length of stay on the Walt Disney World property and to building on "The Vacation Kingdom of the World" resort theme.

Eight years later, on October 24, 1982, Card read the words on the Epcot Center Dedication Plaque that I had co-written with Erwin Okun, Disney's vice president of Public Affairs.

In retrospect, I can clearly identify four principal segments in the development of the Epcot Center that we unveiled in October 1982:

1. Deciding what to do.
2. Creating the concept and convincing Disney management to fund it.
3. Selling it to corporate and international sponsors.
4. Building it.

DECIDING WHAT TO DO

It was easy to know where to begin; we had Walt's comments at the 1965 Florida Press Conference, the twenty-four-minute film I had written (including Walt's four or five minutes of narration), and the secret work of a variety of consultants researching state statutes, federal legislation, government department policies, and interesting new developments around the world. However, most of the latter work was quite literally secret. To this day, to my knowledge, the body of material compiled by the research team for Walt's Epcot Community has never been available to the public or to researchers. However, the major finding of this important work, as it related to land planning and development of the property, had been incorporated into the legislation passed by the Florida State Legislature in 1967, establishing the Reedy Creek Improvement District as the governmental agency with jurisdiction over the Walt Disney World property.

Initially, we determined that "the Epcot idea" was much bigger than one company's internal personnel, no matter how talented, could accomplish. We needed to pick our "sweet spots," and broaden our base of creative contributors, finding talent and ideas from a variety of fields and a diversity of backgrounds.

We launched our effort by creating a series of conferences,

initiated to support the marketing and conceptual development of Epcot Center. The program was split into two primary objectives:

Marketing

- To introduce the concept of the Epcot Center project to top level executives from business, government, foundation, and academic communities.
- To begin a dialogue with these leaders and to stimulate their interest in corporate sponsorship of the project.

Concept Development

- To solicit an exchange of ideas among experts regarding the topical issues Epcot should explore, and the stories it should "communicate."
- To identify experts who would serve as official advisors throughout the conceptual development of the project.

We called these meetings Epcot Future Technology Conferences. The first was titled "Concurrent Forums in Agriculture/Food Production and Energy." It was held at Walt Disney World on May 15 and 16, 1976, bringing together forty individuals from industry, academia, and government in the fields of energy and agriculture. In addition to Disney's Donn Tatum and Card Walker, author and futurist Ray Bradbury gave the verbal charge. Forum panel moderators included Dr. Daniel Aldrich, chancellor of the University of California at Irvine and highly respected in agricultural circles.

Our WED Enterprises staff, led by three of my closest associates—Frank Stanek, Pat Scanlon, and Peggie Fariss—

organized and planned the programs. One of the seven original Mercury astronauts, L. Gordon Cooper, then vice president of research and development at WED, served as conference director.

I created an Epcot Background piece that became our standard introduction in the printed material for the conferences:

EPCOT BACKGROUND

Walt Disney did not go to Florida just to build another "theme park" or even a destination resort. He had something far more important in mind.

Walt was looking far beyond his lifetime . . . to the creation of what he called "EPCOT . . . an Experimental Prototype Community of Tomorrow." This is what he said about EPCOT in 1966.

I don't believe there's a challenge anywhere in the world that's more important to people everywhere than finding solutions to the problems of our cities. But where do we begin . . . how do we start answering this great challenge?

Well, we're convinced we must start with the public need. And the need is not just for curing the old ills of old cities. We think the need is for starting from scratch on virgin land and building a special kind of new community.

We believe today that the creative insight which led Walt Disney to propose EPCOT is as valid as it ever was, and needed even more.

National public opinion polls have made it clear that government and industry have both lost the trust of much of the American public. As a result, democracy and free enterprise are coming under increasing attack, both at home and around the world.

At the same time, the public is becoming increasingly aware of the complex nature of problems facing all people. They have a need to know what is being done to solve these problems.

We have dedicated the achievement of Walt Disney's concept for EPCOT to the belief that public trust can and must be strongly reaffirmed in our democratic institutions, and our free enterprise system.

We think that this is where EPCOT can play a major role in today's society.

CONFERENCE PURPOSE

To introduce the EPCOT concept to noted experts in agriculture/food production and energy technologies and elicit critical reaction to this concept.

To stimulate comment and discussion within the scientific communities and open the door to an ongoing interface between these communities and EPCOT.

To establish EPCOT as an ongoing meeting place where creative people of science and industry, from around the world, may gather to discuss specific solutions to specific needs of mankind.

The conference was extraordinarily successful—beyond our hopes and dreams. The enthusiasm of participants led us to plan and carry out these additional EPCOT conferences:

March 1977: "Good Health in America: Challenge and Choice" (cosponsored by Johns Hopkins University and Johns Hopkins Hospital)

May 1978: "Energy Conservative Techniques for the Cold Weather Protection of Plants" (Frost Protection Workshop) (cosponsored by the Department of Energy through the Argonne National Laboratory)

May 1979: EPCOT Space Seminar

October 1982: EPCOT Center opens

October 1983: "Communications and the Quality of Life: Looking to the Future" (cosponsored by the Annenberg School for Communications at the University of Pennsylvania and the School for Communication and Journalism at the University of Southern California)

Attendance ranged from a high of ninety at the Good Health conference to a select seminar of fifteen professors, corporate executives, and space program directors brought together in a focused discussion about "the story of space that should be communicated to the American people."

In all candor, we at Disney were not prepared for the enthusiasm generated by the Epcot concept. Perhaps it was the popularity of Walt Disney World with the public, or the backstage tours, where we emphasized all the innovative systems already in place. Perhaps it was the attitude and enthusiasm of all the Disney employees, from cast members operating an attraction, to corporate executives and Imagineering designers. Perhaps it was the legacy of Walt Disney, still the master communicator over a decade after his passing.

Whatever it was, the feedback was loud and clear in the conference summaries by the participants:

- The public does not trust what industry, government, and even academia tell them.

- The public *does* trust Mickey Mouse.
- Therefore, you—Disney—have a key role to play, telling the stories and communicating the information that the public needs, in ways they understand and accept.

It was also a thrill to have the opportunity to present our early concepts to President Jimmy Carter on October 1, 1978. That day, the president visited Walt Disney World to address the International Chamber of Commerce convention. We took advantage of the gathering of 2,500 delegates from seventy countries to fill a room at the Contemporary Resort with early artwork and models, and invited the delegates for a preview of Epcot Center. The big bonus came when we were joined by the president and his family, including Rosalynn and daughter Amy.

* * * * * * * * * *

Invariably, we left the Epcot Future Technology Conferences both challenged and exhilarated—and with a folder full of names of attendees who wanted to continue to be involved. Flattering, but how should we implement this? The idea we came up with turned out to be vital to the development of our Epcot pavilions and, years later, of Disney's Animal Kingdom park: we established advisory boards in the key subject areas—energy, health, communications, the land, and the oceans. In several cases, the advisory boards literally changed the direction of our creative development.

There was still another significant outcome of the conferences: the movers and shakers we met from industry, universities, and government who helped bring Epcot to life. Several, like Carl Hodges of the University of Arizona, became key consultants working with our WED team to design and build the major pavilions in Epcot. Others, like Tibor (Ty) Nagy, a vice president at General Motors, became key conduits into their companies, helping us to acquire the necessary sponsors for Epcot. Their involvement was nothing less than absolutely essential as we began our development.

* * * * * * * * * *

CONCEPT DEVELOPMENT

Our Imagineering staff had developed some preliminary concepts, which I presented at the Epcot Future Technology Conferences in Florida. But the real creative thinking was just beginning in Glendale, California. And we were not thinking small.

We started with the aggressive conceit that we would develop two separate and distinct parks—one showcasing countries of the world, their people, cultures, and industries; the other featuring stories about "real world" subjects: energy, food, health, space, communications. Two issues developed as we began our master planning. First, almost all countries are members of the B.I.E. (Bureau of International Exhibitions). Their charter limits official participation by a country in a "World's Fair" or "International Expo" to one a year; no permanent exhibitions are permitted. That meant that multiple sponsors per country would probably be necessary to finance the international pavilions. The king of Morocco could ignore the rules (and did so with his country's pavilion that opened in 1984). But in most cases, industries and their export products—from food to specialty merchandise, souvenirs, and travel and tourism agencies—had to be sold individually on picking up the tab. Thus, except for

Morocco, no nation is represented as such in Epcot's World Showcase.

The second major factor was the time it took to develop a concept for Epcot's Future World pavilions. Almost a decade earlier, it had taken us nine months to weave our way through all the vice presidents at RCA to finally have an audience with Chairman Robert Sarnoff . . . only to be rebuffed and sent back to the drawing board. Now we were dealing with real-world subjects that rarely had a precedent: how would we tell entertaining and meaningful stories about energy, transportation, communications, food? I well remember the day Card Walker asked me how we were going to entertain our visitors in The Land pavilion, on the boat ride we had conceived. The boats would be coursing through domed Living Laboratories, where we'd be growing a variety of food from around the world. "Don't worry, Card," I reassured him. "We'll be watching lettuce grow!" He was not amused.

Of course, that's what concerned Disney's corporate management—that the science and technology would over-whelm the entertainment and storytelling. In a strong sense, we *were* in competition with the Magic Kingdom. If it wasn't fun, why would people come to Epcot when Cinderella Castle, the Jungle Cruise, and Space Mountain were just two miles away?

My "rule book" was clear and direct. I told the Imagineers that our role was simple: create great stories, present them in unique ways (if possible), and don't worry about com-municating everything you learn about a pavilion's subject. Instead, make it entertaining and *fun*. In fact, I said, it's impos-sible for us to be the source of all relevant information about these subjects (we did create other sources as part of the project), so let's concentrate on creating great stories that are "turn-ons," encouraging our guests to want to know more about the subjects of our shows.

There was one more essential point I wanted the Imagineers to remember. Despite IBM's passing on our sponsorship proposal, in my office I pinned up a full newspaper page ad they had run. It simply said: "THE FUTURE IS A MOVING TARGET!" Following that slogan, however, was *not* simple.

Most projects have a turning point or two, when it's "fish or cut bait" time. For Epcot, there was a confluence of several key elements that ultimately made the project jell, and gain the green light we needed from Disney's corporate management. Here are three of the most significant:

- In October 1976, Card Walker delivered a speech entitled "Walt Disney World: Master Planning for the Future" at the fortieth anniversary convocation of the Urban Land Institute. He outlined four major objectives for the creation of Epcot: a demonstration and proving ground for prototype concepts; an ongoing "Forum of the Future"; a communicator to the world; a permanent, international people-to-people exchange.

For the first time, Disney had "gone public" with a strong indication of its plans for Epcot.

- Harper Goff, who had designed the original Jungle Cruise for Disneyland and the iconic *Nautilus* submarine for Walt's movie *20,000 Leagues Under the Sea* created a painting that showed how the diverse architectural styles of countries as different as China and France, or the U.K. and Mexico, could be made to live side by side in our World Showcase area. With one major illustration, Harper sold everyone—from our designers to Disney management—on the concept. As the search for sponsors began in earnest, Harper's rendering spoke volumes in presentations around the globe. With skills developed as a motion picture art director, Harper would go on to lead the design concepts for our Japan, Germany, and United Kingdom pavilions in Epcot.

- From the very first communication about Epcot in his film, Walt Disney had emphasized that *no one company* could accomplish this project alone. In his 1976 speech to the Urban Land Institute, Card Walker had noted "gratifying interest and dialogue" regarding sponsorship with "many of America's leading corporations," specifically citing IBM, RCA, Sperry Univac (now Unisys Corporation), AT&T, General Electric, Westinghouse, Ford, General Motors, Exxon, Gulf Oil, and Kodak. But no one had yet signed up. What we needed was one major corporation to show its faith in the values of participation in Epcot—a ten-year commitment starting with the yet-to-be-established Opening Day. That's where the story of Ty Nagy became so important.

One of the interesting people Peggie Fariss turned up in her research for outside experts to attend the first Epcot Future Technology Conference was the aforementioned scientist at General Motors named Ty Nagy. My recollection is that he, like many others we invited to these Epcot Forums, decided to participate more out of curiosity— "What's a company like Disney doing outside their fantasy kingdom in the *real* world?"—than anything else. (To some participants, of course, spending a weekend at Walt Disney World wasn't exactly the most unpleasant assignment.) But Ty Nagy was intrigued; after the exchange of several notes and telephone conversations, he convinced the chairman of a key GM committee that he served on to let Disney come to Michigan and present the Epcot project. That committee, it turned out, was charged with recommending a future course of action and direction for GM. It was called The Scenario 2000 Advisory Committee, and its chairman was Roger Smith, soon to become chairman and CEO of what was then, in 1977, the second largest industrial company in the world.

This was the opportunity we needed, and we pulled out all the stops.

First, we loaded every model we had under way for the project—an overall concept layout in detail, models of half a dozen pavilions ranging from energy to space, and facades of countries in the World Showcase—into trucks, accompanied by dozens of illustrations, some as large as four-by-eight-foot storyboards. GM allowed us to take over the main rotunda floor area of its Technical Center in Warren, Michigan—a space so large, that the company used it sometimes to introduce their full line of cars within it.

To organize our presentation and maximize the total impact of the Epcot Center project, we brought in one of Hollywood's great talents, John DeCuir. DeCuir had served as art director for The Hall of Presidents in the Magic Kingdom, but more significantly to us (and to GM) were his film credits for art direction or production design. They included *South Pacific*, *The King and I*, *Cleopatra*, and *There's No Business Like Show Business*, among others. We wanted GM's brass to know that "show business is *our* business." Recognizing the opportunity, Card Walker filled the Disney company air-craft—that same Gulfstream I Walt used—with every key executive who might later be involved with GM. Movies and television, consumer products, the parks, educational mate-rials, marketing, and the soon-to-debut Disney Channel—all were represented.

Roger Smith was impressed. As the chief financial exec-utive of GM at that time, he saw an opportunity to take advantage of the excellent year GM was having in 1977, and at the same time continue GM's tradition of leading the way in world's fairs. On the spot, Smith made up his mind that GM should become Epcot's first major stakeholder. His only hesitation was how to present the project to other top GM executives, whose support he would need to commit per-haps $50 million for participation (including Disney fees, a corporate VIP area, and a postshow "product area").

The answer turned out to be simple—for Roger Smith and Card Walker. They agreed that while the rest of the Disney group would depart as scheduled, Marketing Vice President Jack Lindquist and I would be left behind, along with all the models and artwork, so that GM president Pete Estes and other executives could view the concepts early the following morning. Who knew that a corporate president would take a 7:00 A.M. meeting? Jack and I agreed to accommodate Roger Smith's request, on one condition: that we be taken to a local store to buy clean dress shirts for the presentations. Dressed in our new finery, the next morning between 7:00 and 9:00 A.M. we did indeed meet and present to President Estes and other key GM leaders. And by December 31, 1977, General Motors had become the first major Epcot corporate sponsor.

Facing the dilemma of not enough industry sponsors for Epcot's Future World, or international participation in the World Showcase, John Hench and I made a major design decision, literally, about one hour before a key meeting with the Studio brass. With the help of our Model Shop staff, we pushed the project models for Future World and World Showcase together—creating one project with enough potential participants combined to provide the seed money that suggested the sales effort could be a success. Imagineering's model makers set a new record for patching and painting the two models into one complete idea, making it look as though it had been designed that way, and not slapped together in a matter of minutes. Disney's corporate management praised our stealth development of the concept; no word had leaked out about this total reconceiving of the projects. We were lucky it didn't occur to us in time for internal rumors to leapfrog from Glendale to the Burbank Studios. Explaining such a major change by telephone in response to rumors would have been a disaster—especially if one of the ever-present corporate naysayers had beaten us to the key decision makers.

* * * * * * * * * *

All our energies were now focused on leading the Imagineering staff in the development of hundreds of individual pieces of the project. With the two halves of Epcot now one, John Hench and I, in concert with the team that would operate the Epcot Center, recommended that the Main Entrance be located in the middle—between the Future World and World Showcase areas. That way, the two sections could operate together on the same schedule—or the hours of operation could be changed for each, almost on a daily basis, if necessary. The operations team could also monitor the number of guests entering, and direct them to one side or the other, depending on capacities and wait times for attractions.

Excited by the opportunities that our new scheme presented, we hastened to present it to Card Walker for his approval. I'm not sure I ever saw him more agitated than by our Main Entrance proposal. He immediately tossed away his CEO hat and donned the marketing hat he had worn for so many years at Disney.

"There's no way we can do this," Card lectured. "When our guests enter and exit through Future World, our corporate sponsors get two shots at them—coming in, and going out. With your scheme, guests may pass the Future World pavilions only once—or not at all! I'm not going back to Roger Smith or Cliff Garvin (Exxon's chairman) with this plan—the entrance stays at Spaceship Earth!"

And it did. But by the dawn of the 1990s, with the opening of the "Epcot Resort Area" southwest of the park where two Disney resorts (Yacht Club and Beach Club) and the Dolphin and Swan hotels had become major accommodations, another entrance into Epcot was needed. The so-called Epcot International Gateway, opened in 1990, brings guests directly into the World Showcase area, across from the France pavilion. (A third Disney resort, the Boardwalk Inn, opened in the Epcot Resort Area in 1996.)

A second major controversy erupted over the location of The American Adventure pavilion. On a visit to Washington, D.C., John Hench and I had become enamored with the Smithsonian's Hirshhorn Museum on the National

Legends of Imagineering (left to right): Herb Ryman, Ken O'Brien, Collin Campbell, Marc Davis, Al Bertino, Wathel Rogers, Mary Blair, T. Hee, Blaine Gibson, X. Atencio, Claude Coats, and Yale Gracey.

Walt demonstrating the movement he wanted for the Audio-Animatronics figure of Abraham Lincoln.

Me, Welton Becket (head of the architectural firm Welton Becket & Associates), and Richard Irvine (then executive vice president and chief of design for WED Enterprises). Dick is standing on the yellow "X," marking the proposed location of Cinderella Castle, in this photo that was taken on November 1, 1967.

Me with the Animal Kingdom construction team.
Photo taken for the annual report.

Herb Ryman and me reviewing his illustration depicting
the entrance of Epcot Center.

Landscape Legend Bill Evans (pointing) and Imagineering art director
Bill Martin (third from right) at the Walt Disney World site (circa 1967).

Imagineering's Art Kishyama (left) showing Tokyo DisneySea plans to Jim Cora (center), me, and Craig Russell (right).

Rare photo of George Lucas (kneeling and without his trademark beard) reviewing the model for Star Tours with Ed Sotto (also kneeling). I'm at the right looking on.

John Hench (to my left) joined me to review the Horizons pavilion in Epcot with executives from General Electric.

When John Hench (second from left) received the Themed Entertainment Association's Lifetime Achievement Award, he was escorted by previous recipients (left to right) Harrison (Buzz) Price, me, and Don Iwerks.

Mickey and Minnie join Bob Iger and Jay Rasulo at the dinner celebrating my fiftieth Disney anniversary.

Disney Legend Blaine Gibson, now in his nineties, is someone I stay in close touch with.

That's me with one of my favorite field construction leaders, Walter Wrobleski, at Disney California Adventure.

"Disney Day" at Angel Stadium of Anaheim during the time when Disney owned the team. I'm still a big fan.

Celebrating the beginning of construction for
Tokyo DisneySea (left to right): me, Noboru Kamisawa,
Jim Cora, Jim Thomas, and Bill Gair.

Splashdown on the bobsled at Disneyland's Matterhorn
Mountain. If you're not having fun in the fun business,
you're in the wrong business!

Mall. Designed by architect Gordon Bunshaft of Skidmore, Owings & Merrill to house contemporary art, the building is basically a raised, open circle elevated by four major "piers" with its entry located in the central courtyard. "The central plan," wrote Paul Goldberger, architecture critic of *The New York Times*, in 1974, "is not only clear, but also provides a pleasant processional sequence . . ."

That sequence was exactly what John and I wanted. By placing the pavilion at the entrance to World Showcase and elevating it in a manner similar to the Hirshhorn, we envisioned guests walking under the pavilion and emerging at an overlook into the World Showcase. The conceit was as though America was opening its arms and saying "Welcome!" to all the pavilions of countries around the world.

This concept was a wonderful idea—on paper. But a Disney park is a live community of people and events, and often an idea, no matter how eloquently expressed in writing or through an illustration, must take a backseat to the realities of life in that community.

Dick Nunis, Disney's chief of operations for all the parks, pounced on the concept—not the design of the building, but its location. "We have to give our guests a key reason to go all the way around that big lagoon," he argued, focusing on the Promenade, the full circle of walkways around the body of water in the center of the World Showcase. "We need to put the big attraction—like the castle of the Magic Kingdom—at the far side of the lagoon to make people want to go there!" In other words, we needed what Walt Disney called "a wienie"—the beckoning finger that says, "Come this way or you'll miss the fun."

Dick was right; The American Adventure *is* the castle

of the World Showcase, and it is a key incentive for our guests to "circle the world." Of course, it meant a complete redesign of our American Adventure pavilion. A contemporary structure would not fit architecturally among the World Showcase pavilions, all of which feature traditional, iconic designs representing their nations, from the Japanese Torii Gate to the French Eiffel Tower. The home of our American Adventure show thus became a stately example of the Georgian Colonial style prevalent in important structures, and the homes of the wealthy, in the 1700s in America. (Contemporary may have worked for a hotel, but not for this building.)

These fundamental conceptual decisions were in many ways overshadowed by two key aspects of the project: first, determining *what* to build; and second, identifying and selling sponsors (again, in Disney-speak, participants). We knew that the big corporations would want to weigh in with their "suggestions" for a ninety-thousand-square-foot, thematic structure that featured their logo and a PRESENTED BY on the exterior. But we were undoubtedly very naive about how many suggestions they would have—and how vocally they argued for their point of view.

One major example was the Universe of Energy (now Ellen's Energy Adventure), presented by Exxon. Randy Bright, the leader of our show development and writing team, handled this one personally. It took thirty-nine—count them!—versions of the shooting script before we agreed on one for the film portion of the attraction. Let's just say there were a number of "facts" that we thought could be more objective. We made liberal use of the Energy advisory board, composed of key people we met through the Epcot

Forums . . . and of the contract Exxon had signed, along with all the other Epcot participants, giving Disney *final approval* of all show elements.

* * * * * * * * * *

So much of Epcot has depended on the interaction and cooperation between The Walt Disney Company and major corporations that it's difficult to separate the concept phase from the sales phase. Often a final agreement with a participant depended on the Imagineers' ability to create a pavilion concept that convinced a corporation's management, and their board of directors, to sign on the dotted line.

We also knew that Imagineering's reputation, established by Walt in Disneyland and significantly enhanced by the New York World's Fair shows and Walt Disney World itself, was a great trump card. As Colby Chandler, chairman and CEO of Kodak, told the media at the opening of Journey into Imagination: "We knew from the very beginning it would be a challenge to create a journey that would capture the imagination of everyone. But we also knew that if anyone could do it, Disney could . . . Epcot Center itself is a tribute to the reach of human imagination."

In Glendale, we directed our efforts toward developing major pavilions about key subjects: energy, transportation, food, health, space, communications, the oceans, and subjects that responded to sponsor discussions. In one form or another, every one of these subjects ultimately found a home in Epcot, as did several themes that responded to participant interests, such as Journey into Imagination for Kodak, and Horizons for General Electric. We were not as successful in the World Showcase. Even though several of them were some of our best work—such as the concepts that we developed for an African nations pavilion, Israel, Spain, Denmark, Switzerland, Costa Rica, Venezuela, and Iran (there was even a presentation in Tehran to the Shah himself!)—they were not built.

One special thrill for me was getting to know Alex Haley, the author of *Roots*, who consulted on our African Nations pavilion. One night I took the midnight red-eye flight from Los Angeles to Orlando, necessitating a change of aircraft in Atlanta. To my surprise, there was Alex Haley, waiting to board the same flight to Florida—at 5:00 A.M. We had a great conversation, while all around us frenzied parents were chasing their children, already anticipating their trip to the Magic Kingdom I suspect.

It was the extraordinary inventiveness of our Imagineering staff that carried the day, and opened doors to boardrooms that might otherwise be closed. Inventing new ways to present our stories became commonplace. The Universe of Energy ride system carried guests in six huge ninety-six-passenger, wire-guided vehicles single-file through a primeval world of dinosaurs, only to re-form as a group of six for a big screen film about the subject. In Spaceship Earth, visitors experienced a time-travel adventure aboard vehicles that moved up and down an eighteen-story structure, viewing a story about the history of human communications. In Journey into Imagination, guests met two new characters, Dreamfinder and Figment (of your imagination, of course) who became popular stars. Figment still welcomes you to the story, thirty years later. And I believe that we relaunched the 3-D film genre that had been dormant since the 1950s with a film called *Magic Journeys* by Murray Lerner—then almost a lone voice in his belief in the medium.

In The Land, we created a walking tour through several biomes—a controlled environment farm where some of the food and fish are actually served in the Walt Disney World restaurants. In the years after Opening Day came more one-of-a-kind experiences: the largest oceanic environment built at that time, the 5.7 million gallon Living Seas pavilion (now called The Seas with Nemo & Friends); . . . and the Mission: SPACE attraction, where guests feel the g-force actually experienced by astronauts when they blast off to outer space.

Developing these stories and designing the pavilions required a unique combination of talents that brought together age and experience, youth and inventiveness, and talent outside the Disney organization. When I realized the number of films we had to create from scratch, I called Randy Bright into my office and told him they were his responsibility. He responded this way: "Okay, on one condition: that I can build my own team—I don't have to use the Studio's filmmakers." To some, it was heresy. After all, every Disney park film to that time, 1982, had been made—at Walt's directive (even after his passing)—by a producer at the Studio. But those great talents Walt could call on—James Algar, Winston Hibler, Bill Walsh, Don DaGradi—were all retired or had passed away. This opened the door for us, and Randy, to bring in new filmmakers: Jeff Blyth, to make a Circle-Vision film in China; Murray Lerner for the 3-D *Magic Journeys;* Rick Harper and Bob Rogers, young writers and directors, to create a beautiful *Impressions de France.* We also hired wonderful art directors: Disney veterans Harper

Goff (*20,000 Leagues Under the Sea*), Bill Martin (Disneyland and the Magic Kingdom), and Bob Jolley (the supreme field art director who put the finishing touches, including aging, on the World Showcase pavilions). There were also movie industry talents like Walter Tyler, an Academy Award-winning art director, who designed the sets for The American Adventure.

One day, in discussion with a small group working on story, I had an inspiration. I recalled that Disneyland opened with no original songs or music—it was all derivative, primarily from Disney films through the years. Then Walt asked Richard M. Sherman and Robert B. Sherman to write a song "explaining" the Enchanted Tiki Room, the very first show to introduce Audio-Animatronics figures—all birds. Their 1963 ditty for the show where "all the birds sing words, and the flowers croon" was an instant hit. Soon, Bob and Dick were capturing the essence of Disney shows for the New York World's Fair, with "There's a Great Big Beautiful Tomorrow" for GE's Carousel of Progress, and "it's a small world" for the pavilion presented by UNICEF.

Those world's fair shows were featured in Disneyland, and soon thereafter they were joined by two iconic attractions, each of which featured a story-song by X. Atencio: "Yo Ho (A Pirate's Life for Me)" in Pirates of the Caribbean (1967) and "Grim Grinning Ghosts" for The Haunted Mansion (1969). Then the song well went dry. No new songs were created for Disney shows in Walt Disney World or Disneyland for the next thirteen years!

When I realized this, I was incredulous. What were we thinking, in a company where songs have told stories for decades? Such tunes included "Whistle While You Work"

(*Snow White and the Seven Dwarfs*), "Who's Afraid of the Big Bad Wolf?" (*Three Little Pigs*), "When You Wish Upon a Star" (*Pinocchio*), "A Dream Is a Wish Your Heart Makes" (*Cinderella*), "The Ballad of Davy Crockett" (*Davy Crockett, King of the Wild Frontier*), "Feed the Birds" and "Supercalifragilisticexpialidocious" (*Mary Poppins*), and so many more during Walt's lifetime.

In minutes, I was on the telephone to Dick Sherman, and we were on our way to involving half a dozen excellent songwriters to play a key role in Epcot storytelling. Soon, there was Bob and Dick Sherman's "One Little Spark" and "Magic Journeys" for Journey into Imagination; Bob Moline's "Listen to the Land" (The Land), "Canada (You're a Lifetime Journey)" (Canada), "Energy, You Make the World Go 'Round" (Universe of Energy), and the inspiring "Golden Dreams" (with Randy Bright for The American Adventure). More commercial songs were created for participants, especially Bob and Dick Sherman's "Makin' Memories" for a Kodak preshow about photography.

Now we were really rolling; everyone was singing off the same song sheet. It was time to find those sponsors!

* * * * * * * * * *

SELLING EPCOT

No story of convincing major corporations to sponsor Epcot's Future World pavilions would be complete—or accurate—without talking about the CEOs we dealt with. No company, with the possible exception of AT&T (Ed Block never told us how he involved his CEO), became part of our project without the direct involvement of its chairman, president, or CEO.

But first . . . the convoy full of models and artwork we

had shipped by truck and trailer to Warren, Michigan, for those GM meetings did not stop there. As soon as Jack Lindquist and I completed our presentation to GM president Pete Estes, our crew packed up the materials, separating them into well-thought-out portions. Half returned west to Glendale, and half traveled east to New York City. We had already determined that there was no way all the key executives we needed to reach would come to California or Florida to hear our story. We needed a dedicated location in *their* backyard that could be dressed out to feel like visiting our Imagineering headquarters. Thanks to our friends at RCA, we found the perfect location: an RCA recording studio at 1133 Sixth Avenue at 44th Street in New York City.

I'm sure some of the great performers who had recorded there would have been shocked at how we converted the space from a "temple of sound" into a "symphony of tomorrow" for Walt Disney World. We still played music here, but it was already recorded, as part of our presentation film, which was generally one-third of our pitch to potential sponsors. Everything was oriented around the overall park model we had shown to GM. The third feature was, unfortunately, a showman's violation of all the sound-absorbing walls of the recording studio. We filled them with reproductions of the major illustrations depicting the project.

The marketing team manned the Epcot Presentation Center for up to six days each week, for well over a year, so that an explanation and overview of our project could be presented to corporations, advertising agencies, international executives, and government officials, almost on a moment's notice. For key presentations, whoever was needed from the West Coast or Florida would fly in, often for a single presentation—an hour or two with an important prospect. It amazed me how many times my one overnight stay at the Waldorf was spent in a seven-room suite that, apparently, was seldom booked or rented in the late seventies. It always seemed to be available, even though I never requested it.

Meanwhile, Jack Lindquist and the marketing team were especially active on the international scene. In his book *In Service to the Mouse*, Jack shares tales of waiting ten days in the Philippines for a meeting with Imelda Marcos, wife of the president; *six weeks* in Tehran waiting to meet the Shah of Iran (the meeting took place, but the Shah was overthrown a few weeks later); and of being "threatened with being beheaded by a ten-year-old prince in Morocco." I was happy that I only had to make short trips to the headquarters of American corporations.

For the World Showcase, we also continued to leverage Walt Disney World. One weekend, Jack Lindquist worked with Disney's Washington office to bring a dozen senior ambassadors and their families from countries around the world, to enjoy the Magic Kingdom and see the Epcot construction site. Leading the diplomatic parade was the star of the ambassador corps in Washington from 1962 to 1986, Anatoly Dobrynin of the then Soviet Union. My wife, Leah, and I were assigned to host the family of Israel's Simcha Dinitz—the ambassador was suddenly called home to Tel Aviv—but the weekend resulted in a two-week tour of the Holy Land for Leah and me, designer Rick Rothschild, and art director Jack Martin Smith. We were escorted by one of Israel's great guides, Shraga Ben Yosef, as we worked with the government (unsuccessfully) to create an Israeli pavilion in the World Showcase.

This special Walt Disney World ambassadors' weekend was marred for me by one incident: the Swedish ambassador insisted his weekend would not be complete without his tennis game. As the best Disney player around, I was elected to take up the challenge. He was pretty good. When the set ended 6-6, we played a tiebreaker, which in those days ended with "sudden death" if the tiebreaker also reached 6–6, as it did.

What to do? As a good host, I blew it, and the Scandinavian took his victory home.

* * * * * * * * * *

The CEOs we met with were always an interesting challenge. As with Sarnoff ten years earlier, we always needed to send an advance party to check out the corporate spaces. Invariably, that meant sending or renting materials as basic as audio and visual equipment, easels, or pinnable corkboards. And then the fun began. Let me recount:

- I was shocked to see my copresenter, Jack Martin Smith, who'd been nominated for Academy Awards as a motion picture art director, suddenly down on his knees in front of our storyboard illustration of the dinosaurs in the Universe of Energy pavilion. "These," Jack gushed to Chairman Cliff Garvin and President Howard Kauffmann of Exxon, "are the Marilyn Monroes of our project!" This was *not* something we had planned.

- Harry Gray, CEO of United Technologies (UTC), was the most thorough, committed, and involved CEO we dealt with in the development of Epcot. As the head of a technology

186

company—Otis Elevator, Pratt & Whitney jet engines, Carrier air, and other environmental systems for buildings—he had a special concern for all the life-support systems designed for The Living Seas pavilion. When Harry summoned us from California and Florida to UTC headquarters in Hartford, Connecticut, we knew the key moment in our plans (and our schedule) had come.

The controversy was not insignificant—not when 5.7 million gallons of seawater was involved. Kym Murphy, our marine biologist, who had worked at several aquatic and aquarium projects before joining Disney, led our engineers away from a chlorine environment because of the negative effects on the ocean creatures he had observed. But his proposal—the use of ozone—had never been attempted in so large an area.

At UTC, there was a divided house. The senior, retiring head of research and development supported our team's recommendation. UTC's new R & D leader, either not wanting to take a chance or hoping to distance himself from his predecessor, recommended against it—thus Mr. Gray's call for a decisive meeting in Hartford. Tempers flared during the spirited discussion, and Harry Gray pushed and prodded, mostly yanking our chains. I was seated next to Ray D'Argenio, UTC's senior public relations executive. As he listened, he drew a picture that looked like this:

I asked Ray for an explanation. This is what he drew:

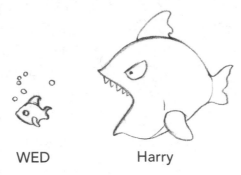

WED   Harry

It was clearly a lesson in who's the boss. There was no question with Harry Gray, as we were to find out over and over again—even though we won this major battle, and ozone became the vital living environment for our sea life "stars."

During a presentation to Kraft of our concepts for The Land in a conference room at our offices in Glendale, Chairman and CEO William O. Beers received a telephone call, which he took in my nearby office. As we walked back to the conference room, Bill Beers stopped for a moment and confided in me:

> *Marty, each of those nine people in that conference room runs a key division of Kraft, Inc.—and they never get together to address the challenges we have. That's why I want to be part of Epcot: it gives each of them a chance to work together on a high-profile project, and focus on communicating our company's leadership in the food business!*

It may have helped when, an hour or so earlier, as we began our concept presentation to a very tense audience of those Kraft leaders, I had instructed Hong Kong-born designer Doris Hardoon Woodward to make the presentation in Cantonese. "But Marty," Doris protested, "they won't understand anything I'm saying!" Doris was correct, as I knew she would be. But by the time I had stopped her and asked for the English version, the tension in the room was gone. Smiles and a bit of laughter replaced those frowns. We made the sale.

When we made our final presentation to GE's chairman and CEO, Reginald Jones, he had asked his three vice chairmen to attend the meeting. Shortly after GE signed its participant agreement, Jones retired, and the vice chairman who had been the most inquisitive and critical of our plan became chairman and CEO. His name was Jack Welch. Although GE was in, our concept was out—as were many of the old ways at General Electric. We didn't have to go through "Six Sigma" training, which became one of Jack Welch's signatures at GE, but we certainly knew who was "bringing good things to life" as we developed the Horizons pavilion, since replaced in Epcot by Mission: SPACE after GE's original participation contract ended.

* * * * * * * * * *

John L. Tishman, the longtime chairman and chief executive of Tishman Construction, has written a fascinating memoir entitled *Building Tall—My Life and the Creation of Construction Management*. Among his interesting reflections is a comparison between New York's World Trade Center—Tishman Construction built the Twin Towers that were destroyed on September 11, 2001—and Epcot Center, for which Tishman Construction also acted as construction manager:

Disney's Experimental Prototype Community of Tomorrow was actually a larger construction project than the World Trade Center had been in terms of the amount of area covered, the number of buildings—each one distinct—and the complexity of all the elements . . .

. . . The whole would cover some six hundred acres, which was to be carved out of very swampy land, including some large sinkholes . . .

Smack in the center of the six hundred acres was a huge sinkhole. Sinkholes are geological formations that can be as old as fifteen million to twenty-five million years. This one had been waiting for us quite a while, and its boundaries were not fixed—regularly, cars and trucks that we thought had been on safe, solid ground would start to sink in and would have to be rescued by a tow truck. The sinkhole was full of organic silt and peat, and the sand underneath went down as far as three hundred feet. Nothing solid could be built on it, since the underlying sand could not support the weight of a building. The most logical thing to do with the largest sinkhole of all was to dig it deeper and make it into the lagoon around which the World Showcase pavilions would be situated.

Simple idea, difficult thing to do. Under our direction, three general contractors specializing in heavy construction worked on the area. First, they had to construct a bathtub containing an area that could be filled with enough water in which to float a dredge to excavate and remove the muck. The muck was five feet thick and there was a million cubic yards of it to be removed so that the underlying sand could properly serve as the lagoon bottom. Complicating the task of removal were two huge "root islands" in the muck.

Unable to get them out, we eventually poured onto them a half-million yards of sand taken from another part of the lagoon. Then, top-heavy with sand, the root islands sank beneath the surface of the water and stayed there. Today, looking at the lagoon, you see no evidence of them. But they are there, beneath the surface . . .

Each pavilion was to appear physically very different from the other nineteen, and many of them were to be quite intricate and unusual, containing such machinery as moving platforms, as well as theaters, restaurant facilities, carnival-type rides, and the largest aquarium in the world.

The way that the Disney Company worked, its "imagineers" first created the basic design for each pavilion, sort of impressionistic sketches for freestanding sculptures and their surrounding environments. Then these sketches were turned over to outside architectural firms that would complete the actual working drawings and details that construction teams could execute. They awarded the design for each pavilion to a different architect . . . For us, this Disney design system meant that for each pavilion in Epcot, we had to deal with separate architectural and engineering firms. . . .

Our production schedules were at the heart of our work for Disney on Epcot. Such schedules are the guts of any construction management job; everything flows from them—the final revisions of drawings, the assembling of bid packages for the multiple contractors and materials, and the development of strategies for contracting, purchasing, and staffing. Eventually we produced hundreds of schedules interrelating about two thousand different activities.

The method of scheduling was the same as for the

World Trade Center towers, but while during the WTC
project the logistics had a vertical axis, at Epcot the need
was to plan the logistics on a horizontal axis. In turns, this
meant such things as having to plan for and carve out
parking lots for the construction workers' cars, some 2,500
of them each day. We had to create those lots, and a
lagoon (where there had not been one) and a major
monorail system, as well as major access roads leading
to and from Epcot to the nearby highways—and all
of this had to be done before any pavilions could be
erected . . .

Design and construction of Epcot was done on a crash
basis—in three years, a very rapid timetable for so
sprawling a project.

* * * * * * * * * *

While Tishman Construction and the general contractors
hired for each part of Epcot struggled with sinkholes and
the delivery of steel, the Imagineers raced to complete
everything from the Audio-Animatronics figures of Benjamin
Franklin and Mark Twain in The American Adventure to the
zoetropes and Magic Palette "hands on" (the term was current at that time) interactive fun in the Image Works area
of Journey into Imagination. There were so many innovations that we stopped counting, from the amazing Leapfrog
Fountains at Journey into Imagination to the largest continuous projection surface in the world for The American
Adventure attraction. Sequentially, it opened from seventy-
two feet early in the show to 150 feet wide during the finale.

At times, there was so much going on that our management lost track.

"We hired Mark Fuller [to create the Leapfrog Fountains] because of his work on laminar flow fountains," Orlando Ferrante, vice president of production, recalled nearly thirty years later, when Fuller received the Themed Entertainment Association's Lifetime Achievement Award. "Soon, Mark came to me and said he would need 'a few engineers' to work with him on Epcot's special water projects. That turned out to be nearly one hundred engineers, plus the production people to produce the designs!"

In concept, Spaceship Earth began as another descriptive written idea: let guests entering Epcot walk under an icon suggesting our planet itself. The engineers were not enthusiastic about this major challenge, but John Hench, Epcot's chief of design, saw the importance of what he called "the geosphere that is the symbol of Epcot." In *Designing Disney*, John wrote:

> *Spaceship Earth offered an impressive invitation to adventure and equally impressive design challenges. We assumed from the beginning that we needed a large sphere for the Epcot icon, and we wanted one with enough space inside for all attraction. We were familiar with architect Buckminster Fuller's experiments with building the geodesic dome he had invented in the 1940s, including the one he had constructed for the Ford headquarters in Dearborn, Michigan, in 1953. Fuller's famous phrase "spaceship earth" also appealed to us. [Fuller actually visited Imagineering during the project's design phase.] But he had never made a complete sphere as large as the one we hoped to build. Our engineers said that if we constructed only three-quarters of the sphere, our dome could support itself on a base, leaving the interior space clear . . .*

At our first design meeting, the engineers showed
a drawing that pictured a dome sitting directly on the
ground. We needed a sphere, however; I asked if the
dome could instead rest on a round platform with legs
underneath to hold it up, which would allow us to suspend
the bottom quarter of a sphere from the underside of the
platform, completing the sphere.

After several days, the engineers concluded that yes, my
idea could work, but that it would be expensive.

The geosphere we built was 164 feet in diameter,
standing eighteen feet off the ground on three sets of
double legs, with more than two million cubic feet of
interior space. It has so far withstood winds of up to two
hundred miles an hour. It wasn't complicated at all, really. I
was simply able to visualize how the self-supporting dome
could be built as a perfect sphere seeming to float on its
legs.

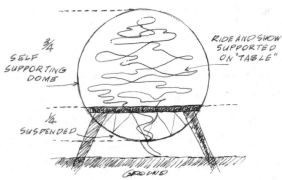

This is the sketch John Hench made for the engineers.
The completed "geodesic sphere" was, when it was built,
the world's largest, encompassing 2.2 million cubic feet of
space inside, with an outside surface area of 150,000 square
feet.

Ray Bradbury's story treatment became the framework for our communication theme, taking us from the cave walls of France to the exploration of outer space. *"Where did we come from? Where are we going? How do we get there?"* Ray began . . . and his first draft answer ran fourteen pages!

One of the key assignments in creating the Spaceship Earth show went to Peggie Fariss. It was Peggie's job to organize the research, including the work of outside academic consultants. What were the key periods and events in world history that advanced our ability to spread communications? What civilizations made quantum leaps forward? What did the people of the times wear, ranging from the royalty of ancient Egypt to the inventor Gutenberg at his printing press?

To assure historical accuracy, Peggie led a research effort that reached out around the country to specialists in the Renaissance, Egyptian hieroglyphics, ancient and biblical languages, and communications. Our primary authority was Fred Williams, founding dean of the Annenberg School for Communication and professor of communications at USC. In addition, Peggie's bibliography of books consulted is nineteen pages long, from Cro-Magnon art to Greek language and "Latin graffiti."

We launched Spaceship Earth with narration recorded by the wonderful voice of television actor Larry Dobkin. Then, in an attempt to create some star power with a voice familiar to our guests, Tom Fitzgerald wrote a great script for a fan of Walt Disney World and Epcot: Walter Cronkite. With changes in the show in the nineties, Tom created a new script for still another amazing voice: that of Jeremy Irons. And finally, with

Siemens becoming the presenter of the new and current show in 2007, Pam Fisher created the current narration recorded with Dame Judi Dench.

The ride system was the most vexing issue of all. There were ride engineers at Imagineering who argued vehemently against the advisability of a ride that would rise 164 feet in the air, and descend backward. The first outside ride vendor selected closed its theme park unit after we chose them. . . . and retreated into transporting supplies in manufacturing operations.

This was one of those classic moments in the development of an attraction when "no" was not in the Imagineering vernacular. Predictably, placing a 180-foot "wienie" at the entrance to a park was so enticing that every guest wanted to know "what's in the ball" (sometimes "golf ball"). There was no getting around solving the challenge of that huge elevation change from ground level to the 164-foot height, which entailed dealing with the dramatically steep slopes and the heavy, endless chain of vehicles needed to achieve the THRC (Theoretical Hourly Ride Capacity) of 2,571 per hour.

Last, but far from least, has been the challenge faced by every design and production team: designing and installing sets and scenes in a limited space environment where the audience is constantly moving upstream or downstream. Don't let that "big ball" fool you: once the track envelope was established, the spaces left for show inside the geodesic sphere were extremely confined, often limited by structural elements, with practically no flat or square surfaces. As one show producer told me, "This building does not conform to easy storytelling!"

The original design and production team thought of loading in the show as a giant jigsaw puzzle. All the scenery was finished three or four months before the freight elevator was installed, so that the elevator shaft could be used to haul all the scenes from ground level to the top . . . because once the freight elevator was installed (and for subsequent changes in the show), all the set pieces had to be built in sections to fit into the limited space.

In so many ways, Spaceship Earth in Epcot represents our desire to communicate the connections all of us share with the past and the future on our fragile planet, expressed so beautifully by poet and statesman Archibald MacLeish. "To see the earth as it truly is," he wrote, "small and blue and beautiful in that eternal silence where it floats, is to see ourselves as riders on the earth together, brothers on that bright loveliness in the eternal cold—brothers who know now they are truly brothers."

* * * * * * * * * *

One of my favorite projects was The Land, presented by Kraft. We had a great relationship with the participant's executives, first with Bill Beers and then, when it became Dart & Kraft, with President and COO Arthur (Bud) Woelfle. (It's now sponsored by Nestlé.)

The original pavilion included two of the major food facilities in Epcot and three main attractions: the film *Symbiosis*, Paul Gerber's tour of the world to review the delicate balance between technological progress and environmental integrity, between man and nature; the Kitchen Kabaret, a humorous musical show devoted to telling the story of the benefits of good nutrition, starring "Bonnie Appetit"; and the Listen to the Land boat cruise. Today, the boat ride is still a major feature, but the main event is one of Disney's most popular attractions in California and Florida: the hang glider–like experience called Soarin'.

Most Imagineers believed the experience that most exemplified "Walt's Epcot concept"—experimental prototype of the future—was (and still is) The Land boat ride. The narrated, thirteen-minute trip in tandem boats carrying forty passengers (over two thousand per hour) travels at a speed of two feet per second through a story of agricultural development in challenging environments around the world—the rain forest, the desert, and the American prairie—then enters a world of agricultural beauty and bounty. There's an Aquacell where fish are raised, and three major Living Laboratories: Tropic, Desert, and Creative or Experimental greenhouses. All told, some forty different food crops and sixteen growing systems demonstrate the potential of CEA (Controlled Environment Agriculture) in a thirty-thousand-square-foot facility where real food from all around the globe thrives, including the lettuce I had teased Card Walker about. Key staples such as rice, corn, sorghum, and tomatoes grow here year-round, and guests often see exotic plants from six continents around the world: African fluted pumpkin, jackfruit, cacao, Java apple, and dragon fruit (from a cactus).

Carl Hodges, then director of the Environmental Research Laboratory at the University of Arizona, was another find by Peggie. Once we visited his labs, located a few steps from the Tucson Airport, we knew that he and his colleagues had to become part of our Epcot team. Hodges and his agricultural scientists' work in halophyte research was especially noteworthy, stretching all the way back in time to the civilization of the Aztecs in Mexico who, it seems, knew more about growing plants in saline soil than anyone. The significance of halophyte research is that more than 99 percent of the water on earth is seawater or ice. The development of plants that can be irrigated with seawater has an important potential for the future.

We charged the University of Arizona group with developing the systems for growing food in The Land pavilion's greenhouse-like structures. To prove the principles, in a controlled environment in Arizona, we had them build and plant a third of the total length of what would ultimately be the Florida boat ride. At the pace the boat would travel, we walked the attraction. We could almost pick the corn, tomatoes, banana squash, pineapples (and lettuce!) as we passed by. It was clear that Listen to the Land would be a winner—it was a thrill just to smell the attraction.

Almost as an afterthought, Carl Hodges asked, "Where do we keep the bees?"

I looked at him incredulously. "Carl, those boats that will be riding through the greenhouse—they will be filled with real people. Bees are out."

"Well then," Hodges shot back, "how do we *pollinate* the plants?"

"Look," I replied, "we are the storytellers. We're in show business. You are the scientists. *You* tell *us* how you are going to pollinate the plants!"

Today, when you ride the boats or take one of the nine backstage Harvest Tours offered daily and walk through the biomes of The Land, you will very likely see a scientist member of The Land's team pollinating each plant, individually, *by hand*. It takes about fifteen hours per week to pollinate the dozens of plants growing in the Living Laboratories, and they have been doing this for thirty years.

At the dedication of The Land in October 1982, Kraft's president, Bud Woelfle, read a quote from the renowned microbiologist, environmentalist, and humanist René Dubos—words that are inscribed at the entrance to the pavilion:

> *Symbiotic relationships mean creative partnerships. The earth is to be seen neither as an ecosystem to be preserved unchanged, nor as a quarry to be exploited for selfish and short-range economic reasons, but as a garden to be cultivated for the development of its own potentialities of the human adventure. The goal of this relationship is not the maintenance of the status quo, but the emergence of new phenomena and new values.*

The dedication speaker followed. We were honored that the speaker was Dr. Norman Borlaug, agricultural geneticist and Nobel Peace Prize recipient in 1970, who is often called a father of the "green revolution."

When the speechmaking ended, I followed Carl Hodges toward the entrance of The Land. Suddenly, he stopped with a shudder, and I worried he might have some kind of physical issue.

"Carl, are you all right?" I asked.

"I suddenly realized what this means for me," he said. "By the end of the day, more people will have seen my work than in the previous thirty years I've been doing it!"

The impact of telling your story to fifteen thousand or twenty thousand people a day, and to millions each year, can be frightening to a scientist—imagine inviting thousands of people into your laboratory. Or it can be a giant stimulus, pushing us to explore new frontiers . . . just as Walt had envisioned the spirit and impact of Epcot.

* * * * * * * * * *

From early in the project development, we had an excellent working relationship with Exxon. To test the impact of working together, Disney produced a comic book called *Mickey and Goofy Explore Energy*. It quickly became the most widely distributed comic book in the history of the medium. Ten million copies were soon in the hands of young readers in schools around the country. A follow-up, *Mickey and Goofy Explore the Universe of Energy*, promoted our Epcot pavilion with an even larger distribution.

What no one knew was what was happening behind the scenes with the brand-new, then one-of-a-kind ride system we had committed ourselves to develop. Each show begins with ninety-six guests seated in each of six electric-powered passenger vehicles—the largest in the world, other than electric trains. Each of the vehicles, eighteen feet wide and twenty-nine feet long, weighs six and a half tons. And, despite the fact that when they leave the guest loading area, they "break apart" into a single file ride-through, the vehicles are driverless.

The vehicles are guided through the Universe of Energy by a small wire (one-eighth of an inch in diameter) buried in the floor. Sensing units mounted under the ride-through vehicles detect signals from a guide wire, and issue commands to the independent steering units on the front and rear axles to keep the vehicles centered over the wire. Inductive power coupling transfers electric power from a source in the roadbed to vehicles by electromagnetic induction across an air gap. Power is transferred without contact only when the Universe of Energy vehicles are stopped in the theaters. A central computer operates the movement of these "traveling theaters," with a secondary computer acting as a go-between for the individual vehicles. Significant changes in direction in the attraction are accomplished by giant turntables, which spin the theater cars on a cushion of air. The two turntable systems, eighty and ninety-two feet in diameter, can handle six cars and a load capacity of eighty-five tons.

I was soon to find out why no one had ever attempted a ride system this complicated. Tony Baxter, senior vice president in the Creative Division of Imagineering, recently reminded me of a call I received and put on my speakerphone, as we were reviewing Tony's design for the ride-through on his imaginative project, Journey into Imagination. The call was from John Zovich, our vice president of engineering, one of the prime people responsible for the ultimate success of Epcot's technology innovations. But on this occasion, the news was all bad.

"We give up, Marty," John said. "We cannot make this system work. It's just too complicated."

"John," I responded, "if you can't make the ride system work, we have no show and therefore no Universe of Energy. We lose our sponsor. If we lose Exxon, it's a domino effect, and what will happen is, the other sponsors we are soliciting will go away. And at the end of the day, we will lose the project—no more Epcot Center. So, John," I said, pausing a few seconds for emphasis, "don't call me again until the ride system is working!" And I hung up on our chief engineer.

I won't say our Imagineering ride engineers were entirely successful. For a full year after we opened, I received a weekly call from Exxon's senior vice president, Jack Clarke, pointing out that the ride and show only operated at 80 to 84 percent efficiency, in contrast to the 98 to 100 percent we target. By year two of Epcot's life, we were in the 90 percentile every week, and Jack Clarke and I could concentrate on an occasional tennis game where, as I pointed out to him, we were both hard-pressed to achieve 50 percent efficiency.

The Epcot advisory boards were absolutely critical to our success. The members were academics and government officials, futurists and history experts, and industry executives and foundation leaders. One of the very best was our advisory group for The Living Seas, which included directors and/or senior scientists from the Scripps Institution of Oceanography and Woods Hole Oceanographic Institution, National Geographic Society president Gilbert Grosvenor, and Dr. Sylvia Earle, who would later become the chief scientist of the National Oceanic and Atmospheric Administration (NOAA).

I'll never forget The Living Seas advisory board meeting that took place shortly after life-forms were discovered around heat-emitting vents at ocean depths never before explored. Dr. Robert Ballard, then the senior scientist at Woods Hole, who had led the expedition that discovered the *Titanic*, approached Gil Grosvenor with this greeting: "You know of course that everything you have printed in *National Geographic* about the potential of life in the deepest depths of the ocean has been incorrect!"

I don't recall how *National Geographic* responded to these new explorations of the deep sea, but for us it meant scrapping a well-defined film show that acted as an introduction to our Sea Base, and starting over to create our scene-setter. And that was just the beginning of our troubles.

Harry Gray, the CEO of United Technologies, let it be known that he wanted the exterior walls of the pavilion to be painted a bright white. John Hench, one of the most knowledgeable designers in the world on the theory and effect of color, visually and emotionally, let Gray know that he did not use a bright white in Florida because the reflection of the sun could be blinding to approaching guests. Gray asked for a demonstration.

While the pavilion was under construction, we erected temporary walls six feet high around the front of the building. On a bright, sunny afternoon, John Hench lined up the painters and, when Harry and Helen Gray arrived, established the parameters of the discussion. "Mr. Gray," John said, "I use thirty-four shades of white in our parks. Which one would you like to see?"

While Harry Gray pondered his response, Helen Gray gripped my arm and drew me aside. "Marty, why are you asking Harry about color?" she asked. "I pick out his ties every morning because he's color-blind!"

* * * * * * * * * *

Harry Gray may have been color-blind, but those eyes were totally focused on his power, which he demonstrated during our meeting about The Living Seas life-support system in the summer of 1985. That day, he saved the best for last.

Our Disney team knew we were in trouble when, having arrived as instructed at 8:30 A.M., we cooled our heels in the UTC lobby until nearly 10:00 A.M. We later learned that the CEO was conducting a pre-meeting with his staff—preparing the "shark attack" I described earlier. Once the meeting began, the discussion was hot and heavy until Gray left us for a lunch break. Harry returned about 2:30 P.M. to inform us that he was sure that he would have all the information he needed to make a final decision by 4:00 P.M. His next question was a total surprise to all of us who were by then looking for a break in the meeting ourselves, so that we could cancel our flight home to Los Angeles. What time, Harry wanted to know, was our flight? When we responded that we were booked on a 5:30 P.M. American Airlines departure from JFK Airport in New York City, Harry immediately turned to an aide. Here's the way I remember the conversation—and the events that followed: "Good—American Airlines—they use our Pratt Whitney engines, and we do lots of favors for them when they have an emergency issue with an engine. Tell them," he instructed his assistant, "that we need a favor in return. There will be five Disney people leaving our headquarters in Hartford [Connecticut] at 4:30 P.M. this afternoon by helicopter. They will not have time to go through the terminal, or security, so what we will need to do is *land the helicopter as close to their aircraft as possible.* American can have their staff meet the Disney people at our helicopter, and take them right on board the Los Angeles flight."

Today, of course, with airport security being what it is, this scenario would be unthinkable. But on that summer afternoon in 1985, we boarded the UTC helicopter on the roof of their headquarters building in Hartford at precisely 4:30 P.M. Shortly after 5:00, we landed at JFK—no more than one hundred feet from that American Airlines craft that would soon carry us to Los Angeles. Two hosts from the airline emerged from the terminal almost the exact moment the helicopter touched down. They immediately escorted the five Disney passengers, myself included, past others waiting to board our flight, directly onto the aircraft. Meanwhile, our luggage was transferred from the helicopter to the airplane. Right on time, at 5:30 P.M., our American Airlines flight departed for Los Angeles.

As promised, Harry Gray had made his decision by 4:00 P.M. He agreed with the Disney Imagineers that ozone, not chlorine, was the correct choice for the life-support system in The Living Seas pavilion at Epcot. He thanked us for "dropping everything" and coming to Hartford for this important discussion, wished us a pleasant flight home, and said goodbye. Harry Gray was gone from the conference room physically, but we all knew who was still in charge. And it was not American Airlines.

Each of the pavilions in Epcot has its own story. In retrospect, it's a miracle that almost every one of these stories had a happy ending. As often happens in a creative environment, imaginative thinking trumps negative attitudes and points the way for technical achievement to follow . . . especially in the World Showcase host pavilion, The American Adventure.

"We never rejected a show concept because someone said it was technically impossible," WED's director of scripts and show development, Randy Bright, related—while admitting that it took six different concepts and five years to develop the show.

Making thirty-five Audio-Animatronics figures—from hosts Benjamin Franklin and Mark Twain to women's suffrage leader Susan B. Anthony and Nez Perce Indian Chief Joseph—move and talk within 13 three-dimensional sets that travel back and forth, up and down, meant developing a complex staging system that rivals or exceeds anything ever designed for a Broadway show. The key is a 350,000-pound automated scene changer that looks like a steel skeleton, and is as long as a railroad box car and twice as wide. On the changer are ten different sets. On either side are other sets hidden below stage on elevators awaiting their cues.

Moving onto the 130-by-80-foot stage, the sets are operated by computer. They glide into place horizontally, then rise into audience view using hydraulic telescoping supports.

Special flexible channels were created to carry electronic wire, electrical connections, air, hydraulic fluid, and water lines, which give lifelike movement to the figures and special effects.

"This is the first 'play' we ever created in our parks, and certainly the first-ever 'play' with Audio-Animatronics actors onstage," according to Show Director Rick Rothschild. But there's one thing missing on the stage—there's no floor. Although the audience cannot see it, "actors" are supported on small platforms surrounded by open space, wires, and pipes. One other thing is missing: although there is a wardrobe room to store standby costumes, there are no dressing rooms. In nearly thirty years, the Audio-Animatronics actors have not complained even once.

* * * * * * * * * *

Epcot today presents the entertainment, food, artisans, and products of eleven countries: Canada, China, France, Germany, Italy, Japan, Mexico, Morocco, Norway, the

United Kingdom, and the USA. Imagineering also designed, on spec, or with preliminary agreements that were never formalized, eight more pavilions: an African Nations show-case, Costa Rica, Denmark, Iran, Israel, Spain, Switzerland, and Venezuela.

Because it was so late in coming into the project, the China pavilion was the most difficult to complete. The first sketch of what became China in Epcot was drawn in April 1981—barely twenty months before Opening Day. It features a Disney Circle-Vision 360 theater that's entered through an elaborate re-creation of Beijing's Temple of Heaven, a struc-ture that dates back to the mid-1400s.

The logistics of shooting a film in China in 1980—just four years after the Cultural Revolution had ended—were incred-ibly complex, made even more difficult by the fact that our crews, directed by Jeff Blyth, were photographing with the Disney-originated nine-camera rig used to shoot Circle-Vision 360 shows—films that place the audience in the cen-ter of each scene. There were only two of these rigs in the world, both built by Disney (until the Chinese copied ours!), utilizing a system originally created by the technical genius of the Disney Studios, Ub Iwerks. The rig weighs in at 396 pounds, and, according to Blyth, at first it "petrified" the Chinese.

"Our Disney shoot was the first coproduction [with a Chinese film company] after the 'Gang of Four' were gone," Blyth recalls. "We had to get permission to film site by site. We started out with 150 potential locations; I spent ten weeks scouting; then our crew—four Americans and eight Chinese, including two translators—spent four and a half months in actual shooting. We filmed the Great Wall in three places, the Forbidden City, the Temple of Heaven, the Potala Palace, the Gobi Desert, Shanghai, Guilin, Yangtze River gorges, the Harbin Ice Festival in Manchuria, and a performance by the Peking Opera. We even filmed in Tibet—at sixteen thousand feet!"

Eventually, the U.S. and Chinese crews became one, except for the aerial scenes. "They let me go up in the air for a pre-scout," Blyth says, "but when the nine-camera rig was mounted on our Messerschmitt helicopter, my Chinese assistant had to handle the shoot. I still have no idea what they didn't want us to see."

Wonders of China was such a big hit that twelve years later, in 1993, Blyth returned for new scenes and updated the film to the present new version, now called *Reflections of China.*

Two other features, consistent with a world's fair context, helped to set Epcot apart from any amusement park. One was Epcot's fine art program, begun with the display of more than $25 million in original art—Mayan artifacts in Mexico, Chinese textiles, Japanese crafts—and later items from the Moroccan royal family, art and artifacts by American artists, and a historical exhibit inside a traditional stave church in Norway. "Art continues to give Epcot a great balance, where you can enjoy high technology and prospects for the future alongside priceless treasures of ancient civilizations," says Van Romans, who has moved on from WED's director of exhibits for Epcot to become president of the Fort Worth Museum of Science and History.

The second world's fair context was Epcot's World Showcase Fellowship Program. Annually, it brought nearly eight hundred representatives from the ten foreign countries showcased in Epcot to work in their homeland's pavilion. They each wore a costume typical of their native land and welcomed Epcot guests on behalf of their countrymen back home. They also lived together in a kind of "world village" a few miles from Epcot.

"We imagined," Dick Nunis said of the program, "that in fifteen or twenty years, these former students would become leaders of their nations and be able to discuss potential ventures or challenges in a friendly way, based on having lived and learned together while working in Epcot." And indeed, even today the European participants in the World Showcase Fellowship Program hold an annual reunion somewhere in Europe, maintaining their fellowship and their connection to Epcot and Walt Disney World.

* * * * * * * * * *

During the eight years of our development of the Epcot Center that opened in October 1982, we met and discussed the concept with many world-renowned people: Buckminster Fuller, whose design and words inspired our Spaceship Earth; *Roots* author, Alex Haley, who worked with us in our unsuccessful attempts to produce an African nations pavilion; the great French chefs Paul Bocuse, Gaston Lenôtre, and Roger Vergé, who brought their gastronomic wonders to the French restaurants; Don Hewitt, producer and creator of CBS's *60 Minutes*, who attended the opening with former New York mayor Robert Wagner and John Tishman, and reminded us of his favorite four words: "Tell me a story!"; and Walter Cronkite, who sent us this note on Epcot's opening:

This universality of Disney carries on after his death, and continues in projects that he had put on the drawing board before he died. Epcot Center in Florida is a case in point— bringing together representatives of international industry, international commerce, and the governments of other countries in a permanent world's fair. It perpetuates that theme of his that we are indeed one people.

We also received this letter from the president of the United States, Ronald Reagan:

Nancy and I are delighted to extend our warmest congratulations and best wishes to everyone gathered for the Grand Opening of Disney World's Epcot Center.

This historical moment marks the realization of a singular vision of the future by a great man and an outstanding organization. Epcot Center stands as a tribute to the technical know-how of American industry and the inventiveness of the human mind. There is far more here than the thrills and delights of amusement, for Epcot is truly a doorway to the twenty-first century and destined to become an integral part of the American experience. In presenting solutions to problems faced by communities and nations around the globe, it will be a showcase for the free enterprise system and optimism of the American spirit.

Walt Disney's achievements brought happiness to the hearts of young and old alike. He once referred to his own work as "imagineering," and he was quick to utilize the talents and creativity of others to take us to a place no one else had ever been, where we would leave the comfort of the familiar and enter the world of the pioneer, and where

imagination and dedication combined to make dreams
a reality.

Epcot Center is the product of a man who dared to
dream and had the courage and drive to accomplish that
dream. When asked for the secret of his success, Walt
replied, "I simply wished upon a star." That star will now
illuminate the lives of youngsters, Americans, and people
from around the world who enter here and experience the
ingenuity, history, showmanship, and hope of Epcot Center.

We join all Americans in wishing you great success as
you point the way to the future.

One of my favorite reviews of what we had accomplished in Epcot was written several years after its opening as an op-ed article in the *Orlando Sentinel* by guest author Herbert London, dean of the Gallatin Division of Interdisciplinary Studies at New York University, and a senior fellow at the Hudson Institute. Under a headline stating, "Epcot Is the True Embodiment of the American Dream," he wrote in part:

Disney World's Epcot Center is advertised as a magic
kingdom for adults, a permanent world's fair, a mecca
for kids of every age. It is all of that and more. Epcot is a
challenge to the future. In a style that is idiosyncratically
American, Epcot dares its viewers to consider the future.
This isn't a future of elitists filled with weltschmerz; this is a
future of hope and opportunity . . .

They also get a message of promise. Energy needs
aren't seen as an intractable problem, but as a challenge.
Car companies aren't resistant to change; they are
searching for the best alternative to the combustion
engine. Food isn't characterized as insufficient to feed

hungry multitudes. It is as bounteous as our imagination. If one can dream, there is hope. Epcot is for dreamers . . .

There aren't any guarantees about the future. The Disney people know that and so do those visitors who pour into the gates each day. But these people know intuitively that the flame of progress must continue to burn if our civilization is to survive. That idea lives in all its majesty at Epcot. It is what children and old folks can share. It is what foreigners find so unique about this land. It is what gives us faith in better days ahead.

* * * * * * * * * *

"Better days" were certainly ahead for many exceptional talents that the Epcot project played an important role in developing. Some of the proudest moments I personally savor that relate to our Epcot days actually occur today, when I meet with or hear about the achievements of some of the young talent who earned their stripes in the trenches on the project. For some, like Monty Lunde, creating special effects for Epcot was his first job after graduating from Stanford; after Epcot he joined with another Imagineer, Rock Hall, to create Technifex. Today, it is one of the industry's premier companies producing attractions, exhibits, and state-of-the-art special effects.

Glen Birket, an admitted "inexperienced engineer," was instrumental in creating the technical systems that still make the complex American Adventure show work. Today his Birket Engineering works for many companies—including parts of four Disney parks around the world.

Two of the highest-profile post-Epcot achievers are Mark Fuller and Bob Rogers. Graduating from the fountains of

Epcot to create WET Enterprises, Fuller has won international renown for some of the most admired fountain installations in the world—in twenty-two countries, in fact. He became a star with The Fountains of Bellagio at the Bellagio Hotel in Las Vegas; built the biggest fountain in the world, The Dubai Fountain (Burj Dubai); and brought his artistry to New York City through the new Revson Fountain at Lincoln Center.

Bob Rogers and his BRC Imagination Arts (he's the chairman) stopped counting their many awards for the films, exhibits, shows, and attractions they have created for clients worldwide. Their creations have been hits at World Expos from Vancouver (1986) to Shanghai (2010), including pavilions representing the United States itself.

I'm proud to say that we put BRC in business in 1981. General Motors had come to us to design their postshow area for the World of Motion pavilion in Epcot; when we could not free up any of our overwhelmed creative staff for the task, I recommended Bob Rogers—and guaranteed GM that Imagineering would look over his shoulder to assure an excellent project. In fact, several of the attractions Rogers and his team developed—notably The Water Engine Show and The Bird and the Robot—were among the most popular with Epcot's guests at opening. BRC continued to work with GM on the development of exhibits and shows for over a decade after their experience in Epcot. And BRC also created the *Back to Neverland* film for the Disney-MGM Studios at Walt Disney World.

Several also have become important leaders in the leisure-recreation industry. Monty Lunde created the Themed Entertainment Association (TEA) twenty years ago;

today it counts more than seven hundred companies around the world as members. In 2011–2012, the TEA president was Rick Rothschild, our show director for The American Adventure pavilion. And Bob Rogers has served on the board of directors of IAAPA, the International Association of Amusement Parks and Attractions.

The incredible requirements of the Epcot project made it almost mandatory that we give experienced hands new challenges, and inexperienced (often young) talent their first opportunity to show what they could do. Their achievements ratified my continuing to "take a chance" on young talent throughout my years as the creative leader of the Imagineers. Sound familiar? It was a Walt Disney tradition I wholeheartedly endorsed.

Melanie Simon, a young planner/scheduler for The American Adventure during her Epcot tenure and now a consultant working with such clients as the Smithsonian Institution and the National Park Service, said it so well in a recent note to me: "One of the real 'miracles' of Epcot is that so many young, inexperienced folks were given the opportunity and responsibility and learned by doing. Gaining the confidence to tackle 'impossible' tasks and not be afraid of new things was life-changing. Sadly, I don't think young people get that kind of education nowadays."

In America, we have the talent to do anything we put our minds and hands to achieving. Let's hope we remember that our young country was founded and has grown into one of the world's greatest nations by creating opportunities for new birds to spread their wings, and fly as high as they can go.

11

"LOST IN TRANSLATION" WAS A LATECOMER TO OUR TOKYO EXPERIENCE.

Surprisingly in a company as public and in the spotlight as Disney, no one has told the real story of Disney's first venture into the international park and resort arena. For several years, I pursued Frank Stanek and Ron Cayo, a Disney strategic planner and a Disney corporate lawyer, respectively—two of the key principals in negotiating the first and most successful foreign venture, Tokyo Disneyland—imploring them to send me notes detailing how it happened.

Several times they said, "Just watch Sofia Coppola's *Lost in Translation* film with Bill Murray. It has all the cultural and language shock we suffered, but it was played for laughs, and ours was deadly serious!"

Finally, I convinced Stanek to help me tell this story; his extensive notes make the beginning of this chapter a primer for one of the most important developments in Disney park history: the "invasion" of Japan and France (and later China) by exported attractions and entertainment. Five parks have already spread Disney style family fun, to audiences across the oceans. A sixth, Shanghai Disneyland, is now being developed for opening in 2015 or 2016.

This is the Tokyo story—one filled with international intrigue, strong personalities, communication challenges, and ambitious executives seeking credit for making it happen as a stepping-stone in advancing their personal careers.

* * * * * * * * * *

Frank Stanek was WED's director of research and planning. His department provided research and analysis related to the expansion of Disneyland and Walt Disney World. This position segued naturally into his assignment to begin the process of analysis for Disney's first park venture internationally. His twenty-five years at Disney involved him in all aspects of new business creation and project development, including the early planning work for Epcot. After leaving the Walt Disney company as vice president of corporate planning in 1987, Frank held key executive positions at Vivendi-Universal Entertainment. As president of International Business Development, he led the international development for Universal Parks and Resorts, initiating the creation of Universal Studios Japan in Osaka, and the acquisition of Universal Mediterranea near Barcelona, Spain.

With Walt Disney World a tremendous success—attracting 10.7 million people in its first year ending September 30, 1972—Disney began receiving inquiries from around the world. Late in 1972, Disney's corporate management directed Stanek to research Japan and Europe as potential locations for "the first international Disneyland." To begin understanding these markets, Stanek focused on receptiveness to the Disney brand, economic stability and growth factors, cultural characteristics, and travel patterns. Ultimately, one succinct sentence from Stanek's summary memo early in 1973 carried the day: "While both Europe and Japan can support a Disneyland project, Japan offers the highest potential for success, even though it may be more difficult to execute."

The energy crisis of 1974 slowed the expansion process, as Florida tourists, then primarily arriving in the Sunshine State by automobile, curtailed their travel, impacting attendance for the first time since Walt Disney World opened in 1971. But in December 1974, a Disney executive team comprised of Card Walker, Donn Tatum, Ron Cayo, Dick Nunis, and WED's Orlando Ferrante and John Hench traveled to Japan to review potential sites.

Initially, two locations were presented to the Disney group. One, at the base of Mount Fuji, the 12,389-foot-tall iconic symbol and most distinctive feature of Japan's geography, was controlled by the Mitsubishi Company. But after visiting the site, the Disney executives were informed that Mitsubishi had "changed its mind," and the property was no longer available. That left a large tract of land in Urayasu, Chiba Prefecture (similar to a county in the USA), about fifteen miles from the center of Tokyo. The main virtue of the location was that it was within a one-hour drive of the resident population of nearly thirty million.

The property was under development by the Oriental Land Company (OLC), a joint venture of Mitsui Real Estate and the

Keisei Electric Railway. OLC had been reclaiming the location, through landfill, developing commercial and residential projects on about four thousand acres on the north portion of Tokyo Bay. In granting the right to reclaim and create this land, Chiba required OLC to devote a portion of the site to the "public good." Bringing Disneyland to Japan would not only meet that requirement, but would do so in a highly visible and popular way.

It took nearly a year of work by the Disney team, spearheaded by Stanek and the corporate lawyer, Cayo, before a letter of intent was signed in July 1976 between Disney and the Oriental Land Company. There followed a year of work, financed by the Japanese at a cost of $1 million, to complete a thorough study of site conditions and construction methods, market feasibility, and attendance projections. The summary result was that a "Tokyo Disneyland" had the potential to attract *seventeen million visitors*—a number the Disney team found "astonishing" on the one hand, and impractical on the other. As Stanek characterized the report, "It was not possible to build a park initially with that kind of visitor capacity, due to both costs and the time required. So we concluded that the park should be sized for ten million, a number we knew was achievable." After all, Walt Disney World, with a small resident base, but a large tourist market, had achieved that result five years earlier.

Early in 1977, negotiations to create a definitive agreement for a Disneyland in Japan began in earnest. Before the agreement was signed on April 30, 1979—four and a half years after the Disney executive team first visited Japan—the project's progress was "like a bottle floating in the ocean, rising and falling as personalities and the issues of negotiating the business agreement moved forward and backward," Stanek says.

"In the end," Stanek remembers, "the key issues of contention were: 1) the unwillingness of Disney to invest in the project; 2) the amount of fees Disney would be paid by OLC; and 3) anything to do with the cost burden to be borne by OLC."

As Disney's chief executive, Card Walker had committed the corporation to building "Walt's dream," Epcot, soon to be under construction for an October 1, 1982, opening. Card Walker was also committed to establishing the Disney parks internationally, but only on the terms he and the Disney board of directors had set.

Compounding Card Walker's attitude toward the Japanese was his World War II experience, when he served as a flight deck officer on the American aircraft carrier *Bunker Hill*. In April and May 1945, desperate Japanese fighters engaged in kamikaze attacks off the coast of Japan. The kamikaze destroyed as many Allied warships as possible by crashing their aircraft directly into the ships, especially aircraft carriers, sacrificing both airplane and pilot in each suicide mission.

In May 1945, the *Bunker Hill* was hit by two Japanese Zeros piloted by kamikazes while it was supporting the invasion of Okinawa. Card's son, Cardon, still a Disney Studio employee today, told me his father had the luck of the draw—a brief five-day leave. The attack killed more than three hundred, including many of his service buddies—and the flight deck officer who was serving in Card's place.

In the 1970s, Disney financed its new projects from internally generated cash, with minimal borrowing. The company's first priority was the Epcot project, already well under way. Card took the position that Disney needed every ounce of capital to build Epcot Center. Therefore, the company's strong position was not to invest in the Tokyo project. On their side, the Japanese could not understand why Disney would advance a very positive view for the success of Tokyo Disneyland, yet was unwilling to invest in the project. The Japanese banks thus asked OLC why they should lend money to a "risky project" in which Disney itself was unwilling to invest.

Finally, Stanek says, a compromise solution was reached to avoid what the Japanese viewed as a deal-breaker. Disney proposed a clause in the agreement that would give it the option of investing $2.5 million into the project for a 10 percent share of the ownership. This language swayed the Japanese banks—implying that Disney "might or could invest" at some point. (The option was never exercised. When OLC went public as a corporation on the Japanese stock market in 1996, it was estimated that by not making that $2.5 million investment, Disney left "over $600 million" on the table, according to Stanek.)

Two long years of drama in these back-and-forth negotiations culminated on April 30, 1979, when Masatomo Takahashi, who had become president of OLC, visited Burbank, and he and Card Walker signed the agreement, allowing the construction of Tokyo Disneyland to begin. By 2011, the project—renamed the Tokyo Disney Resort—now includes a second park, Tokyo DisneySea, and three major Disney branded and designed hotels. OLC, on its own, also designed and built a shopping district, called Ikspiari.

In the fiscal year ended April 20, 2010 (the last full year

before the earthquake and tsunami of March 11, 2011), the two parks combined welcomed 25,818,000 guests. Disney and Japanese engineers devised a plan that allowed the entire site—created on six hundred acres of reclaimed tidelands from Tokyo Bay—to "settle" over time at a constant rate. As a result, the Tokyo Disney Resort withstood the devastating events of March 2011 with no significant damage or serious injury to the forty thousand visitors in the parks at the time.

The parks themselves are extreme contrasts—one launched as a carbon copy of the Walt Disney World Magic Kingdom, the other created as a new "blank page," designed as a "one of a kind" concept by the Walt Disney Imagineers.

The Magic Kingdom reflected a consistent attitude by OLC's executives for the first two decades of their "partnership" with Disney: if it did not exist in a Disney park in the USA, it should not be built in Tokyo Disneyland. Perhaps this reflected the inexperience in the theme park arena of the OLC executive team, but just as likely it was past experience in which copies of foreign iconic product were sold to the Japanese public as representing the original product, when in fact they were poorly designed and made. The Japanese public, by the 1980s, had become discerning about quality, brand name, and true, original product. They wanted "the real thing"; widespread travel had taken many Japanese to Anaheim's Disneyland and Walt Disney World's Magic Kingdom. They *knew* "the real thing."

"Strategically," Stanek recalls, "the framework for the Tokyo Disneyland master plan was set by Florida's Magic Kingdom." As the newer of the two Disney parks, it represented the latest state of the art and was the size necessary to accommodate the ten million–attendance projection.

Cinderella Castle itself was a perfect theme and size, and although Space Mountain was the size of Disneyland's (two hundred feet in diameter rather than the Magic Kingdom's three hundred), once the decision was made not to "Japanize" the park (that is to keep it Western, keep it Disney) only a few major design revisions needed to be made. The most significant was to accommodate the Japanese penchant for shopping and bringing gifts home to family and friends. Together with a concern for rain and cold weather—it occasionally snows in Tokyo—the decision was made to cover and enclose the park's entry. Called the "World Bazaar," it is an international contemporary shopping "street" with Victorian facades. This decision made it the only Disneyland-style park without a train station at the entrance. The 1890-style railroad was moved to "Westernland," where it provides an enhanced show as it circles the Rivers of America area.

The close quarters and crowded conditions that reflect the lifestyle of most Japanese also influenced a major enhancement and special show opportunity in Tokyo Disneyland· expansion of the central plaza or "hub" from which each of the lands fans out. This enlarged area between the World Bazaar and Cinderella Castle has proven to be extremely popular with Japanese visitors, who comprise over 90 percent of the Tokyo Disney Resort's visitors.

The wide open feeling and atmosphere is a great contrast to life in Tokyo, especially. And the increased space has made possible a unique feature for Tokyo Disneyland among the Disney parks around the world: a changeable venue for special seasonal shows that can perform before large numbers of guests, with the castle as a backdrop.

From the beginning there were compelling successes, and abject failures: The candy store in the World Bazaar is one of Japan's most profitable stores on a square-footage basis. Expanded multiple times through the years, the candy store exceeds $100 *million* in revenue yearly.

A major "defeat" occurred when, to ensure that the park could meet the guidelines of the Japanese Education Ministry for school excursions, we created "Meet the World" in Tomorrowland. Based on the historical experiences of foreign visitors (that is Admiral Matthew Perry) and their interaction with the Japanese homeland, the show foundered on its presentation of the empire of Japan's aggression in World War II—avoiding as much of the actual story as possible. A true failure, "Meet the World" was finally closed in 2002 and has been replaced by a very popular Pixar-based show: Monsters, Inc. Ride & Go Seek.

* * * * * * * * * *

A successful project has many fathers, and Tokyo Disneyland (and its sister park, Tokyo DisneySea, opened in 2001) have been unequivocal successes. At one time in the 1990s, before Florida's Magic Kingdom reclaimed the record, Tokyo Disneyland became the first park ever to exceed seventeen million in a single year's attendance—equaling the original 1977 projection that Disney found to be "astonishing."

Following his leadership in successfully managing the negotiating efforts necessary to realize the project, Frank Stanek was appointed by Disney's Executive Committee as vice president, Tokyo Disneyland. He led the Imagineering team truly responsible for building Disney's first international project: John Zovich and Don Edgren, engineering; Orlando Ferrante, production and manufacturing; Edgren and Tom Jones, project management; Dick Kline, design (although the original concepts for a park based on the Florida Magic Kingdom were under the direction of Bill Martin); and John Hench, Imagineering's senior vice president of design, and overall design aesthetic.

Two others were also key project executives. Hideo Amemiya, who had grown up in Japan and become a Walt Disney World hotel executive, came "home" to become general manager of a new company, Walt Disney Productions—Japan. His efforts during the later negotiating phase for the agreement provided an important link in bridging the cultural divide between East and West. Hideo went on to become one of the most respected Disney hoteliers before his untimely death in 2001.

The second was a key Disneyland leader. Dick Nunis, the Disney parks' operating chief, assigned Jim Cora to manage the preopening operations efforts. That included hands-on training of ninety-five key OLC staff members for up to nine months at Disneyland. One of them, Noboru Kamisawa, became a skilled leader of the Tokyo Disneyland operating staff, and a trusted contemporary for both the Imagineers and the Disney operating teams. (Another large group of Japanese employees trained at WED and its manufacturing subsidiary, MAPO, preparing for show installation and maintenance.)

The Grand Opening of Tokyo Disneyland took place on April 15, 1983—six months after the opening of Epcot at Walt Disney World. At this opening, some two hundred Disney team members helped assist and direct the OLC team that met the first guests entering Tokyo Disneyland.

The park was an instant success. Five weeks and four days after opening to the public, the one-millionth guest passed through the turnstiles, on the way to a first year attendance of 10.4 million.

A few weeks before the Grand Opening, Frank Stanek had a new assignment to begin on his return home: investigate a location on the Continent for the first European Disney park and resort.

* * * * * * * * * *

I never read Robert Ringer's 1973 book, *Winning Through Intimidation*, but I suspect it was required reading for the leaders of Richard Nunis's operations teams. By the time Epcot Center and Tokyo Disneyland had opened in the early 1980s, intimidation as a means to an end was high on the list of the Disney operators' "SOP"—Standard Operating Procedures. And Dick was the master.

We all recognized and accepted the fact that Dick Nunis was the elite operator in the park business. He had paid his dues to learn the Disney business as Walt wanted it run in the late 1950s and 1960s. A neck injury in a surfing accident had ended Dick's football career at the University of Southern California, but through his USC teammate Ron Miller, Walt Disney's son-in-law, Dick joined the original Disneyland team, working with the man responsible for the highly respected training program at the park, Van France. Dick soon became one of the top operations leaders, and a favorite of Walt Disney.

After Walt's death in December 1966, Dick seemed to sense that there was a void to be filled, and he aggressively championed his own move up the Disney ladder, ultimately becoming chairman of Walt Disney Parks and Attractions. When Walt Disney Productions became the target of a takeover attempt in 1984, he even turned on his former teammate, Ron Miller, supporting his ousting as Disney's president. (It took twenty-six years for them to engage again, for a program I organized to celebrate Disneyland's fifty-fifth birthday, at The Walt Disney Family Museum in San Francisco.)

One of Dick's major objectives was the "takeover" of the Imagineers. His goal was to make WED subservient to the operators, thereby controlling planning, design, and the selection of new attractions for the parks—a scenario that Walt Disney, Card Walker, and later Michael Eisner and Frank Wells all resisted—but not without continuous diligence. (Walt, and Michael Eisner for much of his tenure as Disney's chairman, believed the tension between the passion and creativity of the designers and the experience and know-how of the operators was healthy in working to achieve the best Disney product for the public.)

Dick's "assault" on the Imagineers began soon after Walt's passing. One of his principal targets was Richard Irvine, WED's design chief, handpicked by Walt as the design leader for park development in 1952. Irvine held the position until a heart attack during construction of Walt Disney World in 1971 prompted his retirement. A widely shared story illustrated the tension. In a meeting taking place shortly after Walt's death, in the office of Joe Fowler, chairman of the Disneyland Operating Committee, Nunis provoked Irvine until the design chief stormed out of the meeting, slamming the door behind him. After several seconds, however, the door opened again, and Dick Irvine emerged, still furious, but now also embarrassed, from Fowler's closet.

Nunis's attempt at a "takeover" of design direction for Epcot Center caused so much confusion ("Who's in charge?" our team wanted to know) that WED's president, Carl Bongirno, and I, as executive vice president of Creative Development, finally demanded a meeting of the two of us and Nunis with Card Walker. We had to have corporate clarity, as well as top management's backing in order to complete the concepts we had worked years to bring to fruition.

Fifteen minutes before the meeting, Card walked into my field office at Epcot Center. "We're almost there, Marty," he said. "Make it work." That was it; Card left. As good soldiers, we did "make it work." I told the Imagineers that our hand over to the operators would take place in October. Until then, we were in charge . . . even when Dick rode around the site in his golf cart, wearing his favorite construction hard hat. While our hard hats were marked "MARTY," "JOHN," and "BOB," Dick's was labeled "SOB1."

Dick was so busy stirring things up in Epcot Center—at the opening, he told one of Imagineering's top art directors, Disney Legend Fred Joerger, "I couldn't have done it without you, old-timer" (Fred was still stifling his laughter years later)—that he almost missed the opportunity to take credit for Tokyo Disneyland (TDL). But in the six months between the openings of Epcot Center in October 1982 and TDL in April 1983, Nunis began campaigning to discredit WED's team with Chairman Walker. In the end, he succeeded, convincing Walker that too many WED executives were "freeloading" at the Grand Opening—even those who had spent as many as three years in Japan building the project. When

Stanek, Zovich, Ferrante, Cayo, John Hench, and myself—those truly responsible for creating the project (or who, as in my case, had assigned a top-drawer creative design team, despite Epcot's demands)—were not invited to the opening, I went to Disney president Ron Miller and convinced him we deserved to be there. Ron agreed, and the conflict was joined.

As the Imagineers left for home, and Nunis's operating team under a respected leader, Jim Cora, moved in, it was clear that "management by intimidation" was at work. The next test would come with the tsunami in corporate management—the arrival of Michael Eisner and Frank Wells as Disney's new leaders.

12

THE ELASTIC E: "I'VE BEEN KNOWN TO CHANGE MY MIND."

Saturday, September 29, 1984, was one of the most important days in the history of WED Enterprises/Walt Disney Imagineering. The date marked the second visit of Michael Eisner and Frank Wells to WED's Glendale headquarters, but the first as a working session to review new ideas. Their first official visit had taken place earlier that week, when the Imagineers gathered to meet the new Disney chiefs for the first time.

They were driven the three miles from Disney's Burbank Studio to the Grand Central Industrial Park in Glendale by Ray Watson, the Disney board member who had just relinquished the chairman's position to Eisner. The new team was late because Watson got lost on the three-mile drive.

That seemed illustrative of his appreciation for Imagineering. Not long before, Watson had proposed reducing WED's staff to three hundred and buying most of the design work on the outside; he had worked that way with Orange County (California) with architects and engineers on housing developments and shopping centers for the Irvine Company, where Watson had built his reputation. That did not sit well with the Imagineers, who knew the difference between building shopping centers and designing theme park attractions.

Obviously, we were hoping for better days; all the news for weeks had been about the potential takeover of Walt Disney Productions by the infamous corporate raider Irwin Jacobs. In fact, along with Jack Lindquist, I had been sent to New York City to assist President Ron Miller and the outside lawyers as they met with potential saviors (we had one meeting with the financial staff of General Motors) who might invest in Disney and thus help fend off the predators. We were all fish out of water; the Disney side seemed not to know what to do. But the Bass family of Texas came riding out of the West to rescue the corporation; together with Roy E. Disney, Walt's nephew, they brought Eisner and Wells into the Disney picture.

Now just one week after becoming chairman/chief executive officer and president/chief operating officer, respectively, Michael Eisner and Frank Wells were at Imagineering to review ideas that we had been working on for the Disney parks. At the time, there were four parks—Disneyland, the Magic Kingdom and Epcot Center at Walt Disney World, and Tokyo Disneyland. Michael and Frank were accompanied by a very welcome fourteen-year-old, Michael's son, Breck.

We knew that we were in the hot seat; with their motion picture and television backgrounds, Michael and Frank had no idea who we were or what we were capable of doing. "When I was at Paramount, I didn't know there was such a group at Disney," Michael later admitted about the Imagineers. So we Imagineers treated the meeting like it was a final exam. We loaded up a huge open space in one of WED's model shops with a show of creativity that reminded some of us of that over-the-top Epcot presentation to General Motors in Michigan: three-dimensional models, artwork big and small, and storyboards loaded with sketches and ideas filled the space. All the key creative talent at Imagineering was on hand to present their projects—in fact *pitch* their projects, which set the actual tone of the meeting.

I was very proud of our team. They were down but not out, with a long list of achievements "after Walt": WED had designed and built Walt Disney World and its Magic Kingdom, Epcot Center, Tokyo Disneyland, and the just-opened new Fantasyland in Disneyland, the first major upgrading in Disneyland since 1969. Yet we were still outsiders in the studio world Eisner and Wells had inhabited. Most of us understood and accepted Walt's premise that you are only as good as your *next* project.

We were fortunate that Breck Eisner had accompanied his father. Breck (who later became a director of advertising commercials, television shows, and motion pictures) was a big Disneyland fan. He was so excited about Tony Baxter's concept for a log flume ride called "Zip-a-dee River Run" that before we left the meeting, it had become one of the first new project commitments of the "Michael Eisner Disney Park Era"—a twenty-one-year period that would add seven new theme parks, two water parks, a sports complex, and thousands upon thousands of overnight accommodations around the world, from the swamplands of Florida to the beet fields of France, and the watery depths of Tokyo Bay and Hong Kong Harbor to the desert that is Southern California.

From day one, we learned about Michael Eisner's creative instincts. The Zip-a-dee River Run log flume ride became "Splash" to promote the DVD release of the Ron Howard-directed movie starring Tom Hanks and Daryl Hannah, which had been released theatrically that year by Disney's new Touchstone Films division. And a Disney park tradition in nomenclature was extended and enthusiastically endorsed by the CEO: in the wake of Matterhorn Mountain, Space Mountain, and Big Thunder Mountain Railroad, Zip-a-dee River Run became Splash *Mountain*. It was soon to be followed not only by the proliferation of these popular thrill rides around the world, but by new adventures such as Mount Gushmore in the Blizzard Beach water park, Expedition Everest (The Forbidden Mountain) in Disney's Animal Kingdom, and Mount Prometheus, site of Journey to the Center of the Earth in Tokyo DisneySea.

The "Elastic E" in Eisner—"I've been known to change my mind"—also came to the fore that first day with the Imagineers. Before the meeting ended, the five-year design and construction time frame for Splash Mountain caused the new Disney bosses to turn to George Lucas to collaborate with the Imagineers on another concept pitched by Tony Baxter and Tom Fitzgerald. It became the popular Tomorrowland simulator adventure, Star Tours. And when Eisner learned that even this show would take three years to complete, he enlisted a singer-dancer named Michael Jackson to work with Lucas and Francis Ford Coppola to create a 3-D fantasy called Captain Eo (more on this later). It opened at Disneyland on September 18, 1986—less than two years after that first meeting with the Imagineers.

Aside from his impatience with new park attraction time frames, Michael Eisner's instincts often amazed me—and sometimes caused significant issues in keeping talented designers motivated. When our Typhoon Lagoon water park in Florida was a major hit (it's still the number-one attended water park in the world), Imagineering was challenged to create a second, separate water park for Walt Disney World. Our teams brainstormed three exciting concepts, each with a distinctive and compelling theme. For the meeting with Michael, we set up the three concepts side by side along one wall in a conference room. My plan was to have each team present its idea, giving each one an equal opportunity to sell their concept. I was all set to give a preamble to the meeting, but Michael walked in, took one look at the wall filled with dozens of sketches, and before I could say a word, pointed to one drawing and said, "That's it!" Meeting over.

I must admit that the Blizzard Beach water park was one of those no-brainers, but we never did get to present the conceit to the boss. The big idea:

A freak storm dumped tons of snow on Central Florida. An entrepreneur rushed to build a ski resort, complete with chairlifts to the highest peak ("Mount Gushmore" of course). But before he could get the ski resort completed, the snow had melted—so the enterprising entrepreneur turned his ski-resort-to-be into a water park.

Its nomenclature tells the story of what quickly became the second most attended water park in the world. There's "Melt-Away Bay," "Runoff Rapids," "Summit Plummet," "Slush Gusher," a kid-sized mountain and slides called "Tike's Peak," a snack stand named "Avalunch," and just one character icon named "Ice Gator."

Writer/story-creator extraordinaire Kevin Rafferty has described part of the Imagineering approach:

> Our best stories are the ones that have a parallel universe—something guests can relate to. They know what a ski resort is, so that allows us to turn the notion on its ear by saying, "What happens to a ski resort when the tropical sun returns, and all the snow starts melting?"

Blizzard Beach is the answer.

My problem was not with this uniquely Disney concept; it was with the two teams that had also conceived excellent concepts that were not even presented to Michael Eisner. But in the creative world the Imagineers live in, no idea can become so precious that its failure to be selected is the end of your career. As John Hench taught me, "It's not an *I* business; it's a *we* business." So many hands touch an attraction that no one can say, "*I* did this."

That's why I always stressed this to all the creative talent at Imagineering: *There is only one name on the door at Disney, and that is still Walt Disney.* "If you want your name in lights," I told them, "you are in the wrong organization."

"Eisner's eye" could also pick out the holes in a story. One instance led to the creation of an innovative 3-D theater experience that has thrilled guests in three parks.

Very late in the design of the Animal Kingdom, it was

decided that the park's icon, The Tree of Life, should become more than just a visual statement. Not much more than a year before opening, we decided to create a show *inside* the tree. The architects and engineers raced to complete their drawings for the contractors and Disney field staff. At the same time, Tom Fitzgerald, Kevin Rafferty, and Joe Rohde struggled with the concept for the new theater's show, also working against a daunting deadline . . . and, of course, seeking Eisner's approval as they presented their ideas. Not satisfied with the latest concept, Michael left the meeting, only to duck back in moments later with a question: "Do *bugs* live in trees?" he asked.

We bit our tongues to keep from laughing at the question, but Eisner was serious. When we responded that "of course they do," Michael asked Tom to call John Lasseter about a new film Pixar was creating called *A Bug's Life*. That broke the creative logjam, and sent the Imagineering team off to develop our own story about the realm of bugs, inspired by the characters in the Pixar film, still in production. The show, called It's Tough to be a Bug!, opened almost exactly one year after that meeting, with a cast of creepy-crawliness taking over the theater, complete with 3-D visual and physical effects such as the stinkiest smells ever experienced in the realm of themed entertainment. Rafferty, the writer, loved the research; he got to consult with some of the country's foremost entomologists (continuing education is a bonus in the entertainment world). Our special effects team reveled in the fact that Tom, Joe, and I had to spend several hours inhaling horrible odors in order to select the number-one stinky.

Tom, Kevin, and fellow Imagineer George Scribner had

a similar experience on a new show for Fantasyland in the Magic Kingdom. To answer guest requests for more characters, Imagineering created a new 3-D film centered around the Disney characters, from Mickey and Goofy to Simba the Lion King and Ariel the Little Mermaid. When Scribner reviewed the storyboards, which featured Tinker Bell as a central figure, Eisner was troubled by its being "too sweet." "It needs some conflict," he told the story team. He suggested giving Donald Duck his irascible role as the forever-jealous antagonist to Mickey Mouse.

By the time Scribner and Rafferty had finished their sessions, Donald Duck was the new star of Mickey's PhilharMagic, an immediate hit across the Disney park world. One of Donald's most electric moments in his illustrious screen history, which began in 1934, is his underwater attempt to kiss Ariel . . . a near-miss that instead connects with an electric eel. It's a shocker for Donald—and a show-stopper for our audiences.

Michael's strengths in finding the holes in our story development were often balanced, however, by some of his wild ideas. One that consumed a lot of effort was his concept for a "Disney car." This was more a marketing opportunity than a design challenge; he envisioned the Disney brand appealing to the family market, with kids clamoring to ride surrounded by their favorite Disney characters. So our designers did some sample sketches, Disney hired a company that does focus groups, and (Michael thought) we would soon have the auto industry bidding for rights to "The Disney Car."

The first focus group we watched was a room full of teenagers. At first, the girls—who liked the idea—seemed to carry the day, but it was the teenage boys who quickly made it clear that they "would not be caught dead" in a Disney car. And when the second group, composed of parents, made that issue the central discussion—"You don't want to read about someone being killed in a Disney car, do you?"—the whole idea suddenly lost its luster. It was clear that branding has a negative side; there's a reason there is no Disney car today.

Especially in the early days of the Eisner years, when only a handful of Imagineers were a known entity (John Hench's pedigree went all the way back to *Fantasia*, for example, and Randy Bright wrote and directed The American Adventure in Epcot), Eisner's instincts were often to reach into the Hollywood star system for key talent. More often than not, that talent had other creative favorites they preferred to work with. So when one of Disneyland's biggest fans expressed interest in doing a show for the park, Michael Jackson said he only wanted to do it if he could work with one of his cinema heroes, George Lucas. In no time at all, *Captain Eo* was born.

When Eisner called to tell me about our new teammates, there was also a deadline: the definitive meeting with Michael Jackson was exactly one week away. Or, said more correctly, *meetings*. We quickly assigned an Imagineering team of Tim Kirk, Joe Rohde, Rick Rothschild, and Richard Vaughn, and they were amazing. Not only did they come up with the story idea that became *Captain Eo*, but their one-week effort produced three show concepts.

At noon on the appointed day, our team pitched the three concepts to Eisner, Frank Wells, and Jeffrey Katzenberg, the head of Disney's motion picture unit. They eliminated one idea. We finished this discussion just in time: at one o'clock, the two remaining concepts were shown to George Lucas, who had to choose which of the two would be shown to Michael Jackson when he arrived for the two o'clock meeting. Captain Eo and his strange band of characters—including Fuzzball and Hooter—were soon on the way to "change the world."

There remained, however, the assembly of a production team for the 3-D film. The easy choice was that both Michael Jackson, the star performer, and George Lucas, who would be the executive producer, wanted Francis Ford Coppola to direct the film. And Coppola wanted the great cinematographer Vittorio Storaro—winner of three Academy Awards, including the Oscar for Coppola's *Apocalypse Now*—to be the color consultant (or as the film's credits listed him, "visual, lighting, and photographic consultant").

With Michael Jackson, as Captain Eo, moonwalking and singing two songs he wrote for the film to Angelica Huston, "the Supreme Leader," you would think this production would set a new standard for 3-D films. But in 1986, when *Captain Eo* was produced, none of the major principals had ever worked in 3-D before. And Vittorio Storaro was known especially for his theories on the "psychological effects of color"—which often tended to produce a darker look. However, 3-D requires more light than a normal film. The result was that the strange and sinister world of the Supreme Leader was very dark and sinister in the theater as well.

As the very first attraction opened in the Michael Eisner regime, *Captain Eo* accomplished two important objectives. First, it was a huge success, establishing the Eisner years as a time of major additions with star power for the parks. And second, the time frame for creating new attractions for the parks had been shortened dramatically. When *Captain Eo* opened at Disneyland in September 1986, it was one week short of two years since the day Eisner and Wells had arrived at The Walt Disney Company. Only "it's a small world" for the New York World's Fair had ever been produced in a shorter time frame as a major Disney attraction.

* * * * * * * * * *

Involving Eisner's family in the company proved to be both successful and popular with the staff—from that first meeting son Breck attended to the enthusiastic participation of Jane Eisner, Michael's wife. In his book, *In Service to the Mouse*, Jack Lindquist writes about one of the major marketing concepts that Jane helped launch:

> In early January of 1987, when we opened Star Tours, the George Lucas attraction, we had a big ceremony with Dick Rutan and Jeana Yeager. In nine days, these two pilots flew the Rutan Voyager around the world nonstop without refueling: they had just finished their flight two weeks before, on December 23. Michael and his wife, Jane, invited Dick and Jeana to be their guests at the Plaza Inn for dinner.
>
> Just after dinner, Michael approached me while I was talking with Tom Elrod, the marketing director for Florida, and said, "Dick Rutan was telling Jane and me about this trip around the world, and at the end of it, Jane asked, 'That's just an amazing story. What are you going to do next?' and Dick replied, 'I'm going to Disneyland.' He said it without hesitation, without prompting."
>
> At that moment, Michael knew we had something big. So did Jane, Tom, and I.

Michael continued, "I want to use that as a major marketing campaign. How can we do it?"

That night, Tom and I talked about the upcoming Super Bowl and if we could gain access to the MVP while on the field at the game's end and ask, "You just won the Super Bowl. What are you going to do next?" And the MVP would answer, "I'm going to Disneyland. I'm going to Walt Disney World."

Almost a quarter century later, "I'm going to Disneyland/ Walt Disney World!" is still going strong. Even GE no longer "brings good things to life," and who can recall why it's so important to have that "pause that refreshes"? Yet Super Bowl heroes, the MVPs of the big game, keep right on telling us, "I'm going to Disneyland!"

Another of Michael Eisner's innovations was the emphasis on each park location *as a resort.* He achieved this with a parade of some of the world's biggest names in architecture, each hired to etch his signature style on "something Disney," usually a new resort hotel. They included:

- Robert A. M. Stern, dean of Yale's School of Architecture, designer of the Yacht Club, Beach Club, and BoardWalk resorts at Walt Disney World; the Newport Bay and Cheyenne hotels at Disneyland Paris; and the Disney Ambassador Hotel at Tokyo Disneyland.
- Michael Graves, now as well known for his product design as for his architecture, who designed the Team Disney headquarters in Burbank (renamed "Team Disney—The Michael D. Eisner Building" in 2006); John Tishman's Dolphin and Swan resorts at Walt Disney World; and The Hotel New York in Paris.

- Peter Dominick of Colorado, whose design of The Wilderness Lodge in Florida was so iconic that it brought him two major assignments: the Animal Kingdom Lodge at Walt Disney World and the Grand Californian Hotel in Anaheim.
- Arata Isozaki, Japan's best-known architect, who designed the Team Disney executive headquarters at Walt Disney World.
- Canadian-born Frank Gehry, designer of the original Disney Village in Paris and the Team Disney building in Anaheim (as well as The Walt Disney Concert Hall in Los Angeles—not a Disney company project).
- French architect Antoine Grumbach, who designed the Sequoia Lodge at Disneyland Paris.
- WATG and its principal architect, Gerald Allison, who worked closely with the Imagineers to achieve one Disney "Grand" hotel—the Grand Floridian at Walt Disney World; and two "Disneyland Hotels": one in Hong Kong and the other at the entrance to the Disneyland Paris park.

It's a fair question to ask why Michael Eisner, with so many in-house designers and others with vast hotel design experience available to him, chose the "star architect" route, even if they had no hotel design background. I think there are three logical reasons.

First was *opportunity*. As CEO of Disney for the first dozen years of Walt Disney World's operation, Card Walker chose to direct the company's finances toward building new attractions and new parks, notably Epcot. This left it to hoteliers outside the Walt Disney World property to meet the demand for accommodations created by the Magic Kingdom and Epcot attendance. And it left Walt Disney World with only two major hotels, the Contemporary and Polynesian—both of which opened in 1971—when Eisner became CEO in 1984.

Second, that truism "there's only one name on the door" meant that the parks themselves would always be linked to one man: Walt Disney. Michael wanted a game he could play in, and win big. It's been said that Victor Ganz, a close friend of Michael's father, was influential in advising Eisner about the potential of making architecture a high-profile priority. The Ganz family and the Eisners, in Michael's youth, lived in the same building in New York City. Ganz was vice president of the Whitney Museum of American Art and one of the country's most astute collectors of twentieth-century art, owning works by Picasso, Jasper Johns, Robert Rauschenberg, and Frank Stella. When the collection was auctioned off on the death of his widow in 1997, it brought in nearly $200 million in sales. Victor Ganz was a man Michael Eisner listened to.

Third, of course, was the media attention these high-profile architects commanded—and not just in *Variety* and the entertainment world. Their buildings got the attention of *Architectural Digest*, *The New York Times*, and other major media. Theme park designers, by contrast, are practically anonymous.

There is a very interesting analysis of this period in Alan Lapidus's book, *Everything by Design: My Life as an Architect*, published by St. Martin's Press in 2007. Lapidus points out that Michael Graves, then teaching at Princeton's School of Architecture, had designed only two large buildings when Eisner selected him for what became the Dolphin and Swan hotels. His two previous buildings were "both client-ego-inspired office buildings . . . and they had exceeded their construction budgets in awe-inspiring terms," Lapidus wrote.

Since the hotels would be owned by John Tishman's company, but were to be built on Walt Disney World property, Eisner and Tishman had to agree on the project. Tishman wanted an experienced hotel designer (Lapidus), so they functioned well as working hotels, while Graves's design "was certainly eye stopping, but could not easily accommodate any hotel function," according to Lapidus. The solution: "Graves and I," Lapidus wrote, "would collaborate on the redesign of his concept to produce buildings that actually functioned as hotels."

Lapidus goes on to describe the interaction between Tishman and Eisner:

> At one meeting, a completely frustrated John Tishman asked Eisner why he was going through this expensive and tangled process. The hotels would look bizarre, which John acknowledged might be a plus, but they would cost a whole lot more and function, even with my input, nowhere near as efficiently.
>
> Peering intently at Tishman, Eisner replied, "John, I'm forty-four years old, I've already made more money than I ever dreamed of. Now I want to be on the cover of Time magazine. By using the most controversial architects in the country, I will establish Disney as a serious patron of the arts." So much for form and function! On a more practical note, Eisner was quoted as saying, "In movies, we use the finest minds, the best writers we can find. I don't see why we shouldn't use the best design minds." Thus, calling in

and publicly crediting renowned outside architects for the first time instead of using his in-house team, Eisner said his goals were to *"build something people can't see at home, buildings that make them smile,"* and to *"create a sense of place that is unique."*

* * * * * * * * * *

It's been said that Michael Eisner and Frank Wells had a working relationship that resembled the time of Walt Disney and Roy O. Disney at the helm of the company, but I never saw it that way. Walt and Roy operated in very different spheres of influence, a clear separation between creating the product and financing and marketing it. Michael and Frank, in contrast, may have thought they were establishing something similar—Michael leading the product development, Frank heading the business side. But in fact, their working relationship crossed all dividing lines, real or imagined. I never heard of a story development meeting that Roy attended with Walt. By contrast, Michael Eisner and Frank Wells were frequently together in meetings, especially in the early years of their partnership at Disney.

In his book *Working Together: Why Great Partnerships Succeed*, published by Harper Business in 2010, Eisner writes of how the relationship began in September 1984:

> *We were headed into the toughest challenge of our professional lives, together. For the next ten years, that journey would be as exciting, enjoyable, rewarding, and triumphant as either of us could have dared to hope. From our first day in the office that fall, my partnership with Frank Wells taught me what it was like to work with*

somebody who not only protected the organization but protected me, advised me, supported me, and did it all completely selflessly.

I'd like to think I did the same for Frank, as well as the company. We grew together, learned together, and discovered together how to turn what was in retrospect a small business into indeed a very big business.

We learned that one plus one adds up to a lot more than two. We learned just how rewarding working together can be.

Michael defined Frank's contributions toward their success in these clear terms:

Now, the most important thing that goes into creative success is having the people who can come up with the great ideas. But the next most important thing is often overlooked: having people who will enable those great ideas, and support those creative people—manage the creativity with real economic foresight. It's not an easy thing to do—in every instance, it is a lot safer to say no, and it takes a special and gutsy kind of leader to say yes. That leader alongside me, that coach and that cheerleader at Disney, was Frank. Together with the countless movie and television show ideas and theme parks that he helped push forward, he supported me on smaller but memorable decisions as well, like the use of top-quality architects for new hotels at our theme parks and other projects, and moving Disney animation into the computer age at a large expense . . .

Frank was the one who helped push, pull, and enable all those ideas, managing the managers of all of creative and

financial in the boxes of our projects. He was the catalyst
who found a way to bring them to life. And he was thrilled
to do it.

Frank Wells had arrived at Disney championed by Roy Edward Disney, the son of Roy O. Disney and nephew of Walt. Roy and his business partner, Stanley Gold at Shamrock Holdings, Roy's family company, had led a revolt that removed Ron Miller, husband of Roy's cousin Diane Disney Miller, as Disney's CEO and president. Before becoming president and then vice chairman at Warner Bros. Entertainment Inc., Frank was associated with Stanley Gold in the entertainment law firm Gang Tyre & Brown.

Frank attended Pomona College in California before becoming a Rhodes scholar for two years at Oxford and earning his law degree at Stanford. He left Warner Bros. in 1982 to realize an amazing ambition: to climb the highest mountain on every continent. Although he failed to scale Mount Everest, the highest mountain in the world at 29,028 feet, he wrote about each challenge in his book, *Seven Summits*. The next adventure he faced was to scale the heights of Disney's Magic Kingdoms.

* * * * * * * * * *

I have great memories of working with Frank Wells. He could be totally focused for a 6:00 A.M. meeting at his home about Euro Disney (he sometimes participated wearing his pajamas, bathrobe, and bedroom slippers), or completely unaware that he was calling you at 3:00 A.M. (Wherever he was in the world, that was the time it was *everywhere* in the world!) I watched him manipulate heads of corporations (he became the best salesman and steward of corporate alliances, signing multimillion, multiyear sponsorships for attractions in the Disney parks). And I was in the right place when he had to borrow $10 to pay for parking at the Century Plaza Hotel because he left home without his wallet. One morning in Tokyo, he asked me and Pete Clark, then responsible for park sponsorships, to jog with him around the Imperial Palace; the four-mile distance, and Frank's slow pace, gave us plenty of time to resolve the issues he wanted to discuss. Pete, a jogger of some note, finally asked if we could pick up the pace for the last mile so we could work up a sweat.

The Frank Wells stories were legendary at Disney. One day he was racing to finish a very important memo when he realized he had to catch a flight to New York. He asked Shari Kimoto, his assistant, to accompany him on the drive to the airport while he finished dictating. Still not finished, he bought Shari a ticket and continued dictating all the way across the country. The next morning, Shari typed a draft at the Disney corporate office. Now it was revision time. On their second morning in New York, the locals asked Shari why she was still wearing the same clothes she had arrived in. Frank, of course, never noticed; he was totally focused on the task at hand.

Frank never let apparent obstacles get in his way. One morning when I was on vacation, Frank called me. "What are you doing, Marty?" he asked.

"Well, Frank, I'm in my bathing suit looking out at the Pacific Ocean—in fact, there are some dolphins swimming past right now."

Frank pretended not to hear me. "How would you like to come to New York?" he said.

"Great," I replied. "I'll be back from vacation next Monday."

"I need you here for a meeting *tomorrow morning*," the voice on the telephone said.

"But Frank," I told him, "my wife and I are going to the Hollywood Bowl tonight with some friends."

"Okay," Frank replied, "but let your friends drive so they can take Leah home—I'll have you picked up at intermission, and get you to LAX in time to catch the midnight flight to New York."

Of course you know what the outcome was. I took the red-eye to New York from Los Angeles at midnight, arriving at JFK just before 7:00 A.M. A driver met me and took me about ten minutes away to a waiting helicopter, which flew me to New Jersey, where another car met me and drove to a nearby hotel. By 8:00 A.M. I had showered and shaved, and was in Frank Wells's suite for a continental breakfast— and my instructions. By 10:00 A.M. we were in a meeting with the president of AT&T, and Frank called on me for the concept and design information he wanted conveyed from the horse's mouth—from the creative leader of Imagineering to the president of AT&T.

By 11:30, I was out the door and the process was reversed: limousine to helicopter, helicopter back to New York, driver to the airport, a 1:00 P.M. flight back to Los Angeles. And then another limousine to another helicopter, which flew me thirty miles to Orange County, where another driver met me and drove to my vacation "hideaway" on the beach, looking out on the Pacific Ocean, where I arrived at 6:30 P.M.—exactly twenty-one hours since I had left the Hollywood Bowl, and about thirty hours since Frank Wells first telephoned me about my new travel plans. "At the end of the day" (one of Frank's favorite expressions), we made the deal. And, I had to admit, Frank Wells did need me there to say my piece and put the deal over the top. But believe me, it was a very long day!

Frank's expression made a big impression on me. It was a metaphor for how he wanted us to leave a meeting—with a decision, with agreement on the next steps. It was the way he wanted to conclude negotiations with another company— you either made the deal or didn't, but you walked away knowing that "at the end of the day" you brought all the resources you needed to the table and gave it your best shot.

Eisner's enthusiasm and Wells's management and business skills were often a magic combination. One of the best examples is the path that led to the launching of the third Disney park at Walt Disney World—the Disney-MGM Studios. (The name was changed in 2009 to Disney's Hollywood Studios.)

When Epcot opened in October 1982—two years before Eisner and Wells came to Disney—our creative team at Imagineering began an analysis of subjects and stories we felt were missing from the Future World area, and countries we especially hoped to include in the future at World Showcase. In our own assessment, we found a glaring omission: there was no pavilion related to show business. Yes, the park itself was all about entertainment and fun—but what about exploring television, the Broadway stage, or how movies are made?

We began development of our "Entertainment Pavilion" for Epcot. By the time we showed early concepts to Michael and Frank, we were all excited about its potential—and they quickly saw a new potential: why not place it *outside* but immediately adjacent to Epcot, and make it into a separate experience—perhaps a half-day park? It would quickly add another key attraction to the Walt Disney World mix, giving guests new reasons to lengthen their stay.

A young designer, Bob Weis, trained as an architect, quickly became the champion of the project. Bob had learned the Imagineering ropes as a design coordinator at Tokyo Disneyland. Suddenly, the idea took off. As often happens with competition, the concept assumed a life of its own when Universal Studios announced that they were going to build a "Studio Park" in Central Florida based on their Universal Hollywood attraction, whose major appeal was its tour of *real* movie sets where movies were actually made. In fact, its true history ("This was Lucille Ball's dressing room") was the major marketing pitch.

Competition is often like a water spigot to a design organization: turn that faucet on, and watch the writers, architects, and engineers run. Suddenly, Michael and Frank were drenching us—and the Imagineers were cranking out drawings as fast as they could. As quickly as you could say, "Let's get there first!" we were off on a sprint to the finish. The "half-day park" died a quick death, but our head start had given us the advantage in creating a much larger park that opened a full year before Universal Studios Orlando.

But development of the concept was not a simple matter in those early days of Eisner-Wells. The widespread belief was that the success of Universal's tour in Hollywood was dependent on the fact that real production took place on those studio back lots. How was a park outside Orlando, Florida, to make that same marketing statement which Michael believed was a must?

The answer was twofold: 1) by building soundstages where TV shows like a new *Mickey Mouse Club* and some movies could be produced while guests watched from enclosed corridors above and at one end of the stages; and 2) by showcasing Disney animators at work as part of a walking tour depicting the animation process. This requirement immediately caused an ongoing conflict between the Imagineers and Disney's Feature Animation group, headed by Peter Schneider. In retrospect, the conflict was understandable. At a time when Feature Animation was building a new organization that would soon produce *Beauty and the Beast* (1991) and *The Lion King* (1994), they also had to create an animation team far from its Burbank leadership . . . one that would work not in obscure offices, but in wide-open spaces, visible to tourists through large windows. It was not an easy sell to the animators, and I believe that credit belongs to Jeffrey Katzenberg, then studio chief, for making it work.

Years later, when interest in viewing artists at their animation boards waned (as often as not, those drawing boards were unoccupied), the animators moved to an adjacent building and were responsible for creating the popular film *Lilo & Stitch*.

The Disney-MGM Studios name itself is an excellent example of the way Michael and Frank worked as one voice. It was Michael who worried that Disney films alone, as of the mid-1980s, did not provide enough variety to create and market the park. Frank, knowing that Warner Bros. (where he once was a top executive), Paramount (Eisner's former employer), Sony, and of course Universal would never license their films to Disney, made a preemptive and convincing pitch to acquire the rights to use the MGM name and a selection of their films in a twenty-year agreement.

Frank Wells worked his side of the street by reaching out to another lawyer. Frank Rothman had built his reputation in sports law (his clients included the National Football League), as well as in the entertainment field. As Rothman was nearing the end of his time as board chairman of the MGM Studios, Frank Wells asked Bob Weis and me to review our concept for the Studio project with Rothman. The name deal, which also included access to certain films (ownership of the MGM library was a confused web, with many films by then controlled by Ted Turner's company) followed quickly thereafter.

Later, it was rumored that Kirk Kerkorian, with his controlling interest in MGM, was not happy that Rothman had signed on with Disney, especially with the inclusion of one of the world's great icons, the MGM lion. But by then, we were off and running, and the Disney-MGM Studios was a *fait accompli.*

For many years, the famous MGM lion roared from the logo of the Disney-MGM Studios, and by the time the licensing agreement ended in 2009, the newly named Disney's Hollywood Studios had become the fifth most attended park in the United States (trailing only its Disney brethren the Magic Kingdom, Disneyland, Epcot, and the Animal Kingdom).

* * * * * * * * * *

One of the most positive aspects of the Eisner-Wells partnership was the adjacency of their offices. If you were meeting with either one, especially Frank, and a question came up requiring the other's opinion, they would simply open the connecting door, ask if the other were available, and, more often than not, you would get a decision on the spot.

A major issue was related to the separation of the creative and operating arms of the Disney parks. As stated earlier, before Eisner took the helm, Dick Nunis, as a member of the Disney board of directors, completely abandoned his former football teammate and supported the removal of CEO and President Ron Miller. In fact, it was broadly reported that Nunis wrote a letter to Chairman Ray Watson suggesting that the company's new president be Richard A. Nunis.

When his offer was not accepted, and the board engaged Eisner and Wells, Nunis sought to increase his power, again attempting to take control over the Imagineers. To their credit, Michael and Frank quickly realized what Walt Disney and later Card Walker had understood: that two points of view are often better than one, and that friction and tension between the creative and operating teams can bring out all the issues *before* a project begins. That tension was the reason Walt had kept Buzz Price as an *outside* consultant. As Buzz put it so succinctly, "I didn't have to be a 'yes man'!"

On one occasion, after consulting Eisner, Frank instructed me to "call Nunis and tell him we want to proceed" with whatever project was under discussion. I realized immediately that my call would start another Attractions-Imagineering verbal war. After all, I had just been through another "discussion" with Nunis, this time to hear him accuse an Imagineer of using drugs. "Give me the proof and I'll deal with it immediately," I told Dick. I never heard from him again on that subject. It was just part of his bullying style.

"Frank," I protested, "doesn't Dick report to you?"

"Of course he does," Frank Wells replied.

"Well, why don't you just call Dick and tell him what you and Michael decided—you know he will call you as soon as he hangs up with me," I said.

"Yes," came Frank's reply, "and I'll be ready to deal with it."

An incident in the early days of the Disney-MGM Studios finally caused me to violate every professional and civil standard I practiced throughout my career. Early in the life of the project, it was clear that the elevated corridors we had designed for the tour had major show challenges. To compensate for a lack of TV or film production, and the fact that setup time on a show set takes up far more time than the actual shooting does, our team produced several short videos that were viewed at strategic points along the corridors.

They included many top stars, among them Warren Beatty, Tom Selleck, Carol Burnett, and Goldie Hawn. Leading up to a theater where guests were seated for the finale of the Backstage Tour were *The Editing Story*, featuring George Lucas, and *The Audio Story*, starring Mel Gibson and Pee-Wee Herman. Then came the finale theater, featuring trailers of Disney films to be released in the near future.

Tom Fitzgerald recalls the presentation:

Working with Feature Animation, we came up with the notion of creating a special piece of film to bookend the trailers. Directed by Jerry Rees, the live-action/ animation film (remember this was in the time of Roger Rabbit *when this technique was new and unique) featured Michael Eisner and Mickey Mouse at the Studio, heading down to the screening room to see some coming attractions. Animated characters and live Studio staff all met in the theater. A highlight moment was when Eisner told Chernabog [the monster from Fantasia] that he was blocking everyone's view. A sheepish Chernabog replied, "Sorry Mr. Eisner, it'll never happen again!"*

The paucity of real production to watch, however, diminished the appeal of the elevated corridors. Eventually, they were abandoned and the space was incorporated into other shows. But in year one, we were in our learning curve, trying a variety of programs and productions, gauging and understanding the public's interest. But that was not good enough for Dick Nunis.

Taking matters into his own hands, he had his maintenance team act as midnight marauders—quite literally, in the middle of the night, they broke through an exterior wall along the corridor and installed doors marked EXIT,—so that guests could leave the tour *before* the "Michael and Mickey" theater finale.

I immediately contacted Frank Wells, and since we all happened to be in Florida a few days after Nunis's actions, Frank arranged for a meeting to take place beginning in the Tour Corridor itself and spilling out into the Animation Courtyard—a very public location in front of the entrance to the Animation Building.

Frank began the discussion by asking Bob Weis to explain the sequence of the attraction; Bob did an excellent job of reviewing the show, making clear why it was important for all guests to see all the pieces of the tour, to and including the finale theater. When he was through, it was Nunis's turn, but rather than explaining his operational reasons for the midnight marauders, he placed a hand on Bob's shoulder and began: "Now young man, when you have been in this business longer, you will understand . . ." It was then that I lost it: I stepped in front of Nunis—he was six inches taller and fifty pounds heavier than I—and said, "F*** you—and don't ever play the 'young man' game with my team again!" It wasn't nice, and I apologize to any guest who may have overheard us. But it was effective; the new exit doors were sealed, and our original sequence continued. Frank had allowed the guests to call the shots, which, within a year or two, they did. As a Disney team—Imagineers and park operators acting together—we agreed that it was not working. The corridor adventure was closed, forever.

* * * * * * * * * *

One of our great triumphs over Michael's early lack of knowledge about Imagineering seems like a no-brainer today. In contrast to the publicity (and egos) attached to talent in movies and television, Imagineers—and their design and storytelling talents—are almost unknown outside the parks and attraction industry. Michael wanted to keep it that way; it was no other studio's business, he reasoned, to know, and potentially try to hire, Imagineering's talent.

It was an impossible dream. Every time we opened a major new attraction, park, or resort, the key Imagineers who created and built the project were onstage for the media to quiz and photograph. Yet it took us until 1996, twelve years after he arrived at Disney, for Eisner to relent and allow the creation of a major hardcover book about Imagineering. Even then, it required a special strategy to convince the Disney CEO.

When "The Book Team"—Imagineers Bruce Gordon, David Mumford, Kevin Rafferty, and Randy Webster—proposed a publication about Imagineering "created and written by the Imagineers themselves," I determined that the way to gain Eisner's approval was to convince him it was an excellent business decision. So we approached Bob Miller, who created the Hyperion book label at Disney. When Bob proved to be enthusiastic about the sales potential, we armed him with illustrative materials, and asked him to make Michael his first sale, based on potential income from the book for Hyperion. Bob was so successful that Michael even agreed to write the foreword.

Our 192-page coffee-table book, titled *Walt Disney Imagineering—A Behind the Dreams Look at Making the Magic Real*, became a favorite project of Wendy Lefkon's, editorial director of Disney Editions. In hardcover and soft-cover, it has sold over 150,000 copies . . . and it now competes in the marketplace with a second 192-page coffee-table edition published in 2010, . . . *Making MORE Magic Real.*

13

EDIE'S CONFERENCE ROOM: "YOU ARE CARRYING MY LOGIC TO TOO LOGICAL A CONCLUSION!"

Frank Wells had been employing his Rhodes scholar Socratic methodology throughout the meeting to counter the arguments of Disney's chief financial officer, Gary Wilson. Finally, Wilson played his hole card: "Frank—You are carrying my logic to too logical a conclusion!"

The next day, I wrote Gary Wilson's quote and the date, 2/12/87, on a notepad, and pinned it on the wall in Edie's Conference Room. I had long been fascinated by seminal advice that seemed to become iconic through repetition. Often it was sage philosophy, like the French poet Paul Valery's quintessential "The future isn't what it used to be" (often attributed to Yankee baseball star Yogi Berra). Or this advice by the great baseball pitcher Satchel Paige. "Don't look back," he advised. "Something might be gaining on you."

At Imagineering, we had our own version of priceless comments, and sometimes million dollar advice, on the pinnable walls of the conference room. Named in honor of Richard Irvine's secretary-assistant Edie Flynn, this conference room, had meetings been recorded there, could have told the history of the Disney park business from the mid-1960s to the mid-1990s—encompassing decisions made by Walt Disney while Walt Disney World was in the early planning stages, through the opening of Disneyland Paris and the early years of Michael Eisner's leadership of the company.

Although no recordings were made, the pinnable walls became my own method of lightening up the serious business of design and decision-making. After a meeting, I would go over my notes and look for excellent bits of advice, attitudes, and direction from our corporate leaders; confessions about mistakes; or wish-I-hads, hopes, and dreams. My criteria was: "Does this shed light on a show or project? Is it something we want to remember? Does it give us insight into the personalities involved?"

Altogether, from the late 1970s to the mid-1990s (when our offices were renovated and we lost the pinnable walls in the process), I probably put up as many as three hundred notes, sketches, clippings, and other items of interest. It wasn't until several years after my retirement in 2009 that I happened upon a large manila envelope in my files. It was labeled simply EDIE'S WALLS, giving no outward hint to the memories that awaited within. Now for the first time, these Disney treasures are unlocked; here are some of the gems.

Sometimes the sage advice on the walls of Edie's Conference Room came from the great outside talents we were privileged to work with. During a meeting about the original Star Tours simulator attraction for Disneyland, someone complained about the "clichés" being tossed around in the story session. That's when George Lucas proclaimed his own advice: "Don't avoid the clichés; they are clichés because they work!" (4/12/86)

Alex Haley, author of *Roots*, worked with the Imagineers on an unrealized African Nations pavilion for Epcot's World Showcase. Perhaps out of frustration, Alex quoted an old African saying: "Never put off 'til tomorrow anything you can put off until the day after tomorrow!" (10/17/84)

While Haley's ageless homily was perhaps not the best advice in terms of construction deadlines, Chairman John Tishman of Tishman Construction set the record straight for Card Walker regarding the opening date for Epcot: "October 1 has never been the problem; *1982* is the problem!" (9/8/81).

Perhaps recognizing the issue, Disney chairman Donn Tatum gave us the answer to speeding up the construction schedule: "We shall certainly support this in a manner yet to be determined." (10/27/81)

It was in Edie's Conference Room that we again heard about Michael Eisner's "Elastic E"; his ability to change his mind—often. Eisner probably held the record with the number of notes I saved throughout his reign as Disney CEO. For example:

"This is so large and impractical—that's what appeals to me!" (11/11/85)

"It has to be magic—but it doesn't have to be seamless." (11/24/87)

"We are committed to acting as though we know what we are doing." (3/3/88)

"I like this because it's being driven by entertainment—and not by office buildings!" (3/23/88)

"We're not going to risk the company on a practical idea—we risk the company on a great idea!" (11/10/88)

"Fantasyland is our company." (6/7/89)

There were also notes related to the often unique language of The Walt Disney Company:

Pete Clark, corporate sponsor executive, on a potential meeting with Mars candy: "I talked to Mars and they can probably come on 5/17."

My response: "I know, I know—and Michael Eisner talks to Pluto!"

Sometimes there were territorial "who's in charge" arguments:

Gary Wilson: "I'm in charge of hotels, and no one has reviewed this with me!"

Frank Wells: "That's because it's a 'haunted hotel' in the Disney-MGM Studio Park, Gary!" (11/9/88)

Some ideas were profound, like designer Tony Baxter's "You can only test a Disneyland when you have one"

(10/1/87), and designer-philosopher John Hench's "Someone has to lay the initial egg. We can't all be egg
counters!" (4/17/81). And designer Joe Rohde's early
assessment of Disney's Animal Kingdom: "This has nothing to do with what's really there—it's all perception."
(6/17/87)

Larry Murphy, head of Disney's Corporate Strategic
Planning function—viewed by John Hench and most of us
who considered ourselves "egg layers" as the most despised
and mistrusted group in the company—was a special
target:

A frustrated designer: "Larry, just make a decision!"
Larry Murphy: "Indecision is the key to flexibility!"
(4/29/92)

Larry could even frustrate his bosses (as noted in this
exchange):

Gary Wilson: "There is some logic to it."
Larry Murphy: "It makes sense!"
Gary Wilson: "I'm not sure it makes sense, but there is
some logic to it." (8/19/87)

In a discussion about the impact of a new attraction
on attendance for existing projects at Walt Disney
World:

Larry Murphy: "What about cannibalization?"
Me: "We handle that in the Animal Kingdom, Larry!"
(7/25/87)

A few more of my personal favorites:

Card Walker, CEO of Walt Disney Productions, to President Ron Miller: "Every time you get discouraged, come over to WED!" (4/29/82)

Teri Rosen, my assistant: "Pat came by and asked that I give you this note: 'Tell Marty that I [Pat] am earning my money today!'" (6/24/81)

Jeffrey Katzenberg, president of Walt Disney Studios, on the key to success of the Disney-MGM Studios: "The thing won't work unless it functions." (8/24/87)

Bo Boyd, head of Disney Consumer Products: "Always try to sell something for more than you paid for it." (6/20/88)

Randy Bright, Imagineering creative executive responsible for production of Epcot films, on the planning of the Circle-Vision production: "China is a big place!" (11/25/80)

Bob Gurr, vehicle designer: "Practice always works because it knows no theory." (2/6/79)

John Hench: "They [guests] don't go out of the parks whistling the lights or the architecture." (2/23/81)

Me, in a discussion about maintaining show quality: "Remember: every day is the *only day* many of our guests will ever visit one of our parks!" (7/6/87)

Gary Wilson, making the ultimate statement about meeting capacity demands when designing attractions and facilities for Disney parks and resorts: "You can't build a church for Easter Sunday!" (11/20/86)

The notes also spoke to the difficulty of *starting* these

meetings. These reminders were pinned on the walls in 1988, 1991, and 1995:

"Frank Wells will arrive in 7 minutes, per Shari."

Re: Eisner/Ovitz New Tomorrowland meeting: "Meeting is moved to 3:00–5:00 on October 31 (rather than 3:30–5:30) "Ovitz will probably arrive closer to 3:15, rather than 3:00 P.M."

Judson Green, then financial executive and later chairman of Disney Parks and Resorts: "Don't worry—you're never too late to be early!" (1/21/91)

Peter's Late Law: "People who are late are always in a better mood than those who have to wait for them." (Quoted from *Peter's Almanac* for April 10, 1983—by Dr. Laurence J. Peter—author of *The Peter Principle*.)

Recently at a memorial service for Barbara Hastings, my longtime executive assistant, I saw Gary Wilson. When I told Gary about the title of this chapter, he laughed and said, "That's Frank!" That's what I always loved about the notes pinned on Edie's Conference Room walls. They were written by real people who were revealing their true personalities in the heat of battle.

14

THE FRENCH HAD A TERM FOR IT: "A CULTURAL CHERNOBYL."

There were strong elements at Disney, led by Dick Nunis, who wanted the first Disney park in Europe to be located on the Mediterranean coast of Spain, where beachfront and the availability of plenty of land might lead to the creation of a European Walt Disney World, a one-of-a-kind resort. But when the French New Town Agency identified a large site in the new town of Marne-la-Vallée, close to the new A4 highway a little more than nineteen miles east of Paris—within driving distance from Germany, Belgium, the Netherlands, and the major population centers of the host country—France won the day.

"Because of its location in a new town," Frank Stanek recalled, "all the services and infrastructure necessary would be assured by the government, and the extension of the RER (Regional Express Network) connecting Paris to the site by rail was also guaranteed. Paris," Frank pointed out, "with a resident population of twelve million and an annual tourist visitation of over twenty million, met our rule-of-thumb metric that indicated a market of thirty million residents and tourists combined would support an attendance of approximately ten million for a Disney park. The other sites in Europe did not meet this metric."

There were plenty of other reasons for Disney's interest in locating in the heart of Europe. Transportation and access to the cultural and business centers of the Continent were prime considerations. With good reason, Eisner saw the opportunity for the new Euro Disney to act as a catalyst for the growth of all the company's businesses, especially television and consumer products, including the new product launched in 1987: The Disney Store. This was to be a quantum leap beyond the scope of the foreign offices Disney had operated in Europe since the 1930s and 1940s. They had been focused primarily on merchandising, publishing, and licensing of the Disney characters and film distribution. Originally, the managers of these offices started as agents representing Disney, but as the volume of merchandising and licensing grew following World War II, most of these agents were converted to Disney employees, reporting through Merchandising/Consumer Products heads in Burbank, and ultimately to Roy O. Disney for many years. The European organization needed a thorough overhaul and updating in the new Disney of Eisner-Wells.

We also needed to better understand the European market for theme parks. To this end, Michael and Frank put the new company aircraft, a Gulfstream II, to the test on a grand circuit of European parks in June and July of 1988. In addition to Michael and Frank (and Jane Eisner and Luanne Wells), the study group also included Peter Rummell, the chief executive of DDC (Disney Development Company), which was charged with master planning of the property and development of the hotels for the new project; Bob Fitzpatrick, a French speaker married to a French woman, who left the presidency of the California Institute of the Arts to head the Euro Disney project; Tony Baxter, Imagineering senior designer who would lead the creation of the park; and me. We visited Alton Towers in the U.K., De Efteling in the Netherlands, Gardaland on Lake Garda in Italy, and a new French water park near Biot in the south of France. Only Efteling made an impression on our group. Built in a beautifully forested region, it was the work of visionary Dutch illustrator Anton Pieck. (We were also impressed—or should I say startled—by the sight of a very well-endowed topless female walking hand-in-hand with her two children across the grounds of the water park in the south of France. The experience did not result in plans to change the dress code at the French Disney park.)

It was clear that none of these parks would offer any competition for a Disney project in Paris. So it's not surprising that by 2011, long after Disneyland Paris had become the number-one tourist attraction in all of Europe (exceeding the combined attendance of the Eiffel Tower and the Louvre), the Themed Entertainment Association (TEA) and the research firm AECOM, in their annual "Global Attractions Attendance Report," published the following visitor numbers for the previous year:

- Disneyland Park at Disneyland Paris: 10.9 million
- Walt Disney Studios at Disneyland Paris: 4.7 million
- De Efteling: 4.1 million
- Gardaland: 2.8 million
- Alton Towers: 2.6 million

Euro Disney, renamed Disneyland Paris in 1994, seemed to be in a cultural recovery mode almost from the day in March 1987 when the formal agreement was signed between Michael Eisner, for the French company Euro Disney S.C.A., and Jacques Chirac, the prime minister of France. The French media reported that "communists and intellectuals" saw the Disney "invasion" of France as an assault on French culture, an unwelcome symbol of America's consumer society. In the single phrase that would not go away, a Parisian stage director called the Disney project "a cultural Chernobyl."

By opening day, April 12, 1992, Disney was embroiled in a variety of controversies, all suggesting an insensitivity to French culture. Staff complaints about long-standing Disney policies related to makeup, facial hair, and jewelry became "attacks on individual liberty," French labor unions protested. The policy Walt Disney established at Disneyland in 1955—no alcoholic beverages are served in the company's Magic Kingdom–style parks—became a *cause célèbre* in a culture where even children are allowed to drink wine with meals. Suddenly, the sushi in Tokyo, grits in Orlando, and even French fries in Anaheim were looking like home cooking to The Walt Disney Company.

* * * * * * * * * *

There was a lesson to be learned from Walt Disney World, and Eisner, Wells, CFO Gary Wilson, Rummell, and Disney's

Strategic Planning group were not about to repeat it. Card Walker had taken the position that Disney was in the park business, not the hotel business. As a consequence, as stated earlier, only those two iconic hotels, the Polynesian and Contemporary resorts, and the smaller Golf Resort, were operated by Disney at Walt Disney World when the new management arrived in 1984. Outside the Disney property, dozens of hotels and motels had sprung up to provide vacation accommodations for tourists, and of course, none of these provided any direct income to Disney. What Walt had sought to avoid by purchasing nearly 28,000 acres—the neon jungle along Harbor Boulevard in Anaheim—did happen in Orlando. This time it was called International Drive, a few miles from Walt Disney World, where every kind of adventure to tempt the tourist has found a home.

The Paris project presented the grandest opportunity yet for Michael Eisner's patronage of the great architects. Disney could control the hotel market in and around Euro Disney by building and operating its own hotels . . . and Eisner could create and bring together some of the world's most renowned architects to design them.

This "council of architects" came together in Glendale and New York in March and April 1988. Listed alphabetically, they included Frank Gehry, Michael Graves, Robert A. M. Stern, Stanley Tigerman, and Robert Venturi. Eisner called the group the "Gang of Five." Fueled by Disney's decision to build 5,800 rooms in seven venues to be ready for the park's Opening Day, they became the principal designers (with several additions) of the hotels and Disney Village— all with American themes: New York (Graves), Newport Bay and Cheyenne (Stern), Sequoia (French architect Antoine

Grumbach), and Santa Fe (New Mexico architect Antoine Predock). Gehry took on the Disney Village.

Only Robert Venturi and Stanley Tigerman did not receive go-aheads from Disney's management. When Eisner indicated we would move forward with a hotel at the very entrance to the park—a first for Disney—and would not proceed with Venturi's Las Vegas theme hotel, Michael sent Venturi to one of our Imagineering buildings to discuss the issues with Tony Baxter and Wing Chao, the liaison to the outside architects. Tony recalls the story of Venturi's visit.

> Michael sent me to review the overall project with Venturi and to talk him out of the Las Vegas-style concept. Instead, I was lectured in language I won't repeat about "how I was destroying" Walt's master plan for the park. Finally, I had enough of his lecture, and told him to get his ass out of our building I didn't realize how famous he was, or I might have lost my nerve!

Despite Venturi's argument that a hotel at the entrance to the park would obscure the view of Fantasyland's castle, Eisner backed the passionate advocacy of Imagineer Baxter and designer Eddie Sotto. Frank Wells had also been anxious about the entrance hotel, for a completely different reason: he was concerned that guests in rooms facing the park might hang their underwear and bathing suits out the windows, making the laundry visible from inside the park. We had many discussions in an attempt to allay Frank's concerns, and, ultimately, these issues informed the design by WATG of Irvine, California, the firm that had recently designed the Grand Floridian Hotel at Walt Disney World. Led by a fine talent, Gerald Allison, WATG turned the idea conceived by Baxter and Sotto into one of the most popular hostelries in Europe—the five hundred-room Disneyland Hotel at Disneyland Paris.

In carrying out the concept that Baxter and Sotto had proposed, architect Allison created a design that serves as the visual and actual entry to the park. All ticketing and entrance gates are located *underneath* the hotel, at the ground level. The result is an icon second only to Le Château de la Belle au Bois Dormant (Sleeping Beauty Castle) at Disneyland Paris. Allison's design placed the VIP Castle Club and suite accommodations as major elements on the park side; neither underwear nor bathing suits have ever been an issue, although guests at the Disneyland Hotel continue to wear both.

* * * * * * * * * *

With fifteen million admissions to its two parks in 2010, Disneyland Paris has been a popular destination with European audiences. Yet it has continued to struggle financially as a business. I have read and heard many analyses and opinions reflecting on the "mistakes" Disney made. Here are two of the most repeated:

Too many hotels, and hotel rooms, were built for Opening Day. While Card Walker had erred on the conservative side and Disney allowed outside hotel and motel operators to feed off Walt Disney World's success, Disney in Paris preempted the market before one was even established. The concepts by the Gang of Five were expensive to build, and often missed the mark on such things as restaurant capacities, in part as a result of Disney having no operating experience in European hotels.

The park itself cost too much to build. Michael Eisner himself has been quoted as saying that certain facilities—especially the arcades behind the shops on either side of Main Street—were too costly and unnecessary. However, the arcades had two major purposes: first, as a hedge against inclement weather (it's cold and wet in winter in Marne-la-Vallée); and second, as a way for guests to enter and exit the park when a major event, such as a parade, makes passage virtually impossible on the open-air Main Street.

Preparing for a talk to the executives and other leaders of Disneyland Paris in 2011, I sent a note asking the key Imagineers responsible for designing and building the park in Paris to share their memories of that period. Eddie Sotto, principal designer of Main Street, sent me this response:

> Sometimes people ask me how the arcades on Main Street got to be so beautiful . . . Prior to the park opening, there was quite a bit of hand-wringing going on as to how guests would circulate during inclement weather. Michael Eisner had issued a mandate to install as many fireplaces as possible to ensure the perception of warmth. The arcades ended up with eighty gaslights. . . . One day Frank Wells was out taking a tour of the construction site, and stepped into one of the arcades. They were nothing more than empty shells with no detail of any kind. The skylights of the arcades were false, and were to be lit artificially so that they amounted to nothing more than just tall dark hallways. . . . Frank . . . pulled me aside and counseled me in a rather demanding tone. He told me that these arcades had better be just as good as the rest of Main Street, because right now they look like

"the Black Hole of Calcutta! . . . Now fix it!" . . . I tried to defend what we did have in store for the space, but my flowery descriptions had no effect; in his mind, he saw a disaster, and was willing to fund any gilding those lilies would require. So when the time came to complete the design, I reminded my superiors of this terse conversation, and there was never any problem with getting the arcades to be as elegant as the rest of the street. . . . I could imagine the result would never have been the same without that famous Calcutta quote. . . .To his credit, when Frank was shown how the final drawings had omitted most of Main Street's detail in their translation to Europe, he was the first one to stand up and fund eight architects being flown in at the last minute, sponsoring a program to add millions of dollars in moldings and ornament to the street to make it the stunner it is. So when people say nice things about the level of detail of Main Street, we have . . . the unlikely hero to thank in Frank Wells, the man who rescued Main Street [and the arcades].

Reflecting on the criticism that the overall financial performance amounted to overspending in the park, Eddie for one has a perspective: "The park has endured for the last twenty years without many major enhancements because of the wisdom of investing in a great show," he maintains.

Eddie Sotto's passion for new ideas and one-of-a-kind adventures was a creative leader's dream. One day he stuck his head in my office and asked me to come out into the hallway, where he immediately lay down on his back, put his hands out as though he were steering a vehicle, and spun his new concept. "Imagine lying on your back inside a vehicle—a space capsule," he pitched. "Watch—I'm handling the controls, because I'm the pilot. But next to me are the other crew members, each with his or her own assignment—and we're *flying* through space, feeling the g-forces the astronauts experience!" We built a full-sized mock-up of the space capsule for a crew of four, consulted with NASA and its Astronaut Corps, designed the capsule's interior, created a story built around a trip to Mars, engineered a new kind of motion simulator, and in 2003, Mission: SPACE opened in Epcot at Walt Disney World. My leadership lesson? Maintain an open-door policy—and make sure your hallways are clear.

Eddie Sotto's view about Disneyland Paris is also mine, and I want to give credit where credit is due for the concept, design, and construction of the park in the face of many obstacles. In fact, our organizational start was headed for disaster until it was rescued by the leadership of one man—my partner, Stanley "Mickey" Steinberg.

Our creative team at Imagineering was absolutely first class. It was headed by Tony Baxter, the originator of Big Thunder Mountain Railroad and Splash Mountain in Disneyland, and co-creator with George Lucas and Tom Fitzgerald of Star Tours. The design leaders were Eddie Sotto (Main Street), Tim Delaney (Discoveryland), Jeff Burke (Frontierland), Chris Tietz (Adventureland), and Tom Morris (Fantasyland). In contrast, the project management and construction organization was a mess—and that's where Mickey Steinberg entered the picture.

In his book *Work in Progress*, published in 1998 by Random House, Michael Eisner remembers Steinberg's impact:

> As our construction problems mounted, Frank's
> solution was to bring Mickey Steinberg into the
> project late in 1988. A big, bluff man with passionate

enthusiasms and a quick temper, Mickey had worked with the architect John Portman for twenty-seven years, running his company and overseeing the construction of its hotels. Now he was executive vice president of Imagineering under Marty Sklar. At Euro Disney, Mickey concluded very quickly that our organizational structure was dysfunctional. "You are headed for one of the biggest failures I've ever seen in construction," he told Frank after visiting the site. "Unless something changes, you're never going to get finished on time." As Mickey analyzed it, the firm we'd hired were construction managers. "What we need are project managers who understand the whole process from construction to design to operations," Mickey said. "If you want to spend more on some aspect of design, the project managers' job is to help you find somewhere else to save money. It's all about trade-offs. That's not happening now."

The situation Mickey Steinberg walked into was actually worse than that, both in terms of the perception of the Imagineering organization in Glendale and the way our hands had been tied by the construction management organization that had been set up in Paris. In the wake of four earlier projects that had gone well over budget, including Pleasure Island at Walt Disney World, Frank Wells had issued a "Black Book" of concerns—and sent Jeff Rochlis to Imagineering to organize and manage the division. Known at Disney as "The Terminator" for his role in firing many longtime employees at the Studio with the advent of the new management team brought in by Eisner and Wells, Rochlis had no background or understanding of a design and construction organization. He became known for issuing the "Triangle of Success," emphasizing the obvious pillars a creative design organization always aims to achieve: "Design, Schedule, and Quality."

The issue Mickey Steinberg found immediately was that Rochlis did not believe the Imagineers could live by these principles. Rochlis's solution had been to turn the management of the park project over to a European construction firm, one that had never built a theme park or its rides before. Essentially, the Imagineers were being turned into "hired help" on a Disney job.

Mickey Steinberg had been recruited to Disney as a result of Frank Wells's Black Book. What he found was a project management organization that had employed a "design-build" system for the projects Wells had analyzed, essentially turning over the project responsibility to outside builders. Mickey took one look and called the giveaway of responsibility for designing and building those projects "nuts."

At Frank Wells's request, Steinberg then focused on the Euro Disney project. In his book, Eisner notes:

> "In the hotel business," Steinberg said, "we concentrate on one icon—the lobby. At Disney, *everything* is a lobby. And only the Imagineers understand how to do it." Mickey spent his first six months on the job making lists of unresolved issues. When his analysis was completed, he concluded that the budget for the park had been underestimated, and that it would require an additional $150 million to finish. He also convinced Frank that we needed to bring a far larger contingent of Imagineers over from Glendale. "I'll take responsibility for keeping to the budget you give me,"

Mickey said, "but our own people are the only ones who have the expertise we need to get this park built."

It took guts—never an issue for Mickey Steinberg—but he also told Disney's corporate management that there would be a one-year delay in the project "so we can finish the drawings." Trained as an architect and engineer, Mickey had built hotels, convention centers, office buildings, and other large projects for the Portman organization, headquartered in Atlanta. He knew that the difference between a project that can be built successfully (you can insert here: "Meets the objectives of the 'Triangle of Success'") could not be accomplished without a great set of construction drawings, especially those that needed to be converted into metrics for building in Paris. The construction organization Rochlis had established had somehow overlooked the importance of completing those vital documents of the construction industry.

With his new responsibilities (and Rochlis gone), Mickey installed a new project management team. A former Portman hand, Fred Beckenstein, moved to Paris to head the field team, and Orlando Ferrante (production), Jim Thomas (estimation), and Matt Priddy (manufacturing) went from hired hands to leading key parts of the Imagineering organization. But it was Steinberg, a Southerner and proud of it, tough as the proverbial construction nails when he needed to be, understanding and supportive when the field team needed it, who saved the day—and the project. As the administrative, financial, and project leader, Mickey was the supreme supporter of the team, enabling me to concentrate on story development and new ideas.

When I asked for those stories from the Imagineers who spent two and three years in France building Euro Disney, I received this "Mickey story that was very personal to me" from Skip Lange, the quintessential rockwork expert, who has built mountains, jungle rivers, and themed environments around the world:

At the end of one grueling "Mickey Meeting," after being beat up pretty good about problems concerning the rockwork effort, I was heading back out to the freezing cold, wet site, pulling on my huge coat, multiple scarves, and ski gloves and mumbling that I was getting blamed and beat up about many things that were really not in my control, being subject more to Project and Construction Management. Halfway out, I decided to make a stand, turned around, and headed back to Mickey's office, peeling all my layers of clothes back off. Luck would have it that Mickey was just finishing up a meeting with most of the managers, and so accepted an impromptu meeting with me. I started making my pitch, which he got the gist of quickly and stopped me midsentence. He went to his support person and asked her to call all of the managers back.

Waiting for them, Mickey made small talk with me while I began to panic as to what I had just done to my Disney career. As soon as all of the managers crowded into his office, Mickey repeated my lament about not being in control of my own destiny and informed all of them that they no longer had to worry about any of the rockwork effort in their respective lands. I would be telling them how rockwork was to be planned, managed, and executed from then on. My elation lasted only a second when he then turned to me with, "Now, Mr. Lange, you do know what this means. I will not be coming to any of them about rockwork anymore, I will be coming to *you*. Do you understand?" With a "Yes, sir" and "Thank you, sir" I left the office (and the amazed managers) and began my trek back to the site, once again pulling the required clothing back on, thinking, "What the heck did I just do?" [and] fearing that I had just alienated the entire management team. It turned out to be the opposite; I think they were glad to be rid of rockwork and they proceeded to help me make it all happen as efficiently as possible. And Mickey, though not easy on me, was very supportive.

All the Imagineers in the meeting still talk about the following bit of "Mickey Magic": in a project review, Steinberg became so incensed at a behind-schedule/overbudget report that he slammed his fist on the conference table. "His coffee cup jumped about two inches in the air," a witness told me, "and the coffee it contained went skyward five or six inches. When the cup came down, it landed perfectly flat on the table, and all the coffee flowed down into the cup as though it was magnetized. There wasn't a drop on the table!" We all took that as a sign from above that he was right. With his drive and leadership, we felt confident we could make that new Opening Day.

Typical of the challenges of the project was the variety of contractors employed. To build the Big Thunder Mountain Railroad, the team had to manage an Italian contractor (steel), a Dutch contractor (ride system), a French contractor (rockwork), and an Irish contractor (electrical). Another Italian contractor met its match when it tried to intimidate Mickey Steinberg.

Another "issue" with some of the contractors was the authenticity of our theming. Knowing how much grand design, some centuries old, was part of everyday living and a prime magnet for tourism in Europe, our designers knew they needed to be inspired by the history and surroundings, but also to create something that was truly one-of-a-kind.

"In the end," Fantasyland show producer Tom Morris told *D23* magazine, this was the result:

> We opted for a fanciful castle that would seem to come right out of a European fairy tale. Mont Saint Michel's manner of reaching for the sky, while coiling up on itself, was an early inspiration. I went on a tour of the castles in the Loire region west of Paris [inspiration for Cinderella Castle at Walt Disney World]. The windows of Chaumont were interesting, the tower at Azay-le-Rideau impressed me, some moats were superb, [and] a specific stained-glass window intrigued me. Inspiration was everywhere. Finally, we wanted to incorporate the "square trees" from Walt's film *Sleeping Beauty* to give it an Eyvind Earle sort of look. [Eyvind Earle, the production designer for *Sleeping Beauty*, had taken inspiration from the tapestries in the Cluny Museum in Paris.] So the story had come full circle.

The dramatic Château de la Belle au Bois Dormant (Sleeping Beauty Castle) blends contemporary French building techniques (concrete, steel, and lots of digging and grading) with local European crafts: plaster-carving, stained-glass window-making, decorative metal work, patterned roof tiles, and tapestries (for the interior). Some of the companies that accomplished the work had been in operation for over five hundred years, notably the tapestry and roof-tile makers. But it fell to contemporary contractors to bring together all the pieces.

Six months before opening, a construction manager warned Mickey that word on the street was that the Fantasyland contractor would soon come to him and state that they couldn't finish the project . . . unless, of course, they were paid a handsome bonus above and beyond the contract they had signed. Steinberg consulted the Disney lawyers, and was told that he could not act unless in fact the contractor did make that threat. As if on cue, the Italian contractor came to Mickey's office and issued their ultimatum. On the spot, Steinberg fired them. The next morning, in their place was a new Irish contractor, Mivan, who'd been waiting in the wings just in case the threat was issued as anticipated. (The Irish turned out to be the best construction workers on the project. The workers brought their families to France, and every Friday night, they celebrated their week's efforts with a giant beer party.)

Living full time in France over the last few months of construction, Mickey and the operations leader, Jim Cora, developed a close working relationship. So that Cora and his staff could train their attractions operating staff by day, the Imagineers took the night shift over the last two months.

"The entire two years that I was there was all pretty much six or seven days a week, ten-plus hours a day, but the last few months got even worse," Skip Lange told me.

"I remember that after the on-site cafeteria was opened, you could go there at all hours of the night and see fellow workers sleeping on the bench seating. Many of us were working twenty-hour days, going home only for just a couple of hours of sleep and a shower."

The combination of winter weather, the schedule demands, and working the night shift caught up with many of our team, who were sick when Opening Day arrived. Yet—and this is true of every international project we have built, from Tokyo to Paris to Hong Kong—the experience of living for one, two, or three years overseas is always regarded as a valuable opportunity by almost every Imagineer I have talked to about this subject. That goes for families, too. Many children of Imagineer "ex-pats" have had formative learning experiences across the oceans, attending the American School, and learning a new language.

Almost without exception, I believe the Imagineers take great pride in their foreign assignments, and love to return to see how the craftsmen they trained in Japan, Hong Kong, and France are progressing in their new fields; many are on the maintenance staff at the park they helped build.

At opening, Mickey Steinberg could report to Eisner and Wells and the Disney board of directors that Imagineering had brought in the Disneyland Park at Euro Disney on time and on (the revised) budget. In other major projects built at the same time in Europe, the new Paris Opera House was completed for three times its projected budget, and the European Chunnel linking France and the United Kingdom under the English Channel cost ten times its original projection.

As the final details were wrapped up, John Verity,

project manager for Frontierland, was proud that his team had made the schedule for the haunted house, called Phantom Manor in Paris. "The show looked great, and we had just finished the punch list, when I got a phone call saying Phantom Manor was 'on fire,'" John told me. "Immediately, I heard the fire engine sirens blaring, and we all ran to the attraction to see what was burning. When we got there, we went to the electrical room where the smoke detector had gone off, only to find two French electricians barbecuing a couple of steaks and splitting a bottle of wine!"

It's too bad our corporate management wasn't invited to this little celebration under the Phantom Manor. I think it would have convinced them from day one that wine was a vital accompaniment to any French meal.

15

THE SUN NEVER SETS ON THE DISNEY PARKS

I am proud to say that because my Disney career began at Disneyland one month before the park business began, I retired in 2009 as the only cast member to have participated in the opening of all eleven Disney parks around the world. Somewhere in the world, there's a Disney park open every hour of every day; literally, the sun never sets on their operation on three continents around the globe. Of course, this has posed major challenges for the Disney cast and management, especially where Disney is not the majority owner (Paris and Hong Kong), or has no ownership stake at all (Tokyo).

While Michael Eisner was fully engaged in the development of Disneyland Paris (he even immersed himself in a weeks-long French language course one summer in Paris), he was far less focused on Tokyo. Michael did mount an all-out effort to convince OLC's chairman, Takahashi-san, that the second park in Tokyo should be a Studio concept, based on the existing popular Disney-MGM Studios in Florida (now Disney's Hollywood Studios). But when the Japanese made it clear they were not interested in the concept (Japanese film and TV studios are not the glamour worlds of Hollywood renown), Michael seemed to lose interest. This opened the way for our Imagineering design team, led by Senior Vice President Steve Kirk, to create a brand-new genre in the Disney park lineup.

Called Tokyo DisneySea, the park was unique in many ways, but had some of its roots in a concept we had worked on for a park at the harbor in Long Beach, California, developed as an alternative to building a second gate in Anaheim. It also took advantage of the success of the Disneyland Hotel at the entrance to Disneyland Paris. Guests enter Tokyo DisneySea by walking under parts of the five hundred-room southern European-style Mira Costa Hotel, which (once you are inside the park) serves as the background for major live shows taking place on the waters of Mediterranean Harbor.

It's my belief that a major reason for the success of the Disney parks has been the depth of detail that has brought storytelling to a level never before imagined in the theme or amusement park world. As I put it in a speech at an International Association of Amusement Parks and Attractions (IAAPA) convention, "In a Disney park, not only is storytelling 'the thing'—every thing tells a story. It's the details, stupid!"

Tokyo DisneySea (TDS) is a grand example of this basic Disney approach. As I marveled at the TDS designs presented by Steve Kirk and the team, I asked Steve and Jim Thomas, senior vice president for Tokyo Resort Development for the Imagineers, how they had convinced the OLC to spend what obviously was a king's ransom on the key attractions and architectural settings of each land. This included the wonderful indoor Mermaid Lagoon, lit as an underwater spectacle; the exterior marquee, a fantastic rainbow of sea life forms sculpted in concrete and covered with shining jewels; Mysterious Island, not only home to the high-speed race Journey to the Center of the Earth, but also containing one of the finest works of three-dimensional art ever created in a Disney park, the fire belching volcano of Mount Prometheus and its amazing central Caldera; Lost River Delta, which was lifted right out of a Central American jungle, with live shows and ride adventures to suit every intrepid adventurer; the Arabian Coast, where Aladdin and his Genie reside in a live magic stage show; and much more.

The grand designs made me wonder how Steve, Jim, and Imagineering's other key project leaders (Orlando Ferrante, Art Kishyama, John Verity, and Craig Russell, the design management executive who lived in Japan nearly four years) convinced the OLC to spend so much money. They never told me, but I can make an educated guess: the OLC executives responsible for the project were not going to "lose face" when Tokyo DisneySea was compared to Tokyo Disneyland. Presuming that was one of their major objectives, they (and we) succeeded big time. In 2002, the year following its opening, Tokyo DisneySea was honored by the Themed Entertainment Association (TEA) with its annual Thea Award, in recognition of its "concept, design, and construction." It was the first time TEA had honored a whole new park, and was one of forty-three awards to Disney projects and individuals in the eighteen years that the TEA Awards have recognized outstanding achievement associated with themed entertainment.

As pleased as I was to see our Imagineering staff recognized again, I also felt the same empathy for the Imagineers working on other new parks that I had felt when Michael Eisner chose the Blizzard Beach concept without even listening to the other water park ideas for Walt Disney World. The three other parks developed in and around the same time frame—Hong Kong Disneyland (2005), Disney California Adventure (2001), and the Walt Disney Studios Paris (2002)—had fallen prey to a new Disney "standard": build it small, for less money, and they will come anyway. Call it "the Paul Pressler phenomenon." I'll explain shortly . . . but the good news is that under Bob Iger as CEO, each of those parks is currently undergoing major infusions of attractions and investment. I'm confident that when completed, these major upgrades in expanded areas for guests, and imaginative new attractions for young and old to enjoy, will fully realize the potential of these "too small, not enough to do" parks.

One example: Disney California Adventure opened with eighteen attractions, right next door to its sister park, Walt's iconic Disneyland, which counted more than sixty attractions by its then forty-sixth year. Yet the admission price for both parks was exactly the same. You have one guess where the public wanted to go!

The Hong Kong project had a special attachment for me. First of all, my initial view of the site was from a boat in Hong Kong Harbor; it was all water, and we were warned not to drift too close to shore, because the small shipyard that was about to be displaced was not thrilled about the coming

Disney park. Some of their boat repairmen were reputed to be excellent rifle marksmen.

Paul Pressler was aboard, and on this park, in fairness to Paul, the contract and budget were negotiated under the previous chairman, Judson Green, and his representative, Steve Tight, who apparently thought we were building an iron-ride, off-the-shelf park.

In one sense only, it was a replica—the first and only time we have reused the design of Walt's Disneyland castle, and the look of its Main Street. Even on my last trip to Hong Kong Disneyland, in May 2012, I was taken aback for a moment as I walked with American operations chief Noble Coker onto Main Street, U.S.A.—Walt's nostalgic turn-of-the-century, middle-America throwback to another time and place. It's an amazing feeling to be 7,241 miles from home, and yet feel right at home in a foreign land. In truth, with the dramatic green hills as a backdrop to the castle, many of my colleagues believe it's even more "magical" than Walt's original Sleeping Beauty Castle. (I've exercised my Fifth Amendment rights, even in China!)

As their creative leader, I was proud of the designers, writers, illustrators, model makers, architects, engineers, and nearly 140 other disciplines that make up Walt Disney Imagineering on these projects. They gave 100 percent effort within what Eisner liked to call "The Box" approved for each of these parks, without worrying that their ride system or architectural facade or special effect would inevitably be compared to those in Tokyo DisneySea, whose budgets were inevitably larger. It made me feel that we had successfully carried on the traditions that Walt and the pioneering Disney Legends had established: that it was a "we" business.

And as I always reminded the Imagineering teams, there was still only one name on the door: Walt Disney.

Individual successes in each park were exported to other Disney parks: Soarin' over California in California Adventure (to Epcot); Moteurs . . . Action! Stunt Show Spectacular from the Walt Disney Studios Park Paris (to the Hollywood Studios in Florida); and the infusion of Disney characters in appropriate parts of the globe at Hong Kong Disneyland to make the message of "it's a small world" even more relevant to young audiences (to Disneyland).

Outside the parks, around the world, Disney has sometimes introduced new products, especially in what became known as "Downtown" areas that combine entertainment, restaurants, and shopping. There were mixed successes like Pleasure Island at Walt Disney World; though popular for years, its club concepts aged with little change, and the area is now closed and being rethought. And the Tokyo Disney Resort's Ikspiari, poorly laid out and designed by the Oriental Land Company (despite a strong critique from Disney). And there are hits, like the Downtown Disney areas at the Disneyland Resort and Walt Disney World, popular with both vacationers and locals for their mix of fun, food, and shopping experiences: ESPN Zone, House of Blues, AMC movie theaters, even a Cirque du Soleil permanent theater show (in Florida).

One disappointment for me was when the company lost faith in a project that still is successful at Downtown Disney West/Side in Florida. Called DisneyQuest, it was created as an "indoor interactive theme park," meant to be rolled out in major cities across the country. When the second one, in Chicago, did not meet expectations—whether because of marketing, location, timing, or concept—corporate Disney canceled its expansion. DisneyQuest's interactive attractions—CyberSpace Mountain, Pirates of the Caribbean: Battle for Buccaneer Gold, Virtual Jungle Cruise, and other interactive adventures inspired by Disney park attractions—continue to excite our guests in Florida. I was very proud of the product, with its strategic and business strategy developed by Joe DiNunzio, and the team's creative concepts, led by Larry Gertz. DisneyQuest also achieved fame when Professor Randy Pausch wore an Imagineering logo shirt during his "Last Lecture" at Carnegie Mellon University. A computer sciences expert, Professor Pausch was a key consultant to our DisneyQuest team. His "Last Lecture," delivered while he was dying of cancer, was widely covered by television, and in a book, *The Last Lecture*, published by Hyperion in 2008. Randy called his talk "Really Achieving Your Childhood Dreams"; it was not about dying—it was about seizing every moment and living life to its fullest.

"It's not about how to achieve your dreams," Professor Pausch said. "It's about how to lead your life. If you lead your life the right way, the karma will take care of itself. The dreams will come to you."

16

RIDING MICHAEL'S ROLLER COASTER

Near the end of his twenty-one years as CEO, I was asked by Disney's Corporate Communications to write an editorial in support of Michael Eisner's creative role in the development of our park attractions. In part, this is what I said in an op-ed piece that appeared in the *Orange County Register* newspaper. I began by referencing that first meeting at Imagineering:

> We didn't know what to expect from the new boss that . . . morning, but the day ended up being fun for all of us. Michael was excited by our creativity and had tremendous enthusiasm for what we did at Imagineering. . . . Ideas and the talent behind the ideas need to be nurtured in order to grow and reach full potential, and no matter how strange one of our ideas seemed on paper, Michael was able to recognize its universal appeal.

By the time this article appeared, Michael's days were numbered, as he came under fire from investor groups and other shareholders, members of the Disney board of directors, and the onetime cheerleaders originally responsible for bringing Eisner and Frank Wells to the company in 1984—Roy E. Disney and his business partner at Shamrock Holdings, Stanley Gold. Stanley, in particular, took great umbrage at what I had written.

There were two important reasons I wrote that op-ed piece, despite the calls from Roy and Stanley and other shareholders. Firstly, Roy had very little to do with what went into the parks and resorts around the world, aside from his previous role as a member of the Disney board of directors. In fact, until the Animal Kingdom park (Roy was a big help in putting together and encouraging the advisory board), I can't recall a creative or story meeting Roy participated in during my tenure as creative leader of Imagineering.

Secondly, Michael's role in working with the Imagineers to create imaginative places and attractions in the parks and resorts was enormous. I have already mentioned a few examples—but there were many highlights: Captain Eo, Star Tours, Mission: SPACE, Mickey's PhilharMagic, Splash Mountain, It's Tough to be a Bug!, Blizzard Beach, and several new parks and resort hotels around the world. No question his enthusiasm and role had diminished and it wasn't the same relationship after Frank Wells's untimely death.

My op-ed piece was in some ways a "thank you." I felt someone who was directly involved should say so.

Despite the loss of Frank Wells, the second decade of Eisner's leadership at The Walt Disney Company had begun auspiciously with the release of a series of animated features from 1995 to 1999 (*Pocahontas, The Hunchback of Notre Dame, Hercules, Mulan,* and *Tarzan*); a new relationship with Pixar that produced John Lasseter's original *Toy Story* (1995) and *A Bug's Life* (1998); acquisition of the ABC Television Network (1996); and the opening of the Animal Kingdom park at Walt Disney World (1998). There was also the forgettable *D3: The Mighty Ducks* (1996) and *George of the Jungle* (1997). But Frank Wells's death left Michael without a true second–in–command whom Michael trusted implicitly, as he did Wells. Michael himself has said, ". . . it was never the same without Frank."

I fully admit to an incomplete view of all the challenges Michael Eisner faced in motion pictures, television, the rapidly changing world of interactive media, and so on. But I did have a seat at the table as the creative leader of WDI in the Parks and Resorts division, which accounted for 25.3 percent of corporate revenue when Eisner turned the CEO reins over to Bob Iger in 2005.

Those of us who were in leadership positions at Walt Disney Productions (as it was then called) in 1984 when Eisner and Wells arrived were excited by the talent they attracted, including Gary Wilson from Marriott as CFO; Jeffrey Katzenberg in motion pictures from Paramount; and Rich Frank, also ex-Paramount, in television. They joined key leaders already in place: Dick Nunis, Attractions; Barton "Bo" Boyd, Consumer Products; Jim Jimirro at the fledgling Disney Channel; Jack Lindquist, Attractions Marketing; and Carl Bongirno, president, and me at WED Enterprises. By the millennium, however, they were all gone except for me. Michael did put in place a number of outstanding new executives: Bob Iger, of course, who came to Disney with the purchase of Capital Cities-ABC and who by 2011, as president and CEO, had acquired Pixar and Marvel Enterprises; Andy Mooney, who brought creative new directions beyond licensing to Consumer Products; and Anne Sweeney at the Disney Channel, now the top executive in Disney Television Enterprises.

In TV and motion pictures, there was George Bodenheimer, president of ESPN and ABC Sports; Dick Cook in motion pictures; and Peter Schneider and Thomas Schumacher, who followed their success in Feature Animation and built the Disney Theatrical Group, creating stage shows for Broadway and theaters around the world based on Disney animated stories (*Beauty and the Beast*, *The Lion King*, *Mary Poppins*, etc.). Tom continues to this day as producer and president of the Disney Theatrical Group.

* * * * * * * * * *

But it was the loss of key talent and the appointments Michael made to key leadership positions that caused many of my colleagues to lose enthusiasm for his leadership of the company. My own attitude mirrored that of most of the Imagineers at several losses and changes in particular.

One, Jeffrey Katzenberg, was missed immediately. Jeffrey's support in signing star talent for our shows, especially for the Disney-MGM Studios, helped Tom Fitzgerald and Bob Weis create some memorable film moments, including two films that opened the Disney-MGM Studios: *The Lottery*, starring Bette Midler and directed by Gary Marshall, and the animated *Back to Neverland*, starring the unlikely combination of Walter Cronkite and Robin Williams. Jeffrey made sure that Disney animation produced these and other animation subjects and staffed the important Animation Studios Tour. He was also enthusiastically supportive of Imagineering in the ongoing conflicts between the creative and operating points of view at the parks.

Jeffrey had asked me to meet with him to discuss a "white paper" he was writing about future directions for the company, which I understood he was preparing at Eisner's request. In fact, we later learned that when Michael fired him, Jeffrey had gone to Michael's office expecting to discuss his assignment and the recommendations in his white paper. (In his book *Partnership*, Michael writes: "Jeffrey Katzenberg, who had done terrific work alongside me for nearly two decades, left the company when he didn't get Frank's job, and after Roy Disney demanded he be fired.")

Losing Jeffrey was a big blow to our staff, especially to Tom Fitzgerald, whom Jeffrey had helped school in working with star talent. We felt Jeffrey's loss even more so with the hiring of Michael Ovitz. We did not know Ovitz, and he did not know our business, or the style of our talent. Imagineers are driven by the success of the project rather than their ego, stature, and future contract negotiations—the world Ovitz epitomized as head of Creative Artists Agency. (Again quoting from his explanation in *Partnership*, this is how Eisner explained Ovitz's "in and out" tenure at Disney after Katzenberg had left: "A year later, we hired Michael Ovitz, the head of Creative Artists Agency (CAA), who had been a business friend of mine in Los Angeles for years, to be Frank's replacement. Fourteen months later, he was gone after the arrangement failed.")

Jeffrey, of course, has gone on to other successes

since Disney, first by forming DreamWorks SKG with Steven Spielberg and David Geffen, and now, as CEO of DreamWorks Animation. Considering his legendary work ethic, leadership, and stature in the motion picture industry, his departure was a big loss for The Walt Disney Company.

Imagineering also lost a key voice at the Disney Studio who understood that "resting on your laurels" was the antithesis of the tradition in innovation Walt established. For the years that Dick Cook, who had begun his Disney career working at Disneyland and loved the parks, served as chairman of Walt Disney Studios, the Imagineering group had a strong bond with the Studios. Cook was later fired by Bob Iger.

Mickey Steinberg was another loss. In a business where complementary leadership skills can build one plus one into a ten, Mickey and I were the perfect fit. Mickey's technical skills as an engineer and architect were impeccable—he had spent twenty-seven years managing John Portman's financing and leading the building of developments around the world. That gave him a respect and deep appreciation for creative talent, and the importance of supporting the dreamers of new ideas. He concentrated on "the doing"—organizing every Imagineering function that contributed to making the project feasible and buildable, and overseeing dozens of functions: project management, of course, but also finance, estimating, engineering, architecture, manufacturing, and production.

Certainly a key part of why we worked so well together was our communication. Everyone at Imagineering knew they could not play Mickey and me against one another—that Mickey respected my leadership of the concept work of designers, artists, writers, storytellers, and everyone who contributed to the creative process . . . and that I was ecstatic that I did not have to spend precious time selling the cost of great ideas internally at Imagineering—when "Uncle Scrooge" (Corporate Strategic Planning at the Studio) was the real audience. Mickey filled that role. He was not always successful. Disney's corporate heads had established a "Good Guy/Bad Guy" system for approving projects; of course "strategic planning" were the "Bad Guys."

It was not always pretty with Mickey Steinberg. You always knew where he stood on an issue—and sometimes that straight-shooting honesty made him a target for more politically minded executives in other divisions, which is why his tenure at the company came to an end.

During the five years or so that Mickey Steinberg and I were a team at the head of Imagineering, we built or set in motion over $4 billion in Disney park projects, including new attractions developed for the existing parks. While Mickey's role in Euro Disney is well documented, his mark on Disney's Animal Kingdom, although it opened four years after he had returned to Atlanta, was just as important. Three examples are especially noteworthy.

When the project was just getting under way, the gurus of Disney landscaping came to us with a passionate plea: give us a big down payment on the trees and vines, shrubs, and grasses that will make or break the environments that are being designed, especially for the main attractions of the Africa area: Kilimanjaro Safaris, Harambi Wildlife Preserve, and Pangani Forest Exploration Trail. As soon as we announce the project, prices for the "show" and "specimen trees," and the "thematic area and backdrop trees," are going to soar, they argued. Give us $3 million now, and we'll collect and store the key elements that will make the adventures that Joe Rohde and his team are planning look real for Opening Day.

The petitioners were Bill Evans, one of the most respected landscapers in the world—a Disney Legend for his pioneering work at Disneyland, Walt Disney World, and Tokyo Disneyland—and his protégé, Paul Comstock, just returned from Paris to join the Animal Kingdom team. Their argument convinced us, and in no time they were buying trees and landscape material throughout the Southeast. One surprise was the discovery of an area in Georgia where a government program years before had helped create farms full of bamboo growth. In addition to their use as windbreaks, the stalks were harvested and sold to furniture manufacturers, but the area had fallen on hard times. The Disney landscapers made a deal: we'll buy the whole field of bamboo plants, roots and all, but (and this was the clincher) you farmers can cut the stalks off and sell them separately to the furniture people. We wanted the root ball itself.

Here's the way Paul Comstock described the purchase to me: the Giant Timber Bamboo we bought in Georgia, just south of Atlanta, . . . is native to China. Our plants escaped from a test planting done in the 1930s by the United States Department of Agriculture. The bamboo was being tested as windbreaks for the protection of agriculture. It thrived in the Georgia test, and quickly spread to cover vast tracts of land within a couple of decades. We offered to "mow" a couple acres of the giant grass to the ground and dig out the root systems. After cutting the sixty-foot tall bamboo to the ground, we then jackhammered the grove into seven feet long by three-feet wide by one-inch thick Georgia clay slabs of bamboo root rhizomes. We stacked the slabs like books on a shelf, thirty slabs per forty-foot-long flatbed trailer, and trucked them to the old Epcot Tree Farm. After two Florida sunshine growing seasons, the transplanted roots had shot up to twenty-five feet, on their way to the height of forty feet plus we see in the park today. We shipped a couple hundred slabs and turned them into thousands of mature bamboo culms, providing food, habitat, shade, scenery, and a "living show set" throughout Disney's Animal Kingdom (DAK).

The second and most important decision was to keep a core team intact during a project hiatus of nearly one year. Although Michael Eisner had originally suggested the idea of a park about animals, the project was stopped and put on hold as a result of other corporate initiatives requiring key financing. But the DAK team had such a great start that Mickey was able to convince Frank Wells to continue working on the drawing packages for Harambi Village, Rafiki's Planet Watch, DinoLand, the Maharajah Jungle Trek, and other key areas. As a result, when the project was "turned on" again, the Animal Kingdom went to the field for construction with what may have been the best drawing package of any Disney project, ever. The influence this had on contractors' bids, and the schedule, was enormously positive.

A third key decision we made was to approve the research travel by Joe Rohde and his key Animal Kingdom creative team. The early Imagineers who came from art direction backgrounds in the motion picture field were older, and had frequently traveled widely; Herb Ryman's early travels in Asia and Europe were typical. They could refresh their memories of design detail with a trip to the research library.

However, most of our younger designers of the 1980s and 1990s had not traveled widely before building their design careers. Joe Rohde was not just their advocate for true "boots on the ground" research; he was a veteran traveler to Asia and Polynesia. Joe's belief that his team absolutely had to experience seeing lions and elephants on a real African safari, and travel to Asian byways far from civilization, carried the day. While the project was still on hiatus, we approved four different research expeditions. In total, before the opening and later additions of Expedition Everest to the Asian area of the park, Joe and his team took a dozen study trips to Africa and Asia. The authenticity of the Animal Kingdom's designs and attractions (as well as the Animal Kingdom Lodge resort) speaks volumes for Joe Rohde's travel advocacy.

So what happened to my favorite working relationship? Why did Mickey Steinberg go home to Atlanta? The answer is, he crossed swords with Peter Rummell, and Peter won. It was not a pretty picture.

Peter Rummell was the real estate developer in Michael Eisner's entertainment court. He left a position as vice chairman of Rockefeller Center Management, which markets, leases, and manages buildings in midtown Manhattan, to become president of the brand-new Disney Development Company in 1985. The charge was to plan and develop Disney's Florida land, and soon Euro Disney, with emphasis on hotel development (some would say "overdevelopment"), and ultimately the community of Celebration, a faux version of the Epcot community, on land de-annexed from the

Walt Disney World property. A deep divide developed over the master planning of Walt Disney World involving new access roads and other infrastructure related to the Animal Kingdom project and nearby acreage. Eisner sided with Peter, and then took a step beyond: he decided to make Imagineering part of the Disney Development Company.

Despite Frank Wells's warning that Mickey would leave the company (and, we were told, Frank's own objections to the new organization), Michael persisted. One day Frank called to ask Mickey and me to have lunch with Peter to see if we could develop a working relationship. We met in the Executive Suite at the Disneyland Hotel. As Mickey and I drove the thirty-five miles back to Glendale from Anaheim, it was clear that his association with Disney was coming to an end. Days later, he was on his way back to Atlanta, and I (along with all of Imagineering) was now reporting to the real estate developers. Peter became chairman of the new organization. I received a fancy new title, which I wrote myself, to make sure I separated myself from the developers: vice chairman and principal creative executive. Ken Wong, also with a real estate development background, ultimately was given the title president of Imagineering.

I cannot remember having one discussion with Peter Rummell about a creative issue related to Imagineering's role in the parks and resorts. And I never had the feeling that Peter really cared what happened inside the parks. By 1997, Peter had moved on, becoming chairman and CEO of Florida's largest landholders, the St. Joe Company of Jacksonville. It seemed as though his major accomplishment from the merger of DDC and WDI was to drop the name Disney Development Company and rename the whole organization Walt Disney Imagineering. Wouldn't you want to say to people, "I was a Disney Imagineer" rather than "I was a Disney developer"?

* * * * * * * * * *

When I think of Paul Pressler today, what comes to mind is this expression: "You can fool all of the people some of the time, and some of the people all of the time, but you can't fool all of the people all of the time." In retrospect, he certainly fooled Disney management a lot of the time.

Pressler joined the Consumer Products division in 1987, moving from Kenner-Parker Toys to become senior vice president of Disney's Consumer Product licensing. Soon after the launch of the Disney Stores, led by Steve Burke, now chairman of NBC-Universal, Pressler became executive vice president and general manager, then president, leading the worldwide rollout that topped out at over 650 stores. Imagineering designers worked with Pressler on a number of special iconic stores, notably in San Francisco, Las Vegas, and on Fifth Avenue in New York—a gem of a design and representation of the company and what we thought was the direction of the Disney Stores' business. The stores capitalized on the renaissance of Disney animation and the popularity of *Beauty and the Beast*, *Aladdin*, and *The Lion King*. Ultimately, however, as the quality and variety of the merchandise declined (or perhaps there are only so many Disney character T-shirts a family wardrobe needed), the stores went into steep decline, until the company sold those remaining. By then, Pressler was long gone—from both Consumer Products and The Walt Disney Company.

In 1994, with the retirement of Jack Lindquist, Michael

Eisner made Pressler the president of the Disneyland Resort. Four years later, with the retirement of Dick Nunis, Pressler became president of Disney Parks and Resorts worldwide. After two more years, he was named chairman, with an additional prize: forty-eight years after Walt founded WED Enterprises, we had become not just part of Disney Parks and Resorts (technically, The Walt Disney World Co.), but we now reported to the division chairman, Paul Pressler— along with all the ticket takers, ride operators, marketing, and other guest service functions.

It was interesting the way Michael Eisner chose to inform the leaders of Imagineering about this sea change. About a year earlier, responding to an issue I had raised, Michael had assured me that he would never have the creative organization—Imagineering—reporting to the operators. At Imagineering, we sometimes used the metaphor that this would equate to a movie director reporting to the manager of a movie theater in your local mall.

To keep some of our key talent working during a slow development period for our parks attractions and exhibits, we had taken on the design of a new children's museum called "Port Discovery" in Baltimore, Maryland. The museum's grand opening took place in December 1998. Ken Wong and I were there to celebrate the work of Doris Woodward and the Imagineering design team. Suddenly Ken and I were given an urgent message to call Michael Eisner's office ASAP. As it happened, the only telephone we could find with any degree of privacy was an outdoor pay telephone nearby. It was there that Ken and I took turns being informed by Disney's CEO that we—and Imagineering—now reported to Paul Pressler.

I was the frequent subject of character sketches. Some of my favorites (clockwise from top left) were by: John Graziano for *Ripley's Believe It or Not!—Amusement Park Oddities & Trivia* (a book by Tim O'Brien); Don Lowe, *Mickey's Ten Commandments*; Seisaku Sato, *The Wise Bird* (Oriental Land Company); and T. Hee, *Sayonara!* (on leaving for Japan).

MARTY SKLAR - June 3, 2006
Recognizing 50 Magical Years with The Walt Disney Company

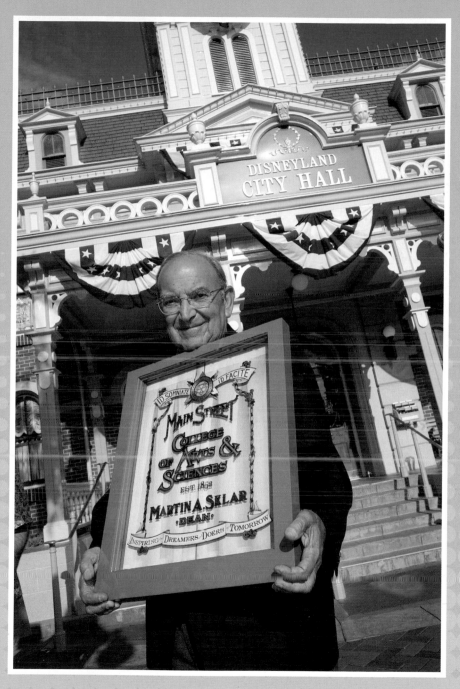

My fifty-year Disney Service Award (upper left), and my window dedication at Disneyland, July 17, 2009 (lower left and above).

Many Disney colleagues, friends, and family celebrated my window dedication, including Wing Chao, executive vice president, Master Planning, Architecture, and Design (upper left). Ed Grier, president of Disneyland (center, right) made the presentation. Leah joined me (center, left), as she has done in all my Disney adventures since 1957.

Thanks to all the Imagineers (and especially the humor of writer Kevin Rafferty), my retirement party at Walt Disney Imagineering was a true blastoff! Highlights: Richard Sherman performing his Supercalifragilisticexpialidocious parody (see book's Foreword, top right); comments by Craig Russell (center, right), now chief design and project delivery executive of Walt Disney Imagineering; part of the Finnish delegation (far right), grandson Gabriel and son, Howard; and (lower left) presentation of a check for $250,000 from The Walt Disney Company to establish the ongoing Ryman Sklar Intern Program at Imagineering and Disney Animation.

Many of my longtime Disney colleagues spoke and made presentations at my Imagineering retirement party, including (top) Bruce Vaughn, chief creative executive of Walt Disney Imagineering; Academy Award–winning songwriter Richard Sherman (center, right); Tom Fitzgerald, senior vice president of creative development at Walt Disney Imagineering (lower left); and my favorite partner, former executive vice president Stanley "Mickey" Steinberg (lower right).

Pressler's meteoric rise through the Disney ranks was the subject of much speculation, especially by the blogs. One of the most specific views was published two years after Pressler left Disney, credited to a "Tom Morrow." The 2004 piece was entitled "The Fall of Walt Disney Imagineering." It read in part:

> From 1995 to 1999, [Pressler] squeezed every penny out of Disneyland, making dramatic budget cuts and focusing attention on merchandise promotions and suggestive-selling programs. Hard selling was never the Disney way—in fact it was the antithesis of Walt's philosophy. Just like at the Disney Stores, Paul Pressler would impress his bosses by achieving short-term gains at the expense of the long-term health of his business unit. Stores became more important than attractions.
>
> Some of Disneyland's classic attractions would be shuttered to save costs, among them Skyway and Submarine Voyage; both closed without replacement. . . .
>
> Many of the most significant budget cuts affected Disneyland maintenance. The financial price of these decisions is being paid today. Disneyland, long regarded for its cleanliness and efficient maintenance practices, is being forced into a dramatic refurbishment program to bring the park up to its old standards—including a twenty-eight-month refurbishment of one of its signature attractions, Space Mountain . . .

Pressler left Disney in September 2002 to become president and chief executive officer of Gap, Inc., the San Francisco-based retailer, operator of The Gap, Banana Republic, and Old Navy chain stores. During his last year at Disney, our Imagineering design staff at Disneyland had compiled list after list of maintenance items that had reduced show quality in the park to the lowest level any of us could remember. No argument to Byron Pollitt, Pressler's chief financial officer, or Cynthia Harriss, Disneyland's president, opened the purse strings. Wherever you looked—at paint, woodwork, iron railings, paving surfaces, etc.—the park set a new low in Disney quality.

Byron Pollitt had his Disney training in the "no" business with the corporate Strategic Planning group. Typical of his attitude was a discussion we had about the impact of new attractions. Byron claimed that it was marketing of the new attractions, not the experiences themselves, that drove attendance—even in the case of Pirates of the Caribbean. I pointed out that Buzz Price, the most respected economist in the parks and resorts business worldwide, had claimed that "the most impactful attraction" in the modern history of the park business—by far—was Pirates of the Caribbean. After all, without the adventure, what drove the marketing campaign? (Recall my earlier note that Disneyland's attendance increased from six million to over nine million from 1966 to 1969 with the additions of Pirates of the Caribbean and The Haunted Mansion.) I received no response from Byron, but the company's response since the departure of Pressler and his team has been to create blockbuster after blockbuster new attractions around the world, including the enormous Cars Land opened in 2012 at California Adventure; a whole new Fantasyland at the Walt Disney World Magic Kingdom (to be completed by next year); and major new areas in Paris, Hong Kong, and Tokyo. And to market the heck out of each one!

Cynthia Harriss had joined Pressler's staff at the Disney Stores in 1992 after nineteen years with the Paul Harris Stores, a women's clothing chain. Pressler named her executive vice president of Disneyland in January 1999, and by December she had been promoted to president of the resort.

I liked Cynthia, and thought she meant well—but she was truly a fish out of water in the park business. To support her, Walt Disney World sent Disneyland several of its best operating executives. Every one of them wanted out of the Disneyland Resort environment, where they felt top management lacked a basic understanding of the way a Disney park should be operated. They also were forced to make personnel decisions they felt were unfair to cast members.

Imagineers—especially Tony Baxter and I—were especially upset by the decision the Pressler regime made to close down the Submarine Voyage in Tomorrowland. Launched in 1959, Disneyland's eight-vessel fleet was originally promoted as "the eighth largest submarine fleet in the world." By the time of its closing in September 1998—Pressler promised a new attraction by 2003—more people, by a substantial number, had gone underwater in a submarine at Disneyland than anywhere else in the world!

The decision to shutter the attraction, leaving a big, empty lagoon as the centerpiece of Tomorrowland, was actually based on one factor: the cost of maintenance, reportedly nearly $3 million per year. Not too long after its closing, Disneyland's management came after us to jettison the whole submarine fleet because of the cost and space required for storage. At that point, the *Orange County Register* correctly quoted me as saying that before we allowed the submarine vessels' demise, "I would throw myself across Harbor Boulevard!" (Harbor is the main thoroughfare running north-south adjacent to Disneyland.)

If those eight submarines had been destroyed, today there would be no Finding Nemo Submarine Voyage, where the iconic Pixar character takes you on a journey to the East Australian Current, mirroring the story of the clown fish, his father, Dory, and Crush the sea turtle.

It was no surprise when Pollitt left in January 2003, and Harris in October of that year, both joining Pressler at The Gap. Fortunately, those long lists of show-quality-related maintenance items our staff made, as frustrating as that process was, were ready to go when a new leadership team replaced Pressler's as Disneyland's fiftieth birthday approached.

I made the argument on several occasions that while the fiftieth was an important celebration, we were really talking about the next fifty years in Disney fan attitude. We knew that the marketing campaign would make the fiftieth year a success, but the experiences our guests would have that year—including the visual appearance of the park as a result of the lack of maintenance—would set the tone for many years to come. The peeling paint and rotting wood on Main Street had to be fixed. "What would Walt think?" was a valid question. We all knew the answer.

The good news was the arrival of two top executives from other Disney assignments to run the Disneyland Resort. Number one was Matt Ouimet, who became president of the resort. His Disney career began as chief financial officer at Disney Development Company, but his reputation was based on his roles as chief executive officer of the Disney

Vacation Club and president of the new Disney Cruise Line. Matt had led the staffing and operation of the two cruise ships, the *Disney Magic* and the *Disney Wonder*. Not only was the business a financial success from day one, but the ships became known as the "quintessential Disney experience."

Many guests said it was a step beyond the parks and land resorts in service and quality. In the Disney business, there was a new number one.

No one will say how much investment it took to bring Disneyland up to Disney standards, but if you said "tens of millions of dollars" (probably close to $70 million), you would be a good guesser. With Matt Ouimet's leadership, the funds were made available, and the partnership of Disneyland's new maintenance and operation teams with Imagineering (and those lists!) led to the assignment of a major project team. Complete with a new schedule and budget, their assignment was to make Disneyland the spiffy place it became for the park's fiftieth anniversary "Homecoming" in 2005.

There was still another issue to make the fiftieth anniversary a success: rebuilding the morale and training of the Disneyland staff. That responsibility was given to one of my favorite operations leaders from Walt Disney World. Imagineering had enjoyed a great working relationship with Greg Emmer for many years, especially when he was the top operations leader for Epcot. Now he became Matt Ouimet's operating partner, and together they made themselves the most visible of executives. It seemed that they were always inside the parks—Disneyland and California Adventure—walking, observing, talking to cast members and guests.

It was "management by walking around"—and it paid big dividends in motivating the cast and creating the spirit of friendly, helpful, dedication that made the fiftieth year a soaring success.

I especially appreciated the invitation from Matt to participate in the July 17, 2005, dedication of a window on Main Street honoring the Disneyland cast. The simple words I wrote for that window say it all:

OPEN SINCE

'55

DISNEYLAND CASTING AGENCY

"It takes People to Make the Dream a Reality"

Walter Elias Disney

Founder & Director Emeritus

* * * * * * * * *

One last personal issue related to "riding the Michael Eisner roller coaster": whatever the personal animus that grew and festered between Michael and Steve Jobs and consumed the Pixar-Disney business relationship, the creative teams throughout Disney had enjoyed a chance to work with John Lasseter and his Pixar colleagues. We prayed that it would continue. The fun, the passion, the love of story, the technical know-how we found in John and Ed Catmull and their Pixar associates was just too good to lose. We were all ecstatic when, as one of his earliest major decisions as Disney's CEO, Bob Iger agreed to purchase Pixar from Steve Jobs.

I can't believe it would ever have happened if the old Strategic Planning process had still been in place. "No, because . . . ," as Buzz Price said, is the language of a deal killer. "Yes, if . . ." is the language creative people love . . . especially in an industry called "show business."

* * * * * * * * * *

I experienced one more highlight—and honor—as the fiftieth anniversary year began. When the Pasadena Tournament of Roses chose "Celebrate Family" as the theme of the 2005 parade on New Year's Day, Disneyland was invited to create a float and entertainment, and to lead the entire parade down Colorado Boulevard. In fact, the grand marshal was none other than Mickey Mouse himself—adding to a Disney tradition on New Year's Day: Walt was the grand marshal of the 1966 parade, and Roy E. Disney enjoyed the same honor in 2000.

When the Tournament of Roses approached Disney to recommend someone with creative and artistic credentials to become one of the three judges charged with choosing the award-winning floats, Disneyland's liaison to the parade, Brian Whitman, suggested me, as the longtime creative leader of the Imagineers.

It turned out to be an extraordinary experience, beginning four days before the January 1, 2005, event—the 116th parade in the storied history of the Pasadena tradition, now broadcast around the world as a New Year's Day event—with far more viewers, I'm sure, than all the New Year's Day football bowl games combined. My fellow judges and I traveled many times to multiple locations in Pasadena, and miles and miles to surrounding communities, to evaluate the floats as they were being built through the vision and labor of talented artists, professional float builders, floral designers, and thousands of volunteers who install each flower by hand, to achieve the designer's vision.

Even after our "final" voting had taken place New Year's Eve, the judges were given one more opportunity—as the sun was coming up at 5:00 A.M. New Year's Day—to see the floats lined up on Orange Grove Avenue, awaiting the start of the parade three hours later. My fellow judges and I were steadfast and unanimous in the choices we had made, selecting the beautiful entry of the Rain Bird corporation to receive the Parade's Sweepstakes Award. (A bonus: the parade's quintessential designer, Raul Rodriguez, who has created the concepts for several hundred Tournament of Roses floats, was the designer of Rain Bird's award winner. One of Raul's earliest jobs was at Walt Disney Imagineering.)

After a good night's sleep or two to catch up after my exciting start to 2005, it was again time to move on— to Disneyland's fiftieth celebration, and my new career challenges.

17

"YOU ARE THE HARDEST WORKING AMBASSADOR IN THE WORLD!"

Jay Rasulo's handwritten note of August 1, 2008, was sweet music to my ears. "This update makes me very happy—all the stuff we talked about is happening in spades!" Jay wrote. "You are the hardest working ambassador in the world!"

Jay was the chairman of Walt Disney Parks and Resorts. At the end of 2009, he "traded" positions with Tom Staggs and became Disney's chief financial officer. Early in 2006, Jay had asked me to move my office from Imagineering in Glendale to the Walt Disney Studios in Burbank—the three-mile separation that had so confused Ray Watson when he first brought Michael Eisner and Frank Wells to WED in September 1984. Although I did know the way, it was a true culture change for me.

Traditionally, the creative leader of Imagineering had occupied a good-sized corner office at 1401 Flower Street, adjacent to Edie's Conference Room and the office of the number-one designer at Imagineering, Senior Vice President John Hench. Only Dick Irvine, the original occupant of the office, and I had been occupants of that corner office from the day WED moved there in 1963 until my departure to the Studio in 2006.

As my seventy-second birthday approached in February, Jay had asked me to take on a new role, as he began the search for a new creative leader for Imagineering. I had actually stepped aside many months before so that Tom Fitzgerald could lead the creative team in story development. But Tom's skill at storytelling, and his aversion toward time spent in managing the creative group, cried out for setting him free to maximize his considerable talent. Compounding the problem was the fact his intended administration "partner" had no real interest in sharing. Don Goodman, another graduate from Disney Development, was clearly in charge—which meant that the right-brain creative skills were clearly secondary to the left-brainers in Project Management, reporting directly to Don.

Unable to influence the situation, I was clearly ready for a meaty new assignment to round out and, as it turned out, complete my fifty-four years at Disney. On February 15, 2006, in a memo I titled "Change Is Just Around the Corner," I informed the company of my new role. "Jay has asked me," I wrote, "to become Imagineering Ambassador for the Parks and Resorts segment, communicating the Disney difference. I will be representing the energy, passion, and talent of the Disney Imagineers I have helped to lead creatively and symbolically for so many of those fifty years."

It was great timing, I said. "Several years ago, as I looked ahead toward my fiftieth year at Disney, I set two major goals for myself: first, to play a key role in the development and achievement of a spectacular fiftieth celebration for Disneyland; and second, to complete more than four years of creative support and leadership with the opening of Hong Kong Disneyland." Now, I wrote, "I was 'all ears' to a challenging proposal Jay made. . . . It was clear to me that I am the perfect casting (perhaps the only) candidate capable of originating and organizing this assignment. (I do have an ego, even if I hide it 99 percent of the time!)"

I immediately set out to define the role, sending Jay a memo listing six specific areas I planned to concentrate on:

1. Attract the best young talent.
2. Develop/participate In outside programs/events/projects.
3. Motivate Disney cast members re: legacy of creativity and innovation.
4. Liaison with other Parks and Resorts initiatives.
5. Potential new initiatives.
6. Marty's "Personal Projects" (to be determined by Marty).

In many ways, I consider the three years and five months I spent as executive vice president of Parks and Resorts and Imagineering Ambassador among the most important of my fifty-four years at Disney. As I told Jay in the note I wrote in response to his "hardest working ambassador" comment, "I think what we've found is there's a need and a hunger for the kinds of things I've been doing—both inside and outside the company. When you feed off other people's reactions, it's great to feel you're touching the right buttons."

When I look back at my twice-a-year reports to Jay Rasulo during those three years, it's hard to believe how much my tiny three-person staff—my assistant Jim Clark, my administrative assistant Steve Cook, and me—accomplished. The good karma began with our move to the first floor 1D wing of the Old Animation Building at the Walt Disney Studios.

Our three-room suite turned out to be somewhat of a "shrine" at the Studio. Feature Animation had long before, in 1995, moved into its own Robert A. M. Stern designed building on Riverside Drive, a gift of *The Lion King* and *Beauty and the Beast*. No history there, but our offices on the Studio lot were rich in Disney animation tradition: they had been the working spaces for Frank Thomas, Ollie Johnston, and Milt Kahl in the heyday of *Snow White and the Seven Dwarfs*, *Pinocchio*, and *Fantasia*.

My corner office, not far from the intersection of Mickey Avenue and Dopey Drive, seemed to have a special place in the memory of some of the current stars of Disney animation. One day I returned from lunch to find a pencil drawing of a beautiful girl on my desk, and a note from her creator: "I hope you know you are sitting in a very special place," it read. "Ollie Johnston's old office." The girl Glen Keane drew was the one he created for her namesake movie, *The Little Mermaid*. Glen was reminiscing about the old days and one of his mentors. In fact, "Frank and Ollie," creators of such characters and scenes as Pinocchio, Bambi and Thumper on the ice, Lady and the Tramp eating spaghetti, the evil stepsisters in *Cinderella*, Alice of Wonderland, King Louie in *Jungle Book*, and the dancing penguins in *Mary Poppins*, were two of Walt's "Nine Old Men," the kings of Walt's animation world of the 1930s through the 1960s. They also wrote the books that explained and memorialized the medium, including *Disney Animation: The Illusion of Life*; *Too Funny for Words: Disney's Greatest Sight Gags*; *The Disney Villain*; and *Bambi: The Story and the Film*.

A few examples illustrate the highlights of those three-plus years, for me personally as well as for the Disney Parks and Resorts division. To attract young talent, I made speeches across the country, and talked to student groups from Carnegie Mellon, Florida State, UCLA, Cal State Los Angeles, University of California Davis, the University of Illinois at Chicago (U.I.C.) College of Applied Health Sciences, and interns from many schools working summers at Imagineering and in the College Program at Disneyland. It turns out that U.I.C. has one of the premier programs in biomedical visualization in the country. Professor and program director Scott Barrows is a protégé of artist Frank Armitage, whose work ranged from set design on the iconic film *Fantastic Voyage*, to Disney animation (*Sleeping Beauty*) and the parks (his illustration of the Château de la Belle Dormant for Disneyland Paris was an inspiration). Frank also studied medicine, and crafted a second career as one of the country's best medical illustrators. In his honor, the U.I.C. Medical School created the annual Frank Armitage Lecture. I was honored when Frank and Scott Barrows asked me to be the speaker at the inaugural event in 2007.

We also organized the first-ever "Imagineering Day at CalArts." There was a CalArts connection to Disney animation, but the panel of talents we brought to the school was the first to communicate about all the disciplines in the arts at Imagineering—we like to say there are 140 different disciplines when you add the engineers, architects, and other technical skills. I was surprised at this omission, given the fact that Walt had inspired this "school of all the arts" with his endowment, and given the number of Disney executives who have served on President Steven Lavine's board of directors at CalArts. Several CalArts graduates were members of my panel, which included a variety of disciplines. The Imagineers presented examples of their work, often indicating how their CalArts training had prepared them for the challenges they now face.

Events and programs outside the Disney sphere revealed a real hunger to know more about everything Disney. I made keynote speeches at the conventions of the American Creativity Association, the California Association of the Gifted, and at a conference we helped put together called "Courageous Creativity." Organized by Kristine Alexander, executive director of The California Arts Project, and now approaching its seventh year, Courageous Creativity annually brings together 125 teachers and administrators from throughout California at the Disneyland Resort. There, the group interacts with Disney talent, and discusses ideas and techniques they can implement with young people in the schools of their communities.

Personal favorites for me were the annual programs I presented with Bob Rogers, chairman of BRC Imagination Arts, at the convention of IAAPA, usually at the Orlando Convention Center. Our sessions have been rated number one or number two for a decade at this weeklong convention of attraction industry practitioners; with an annual audience of four hundred to five hundred people. My favorite of all the sessions Bob and I have presented was entitled "Tell Me

What Is Never Old." It began with a twenty-minute recorded session in which Bob interviewed me and Buzz Price. To this day, I review it from time to time to hear the wisdom of Buzz, who passed away at age eighty-nine in 2010. (On a scale of 1.0 to 5.0, Buzz and I were rated 4.89 and 4.93, respectively, by the IAAPA attendees at that session.)

And who would not count as favorites three programs onstage with the great author Ray Bradbury? Two were for standing-room-only programs at the beautiful Cerritos (California) Library, created by our friend, Waynn Pearson. The third, with moderator Leonard Maltin, was a discussion at the annual convention of Science and Technology Centers at the Los Angeles Convention Center. (When Ray turned ninety-one in August 2011, I sent him a note saying that adding the nine and the one made him a perfect ten. What an inspiration!)

Much of my Ambassador years' efforts were spent on the third category: "Motivate Disney cast members re: legacy of creativity and innovation." I made talks to Disney audiences in Paris, Tokyo, and Hong Kong, plus at Walt Disney World, Pixar, and, of course, in Glendale to Imagineering's staff. I organized and acted as moderator for Disney Legends panels that included some of the company's great talents, all retired: X. Atencio, Harriet Burns, Rolly Crump, Dick Sherman, Don Iwerks, Blaine Gibson, Alice Davis, Bob Gurr, and Orlando Ferrante.

But it was my talks at three Disney Leadership Conferences, held on both coasts in 2004, 2006, and 2008, that seemed to elicit the most favorable reaction from my fellow cast members. It was a little embarrassing to read that my talks about "Mickey's Ten Commandments" were rated number one at these Leadership Conferences, when highly paid speakers from outside the company and top division executives also made presentations and were also rated.

One of our most important programs came about when Jay Rasulo told me about a discussion with Bob Iger, in which the Disney CEO suggested that employees on the Disney Studio lot, and in the Burbank-Glendale area, should learn more about the people and projects of Imagineering. With the help of Jim Clark, we created "Imagineering Week at the Studio," which became a popular feature for three years, 2007–2009. All week long, we featured Imagineers and their projects and Disney Legends in lunchtime presentations, culminating in a special Friday event that ran from 11:00 A.M. to 2:00 P.M. It was like a county fair, with games, music, an opportunity to meet key Imagineers, prizes, live entertainment, and a major feature in the Studio Theatre. Attendance for the noontime presentations totaled 650, and more than 2,500 employees attended the Friday "fair."

My reports to Jay, of course, were accompanied by as much feedback as I was able to gather, and every item included some commentary so that he had a clear picture of what it was, and why I spent time doing it. One note in my August 12, 2008, report under the "Personal" category was especially important to me. "The very happy personal news," I wrote, "is that Leah and I will be in Finland in October, joining son Howard and his family when he receives his PhD in English Literature at the University of Helsinki."

For this ambassador, it was a very special ceremony, especially when Leah and I watched the awe on then seventeen-year-old grandson Gabriel's face as he watched and listened to his father's defense of his PhD dissertation.

* * * * * * * * * *

When Jay Rasulo first approached me to move from Glendale to Burbank, it was partly to free up those office locations along "the Gold Coast" at Imagineering in preparation for new leadership. As it turned out, it took well over a year to achieve, and in the final analysis, it turned into a nice compliment for Mickey Steinberg and me. Disney's corporate management, on Jay's recommendation, determined that Imagineering's best leadership format had been the Mickey-Marty partnership of administration-financial and creative talents. So in May 2007, Jay announced the appointment of Bruce Vaughn as chief creative executive and Craig Russell as chief design and project delivery executive for Imagineering—a partnership of equals with complementary leadership skills.

18

MICKEY'S TEN COMMANDMENTS

It has been almost forty years since the word "writer" appeared on my job description. For thirty of those years—from 1974 to 2004, the period of my creative leadership at Walt Disney Imagineering—I had the final word on what the Imagineers presented to Disney corporate management or, for a few years, to the Parks and Resorts leaders before a project reached Card Walker, Ron Miller, or Michael Eisner.

I did, however, continue to work in the realm of the written word, often invisibly, in keeping with the "we" and not "I" theme. Because of my background in creating slogans like "The Vacation Kingdom of the World" (Walt Disney World), and "Imagineering is the blending of creative imagination with technical know-how" (a favorite statement of Walt Disney), I had an opportunity to ghostwrite dedication plaques, honorary window copy, introductions to a myriad of

Disney parks and Imagineering books, tributes, and memorials to the great Disney Legends on their passing, and even the copy line that appeared at the bottom of the stationery for every division of the company: PART OF THE MAGIC OF THE WALT DISNEY COMPANY.

One of my favorites was the sign that stood outside Disneyland's empty Haunted Mansion for about five years before the interior show was created in 1969. The sign invited AN ACTIVE RETIREMENT to enjoy ALL GHOSTS AND RESTLESS SPIRITS where they could continue to practice their ghostly specialties. YOU TAKE CARE OF THE INSIDE, the sign copy promised. WE'LL TAKE CARE OF THE OUTSIDE.

But it was "Mickey's Ten Commandments" that established me as a speaker and creator of my own ideas, and gave me the opportunity to communicate them to audiences inside and outside Disney. Although I created the commandments, the first speech was actually written by Imagineer Paul Goldman. It launched a career of speechwriting for Paul, first for executives at Walt Disney World, followed by ten years writing for the chairman and CEO of New York Life Insurance Company.

My initial presentation of "Mickey's Ten Commandments" was actually a double—two speeches that began in the Twin Cities in Minnesota at the national convention of Science and Technology Centers. Two days later, I made the same talk at the Art Directors Club of Boston.

I developed, refined, and practiced these key principles of leadership, based on what I learned from Walt Disney and my mentors, the great Imagineering Legends, especially designer John Hench. I crystallized these "learnings" into the first of what I called *Mickey's Ten Commandments*:

1. Know your audience

Identify the prime audience for your attraction or show before you begin design.

2. Wear your guests' shoes

Insist that your team members experience your creation just the way guests do it.

3. Organize the flow of people and ideas

Make sure there is a logic and sequence in your stories and in the way guests experience them.

4. Create a wienie (visual magnet)

Create visual "targets" that will lead visitors clearly and logically through your facility.

5. Communicate with visual literacy

Make good use of color, shape, form, texture—all the nonverbal ways of communication.

6. Avoid overload—create turn-ons

Resist the temptation to overload your audience with too much information and too many objects.

7. Tell one story at a time

Stick to the story line; good stories are clear, logical, and consistent.

8. Avoid contradictions—maintain identity

Details in design or content that contradict one another confuse an audience about your story or the time period it takes place in.

9. For every ounce of treatment, provide a ton of treat

In our business, Walt Disney said, you can educate people—but don't tell them you're doing it! Make it fun!

10. Keep it up! (maintain it)

In a Disney park or resort, everything must work. Poor maintenance is poor show!

These principles quickly became a kind of gold standard in the park andmuseum business. Today you will find this list pinned on the office wall of many Imagineers, and more throughout the leisure-recreation industry. In fact, *Funworld* magazine, published by the International Association of Amusement Parks and Attractions (IAAPA), called them "a classic—perhaps the best guide to the creation of themed entertainment."

The inauguration of an excellent program to train and motivate leaders at Disneyland and Walt Disney World gave me an opportunity to communicate the ideas and principles I utilized to lead the Imagineers. At these Leadership Conferences, I presented two different programs on leadership and one speech I called "Followership: How to Be a Great Team Player and Help Your Leaders Succeed."

After the original list, I have added another thirty. The basic points from my now forty commandments are below, with apologies to God and Moses, who somehow managed to stop at ten:

MORE
"MICKEY'S TEN ^ COMMANDMENTS"
(The Leaders' Bible)

1. Create and maintain a climate of trust.
2. Be responsive and make decisions—that's what leaders do!
3. Empower your teammates—it takes many hands to bake a success.
4. Create opportunities for new birds to fly.
5. Remember: experience is *not* a negative.
6. Make sure yours is not the only voice you are listening to.
7. Celebrate diversity and different points of view.
8. Never rest on your laurels—the next at-bat is your most important.

9. Take a chance—support risk-taking.

10. Provide plenty of blank paper.

MORE
"MICKEY'S TEN ^ COMMANDMENTS"

(The Leaders' Bible—Part 2) *Leadership is earned and must be exercised daily!*

1. Be optimistic—if *you* are not *positive,* who else will be?

2. *Courage* and *confidence* are major cross streets on the road to success.

3. Make *curiosity* your search engine.

4. Learn to *love* your next assignment—be *passionate* about *whatever* you do.

5. Provide time to explore—but deadlines are great motivation and *discipline.*

6. Take time to teach—*mentors* are *mensches.*

7. Forget the politics—it's not an election!

8. Traditions are important—but *change* is *the great dynamic.*

9. *Team* and *work* are four-letter words—but together they spell *"winner."*

10. Remember: the last three letters of *trend* are *E-N-D!*

MORE
"MICKEY'S TEN ^ COMMANDMENTS"

(Part IV—Followership)

How to be a great team player and help your leaders succeed!

1. *SPEAK UP!* Great teammates raise issues *before* decisions are made!

2. Never be afraid to ask questions. That's how we learn our parts—onstage and backstage.

3. Make your experience count (that's why you're on the team).

4. Help the rookies succeed—you were "new" once, too.

5. Understand your role—everyone has a job to do.

6. Never fear failure—winners sometimes fail, too!

7. But—know *when* to take a chance (and always let your leaders know you're doing it).

8. Play by the rules. If you disagree, work to change them *after* the game.

9. Share the joy of success—you didn't do it by yourself!

10. Support your teammates—at Disney, there's only one name on the door.

* * * * * * * * * *

In the spirit of those commandments, I looked back over my Disney career and selected ten of the most significant written communications I was privileged to develop. There were many more to choose from, but for reasons I will explain as I introduce these ten, they all have special significance in time and place in Disney lore.

1. Walt Disney's last message to Disney shareholders—1966 Annual Report.

I developed four annual reports with another Disney Legend, Creative Director for Publicity Art and Marketing Bob Moore, and graphic designer Norm Noceti. We created a theme, reviewed it with Card Walker, and then met with Roy O. Disney, Disney's president and chairman of the board, to secure his go-ahead. Our theme for 1966 was "The Disney World." Roy's message, which I also wrote with a big assist from Roy's financial staff, was entitled, "Wherever We Go, the Organization Is Prepared." Walt's was called, "A Look to the Future":

THE DISNEY WORLD:

A look to the future

The past year has been one in which many groups around the world, both inside and outside the entertainment industry, have paid high tribute to our creative staff. For all these honors, we are all very grateful indeed.

In accepting the "Showman of the World" award from the people who own and operate the nation's theatres, I looked to the past, recalling some of the wonderful people in the theatre business who helped us get where we are today because they had faith in the things we did, from *Steamboat Willie* to the present day. There was always someone — some wonderful exhibitor or an understanding banker — willing to take a chance on another crazy Disney idea.

Today, I propose to look to the future . . . to tell you about some of the plans, and some of the philosophy, that makes us tick here in the Disney organization.

Many people have asked, "Why don't you make another *Mary Poppins?* Well, by nature I'm a born experimenter. To this day, I don't believe in sequels. I can't follow popular cycles. I have to move on to new things — there are many new worlds to conquer.

As a matter of fact, people have been asking us to make sequels ever since Mickey Mouse first became a star. We have bowed only on one occasion to the cry to repeat ourselves. Back in the '30's, *The Three Little Pigs* was an enormous hit, and the cry went up —"Give

us more Pigs!" I could not see how we could possibly top pigs with pigs. But we tried, and I doubt whether any one of you reading this can name the other cartoons in which the pigs appeared.

We didn't make the same mistake with *Snow White*. When it was a huge hit, the shout went up for more dwarfs. Top dwarfs with dwarfs? Why try?

Right now, we're not thinking about making another *Mary Poppins*. We never will. Perhaps there will be other ventures with equal critical and financial success. But we know we cannot hit a home run with the bases loaded every time we go to the plate. We also know the only way we can even get to first base is by constantly going to bat and continuing to swing.

And so we're always looking for new ideas and new stories, hoping that somehow we'll come up with a different kind of *Mary Poppins* . . . or even a different kind of Disneyland.

As 1967 begins, we have high hopes that some of our current projects may measure up to this exciting challenge. Perhaps it will be a motion picture like *The Happiest Millionaire*. Perhaps it will be our so-called "Disney World" in Florida. Or perhaps it will be our year-round recreation facility in the High Sierra of California, Mineral King. On the pages that follow in this Annual Report, we'll try to tell you why we believe so strongly in each of these fascinating

projects, and many more our creative staffs are now producing.

You know, the Disney organization today has more than four thousand employees. Many have been with us over 30 years. They take great pride in the organization they helped to build. Only through the talent, the labor and the dedication of this staff could any Disney project get off the ground. We all think alike in the ultimate pattern.

We're all proud of the honors that many groups around the world have given us. And we're even more proud that the public — whether in theatres, at Disneyland, or in their own homes — continues to express its faith in the kind of family entertainment we produce.

I promise you that all the honors in the world won't go to our heads — we have too many projects for the future to take time out for such a thing.

2. Cover letter from Roy O. Disney—1966 Annual Report.

When Walt passed away on December 15, 1966, the company's annual report was already printed and ready to be mailed to shareholders after the first of the new year. However, several key corporate executives expressed concern at mailing a document containing Walt's message; in fact, they argued that we should scrap the whole report and develop a new communication.

I vehemently disagreed.

Ultimately, as distraught as he was at his brother's death, Roy listened and agreed. I wrote this letter for Roy; when it was mailed to shareholders, it covered the already printed front of the 1966 Annual Report:

AN IMPORTANT MESSAGE
TO OUR SHAREHOLDERS AND EMPLOYEES:

THIS ANNUAL REPORT WAS PREPARED PRIOR TO WALT DISNEY'S PASSING. The keynote of these pages is optimism for the future of the company, whose creative energies he directed for more than 40 years.

This enthusiasm for the future stemmed directly from Walt. You will find it in the message he prepared for this report, and in the story of our company's world-wide operations. And you will find it reflected by our key creative and management people, in every area of the company. We believe, as Walt did so strongly, in the future of Walt Disney Productions.

Walt would have wanted you, our shareholders and employees, to know and share this enthusiasm. That is why this report has been sent to you exactly as it was prepared early in December.

In this report are the facts which support this enthusiasm. It should confirm for you the substantial values — Motion Picture properties (completed and yet to be produced), real estate, Disneyland, Character Merchandising, Music, Publications and the world-famous Disney name — which we have confidence will result in a successful future.

Now, in view of Walt's passing, it is vitally important to the future growth and development of your company that key executive, management and creative personnel have an even greater stake in our continuing progress. To provide this additional incentive for those key people charged with carrying on the Disney tradition of quality family entertainment, we have developed a new Stock Option Plan, which has been mailed to you separately, along with the Company's Proxy Statement. I strongly urge your favorable action to approve this most important Stock Option Plan.

It was Walt's wish that when the time came, he would have built an organization with the creative talents to carry on as he had established and directed it through the years. Today this organization has been built, and we shall carry out this wish.

Walt Disney's preparation for the future is a solid, creative foundation. All the plans for the future that Walt had begun — new motion pictures, the expansion of Disneyland, television production and our Florida and Mineral King projects as outlined in this report — will continue to move ahead.

Roy O. Disney.

President and Chairman of the Board
Walt Disney Productions

3. Disney Image Presentation—November, 1965

Little did I ever dream that Walt's first reaction to something I had written would be, "I didn't know anyone was writing my obituary!" It was actually one of two presentations prepared for the Florida Press Conference in November 1965, where Governor Hayden Burns introduced Walt and Roy, and formally announced that Disney was coming to the Sunshine State.

The first presentation was the "meat and potatoes" variety, describing the engine for economic growth that Disneyland had created in Anaheim and Orange County, California, in its first decade. The second was my nineteen-page script that attempted to describe the impact of Walt's entertainment on people around the world. Despite his comment, I *had* recorded about three minutes of dialogue with Walt. I still regard "The Disney Image," as produced with its wonderful visual content, as among the very best writing I created at Disney. The following pages give the flavor of the introduction in Walt's dialogue that followed a line reciting his "thirty-two Oscars"—his Academy Awards.

FOR: "DISNEY IMAGE PRESENTATION"

WED ENTERPRISES, INC.
June 30, 1965 - Revised

SLIDE PRESENTATION SCRIPT

                    MUSIC
        Open with an orchestra medley of tunes from Disney
        motion pictures and TV -- from Mary Poppins, Snow
        White, Davy Crockett, Cinderella, etc. etc. -- some
        of Walt's most familiar tunes. Along with the music,
        introduce the first series of slides.

1 - 12   MASS SHOTS OF PEOPLE - AROUND THE WORLD

            doing things Disney -- to show the impact of Disney
            in so many aspects of our lives throughout the world.
            Crowds in theatre lines in the U.S.A. and foreign lands,
            at World's Fair, at Disneyland, crowds around Walt, etc.

FADE MUSIC UNDER as narration begins.

In the following pictures, we back away from the mass and focus
mostly on individuals and family groups. Shots to match the
narration.

13.   CLOSE-UP - CHILD WITH MICKEY MOUSE

            from Disneyland newspaper supplement

                        NARRATOR
                These are the people ...

14.   FARMER - MIDWEST AMERICA - READING DISNEY BOOK TO
            CHILD

                        NARRATOR
                People across the face of
                America ...

15.   FOREIGN FAMILY WATCHING TV - VON DRAKE ON "WORLD OF
            COLOR"

                        NARRATOR
                And people across the
                Seven Seas.

16.   AMERICAN FAMILY WATCHING SAME SCENE, SAME SHOW.

                        NARRATOR
                People in homes around
                the corner ...

331

17.   LINE FOR "MARY POPPINS" IN FOREIGN THEATRE

      with foreign language marquee visible

                     NARRATOR
               And people in theatres
               around the world.

18.   ADULT READING NEWSPAPER COMIC STRIP TO CHILD

                     NARRATOR
               People who read newspapers

19.   TEENAGERS - DANCING IN FRONT OF WALL PLASTERED WITH
      PICTURES

      of Annette, Hayley Mills, Tommy Kirk, Dean Jones, etc.

                     NARRATOR
               And people who listen to
               or dance to records.

20.   GRANDMOTHER (OLD) PICKING OUT MICKEY MOUSE T-SHIRT
      FROM STORE - DISNEY DISPLAY IN BACKGROUND

                     NARRATOR
               People who shop for clothes
               and toys and books and games
               for children.

21.   MEN WORKING - DISNEY CHARACTER SAFETY SIGN PROMINENT

                     NARRATOR
               People in industry ...

22.   CLASSROOM - CHILDREN - WATCHING DISNEY FILM IN SCHOOL

                     NARRATOR
               And people in schools.

23.   FAMILY WATCHING TV - SHOT FROM BEHIND TV, THRU RABBIT
      EARS ANTENNA - CHILDREN ARE WEARING MICKEY MOUSE HATS,
      CHARACTER SHIRTS.

                     NARRATOR
               People alone with their
               families in remote hamlets

332

24.   GRANDFATHER WEARING DONALD DUCK HAT - ARM AROUND KID
           ALSO WEARING DONALD DUCK HAT (in G.E. presentation)

                          NARRATOR
                    And people surrounded by
                    strangers in bustling cities.

25.   EXTERIOR SHOT - "SMALL WORLD" MARQUEE

           to read "Walt Disney's It's A Small World" on sign
           (background) with character and people (foreground)
             from G.E. presentation

                          NARRATOR
                    People in boats and cars and
                    theatres at a World's Fair.

26.   FATHER AND CHILDREN FLYING IN DUMBO

                          NARRATOR
                    And people in flying elephants
                    and submarines and horseless
                    carriages at a Magic Kingdom.

27.   FOREIGN GUESTS IN DISNEYLAND - CASTLE I.D.

                          NARRATOR
                    <u>Wherever</u> they are, <u>Whoever</u> they
                    are, these people speak and
                    understand an international
                    language

28.   CHILD WITH DISNEY COMICS AND MAGAZINES - VARIETY OF
           FOREIGN PRINTING

                          NARRATOR
                    A language that knows no
                    ocean and no iron curtain

29.   HAPPY FATHER AND SON - THEATRE AUDIENCE SHOT

                          NARRATOR
                    A language that forms an
                    invisible common bond.

30.   PICTURE OF KING OR PRESIDENT IN DISNEYLAND

                        NARRATOR
                  For people everywhere --
                  king and president, child
                  and adult --

31.   SHOT OF WALT

          surrounded by kids and adults - the NATIONAL
          GEOGRAPHIC shot of Walt signing autographs.

                        NARRATOR
                  --people everywhere Look to
                  the name Walt Disney for the
                  Finest in Family Entertainment!

32.   "LOOK TO THE NAME WALT DISNEY FOR THE FINEST IN
          FAMILY ENTERTAINMENT"

The script then transitioned to Walt's narration.

113.   WALT - WITH MICKEY AND THE FIRST OSCAR

                        NARRATOR
              WALT: "That first Oscar was a special
                      award for the creation of Mickey
                      Mouse. The other Academy Awards
                      belong to our group, a tribute
                      to our combined effort."

START BEHIND THE SCENES COVERAGE OF THE DISNEY TEAM

(Slides 114 - 127, various shots to show actors, writers,
    musicians, art directors, management, engineers,
    etc. etc. <u>at work</u> on the multiple projects at the
    Studio, at WED, at Disneyland. While these slides
    are being viewed, Walt's words tell about the
    company and some basic philosophy:

114.   MANAGEMENT SHOT

             WALT: "The whole thing here is the
                     organization. And the big
                     problem was putting the organ-
                     ization together. Look at
                     Disneyland - that was started
                     because we had the talent to
                     start it - the talents of the
                     organization.

115.   ACTORS - WORKING ON SET WITH DIRECTOR

             WALT: "You know, people are always
                     analyzing our approach to
                     entertainment. Some reporters
                     have called it the "special
                     secret" of Disney entertainment.

116.   BEHIND THE SCENES - BUILDING OF SPECIAL EFFECT
             (such as Giant Squid, or Flying Model T)

             WALT: "Well, we like a little mystery
                     in our films - but there's really
                     no secret about our approach. We
                     keep moving forward - opening up
                     new doors and doing new things -
                     because we're <u>curious</u>...

117.   SCIENTIFIC-TYPE SHOT - RESEARCH

             WALT: "... and curiosity keeps leading
                     us down new paths. We're always
                     exploring and experimenting. At
                     WED, we call it 'imagineering' -
                     the blending of creative imagination
                     with technical know-how.

118:    EARLY CONSTRUCTION SHOT AT DISNEYLAND - WALT ON
        SITE WITH ART DIRECTORS

               WALT: "When you're curious, you find
                       lots of interesting things to
                       do. And one thing it takes to
                       accomplish something is <u>courage</u>.
                       Take Disneyland for example.
                       Almost everyone warned us that
                       Disneyland would be a Hollywood
                       spectacular - a spectacular
                       failure.

119.   WALT AND ART DIRECTORS INSPECTING DISNEYLAND -
        TODAY

               WALT: "But they were thinking about
                       an amusement park, and we believed
                       in our idea - a family park where
                       parents and children could have fun
                       - <u>together</u>.

120.   WED MODEL SHOP

               WALT: "Now Disneyland has begun its
                       second decade, and already we are
                       creating and designing new attract-
                       ions for almost every year in the
                       <u>next</u> ten.

121.   DICK VAN DYKE - WORKING ON SET

               WALT: "We have never lost our faith in
                       <u>family entertainment</u> -- stories
                       that make people laugh, stories
                       about warm and human things,
                       stories about historic characters
                       and events, stories about animals.

122.   LAUGHING SCENE FROM "MARY POPPINS"

               WALT: "We're not out to make a fast
                       dollar with gimmicks. We're
                       interested in doing things that
                       are fun - in bringing pleasure
                       and especially laughter to people.

123.   WALT - LAUGHING WITH GROUP OF ACTORS

             WALT: "And probably most important
                     of all, when we consider a
                     new project we really study
                     it - not just the surface idea
                     but everything about it. And
                     when we go into that new project,
                     we believe in it all the way.
                     We have confidence in our ability
                     to do it right. And we work hard
                     to do the best possible job.

124.   WALT - WITH ROY AND OTHER MANAGEMENT

             WALT: "My role? Well, you know I
                     was stumped one day when a little
                     boy asked, 'Do you draw Mickey
                     Mouse?' I had to admit I do not
                     draw any more. 'Then you think up
                     all the jokes and ideas?'

125.   WALT - WITH SONGWRITERS - AT PIANO

             WALT: 'No,' I said, 'I don't do that.
                     Finally, he looked at me and
                     said, 'Mr. Disney, just what do
                     you do?' 'Well,' I said, 'sometimes
                     I think of myself as a little bee.

126.   WALT - ACTING OUT POINT IN STORYBOARD MEETING

             WALT: "I go from one area of the Studio
                     to another and gather pollen and
                     sort of stimulate everybody.' I
                     guess that's the job I do."

127.   AN AUDIENCE IN A THEATRE - LAUGHING AT SAME SCENE
       AS ABOVE, THIS TIME PERFORMED ON SCREEN BY ACTOR.

The script then segued back to a wrap-up ending.

4. The Many Worlds of Disneyland (1965)

The year 1965 was a celebration of Disneyland's first decade—what Jack Lindquist called the "Tencennial." The twenty-four-page, full-color section we created in the *Los Angeles Times* celebrated those first ten years, and of course looked at the new attractions soon to open: Great Moments with Mr. Lincoln in the Opera House on Main

THE MANY WORLDS OF DISNEYLAND

In all the world, there is but one Disneyland. Here, in a decade's time, 50 million guests from the Earth's four corners have come to participate in adventures unique in all the world. For here, tomorrow is today, and yesterday is forever. ⊕ ⊕ ⊕ In all the world, there is but one Disneyland. Yet Disneyland is many different worlds, by day and by night, for every age and every mood. It is 1890 again on Main Street U.S.A. and 1980 in Tomorrowland. It is the pioneer's hardy realm, Frontierland, and a jungle safari to far-off worlds in Adventureland. And it is a castle full of dreams — the classic tales of childhood "come to life" in Fantasyland. ⊕ ⊕ ⊕ To Walt Disney's Magic Kingdom in these 10 years has come a royal procession of kings and queens, a diplomatic corps of presidents and prime ministers. And with them, from more than 100 nations and America's 50 states, you have come — the young in heart of all ages to join in the daytime fun and nighttime magic of Walt Disney's Magic Kingdom. ⊕ ⊕ ⊕ If you, too, are among the young in heart, come with us on a journey 'round this world . . . the Many Worlds of Disneyland.

Street and the Plaza Inn (1965); "it's a small world" and New Orleans Square (1966); and Pirates of the Caribbean (1967). For me, it meant editing and producing the newspaper section, and writing one of my favorite descriptions of the park.

5. *"I remember . . . because I was there with Walt Disney at Mineral King" (1972)*

In 1965, Bob Moore, Norm Noceti, and I had created the presentation that Walt, Card Walker, and other Disney executives and consultants (including the legendary Willy Schaeffler, director of ski events for the 1960 Winter Olympics in Squaw Valley, California) used in order to win the approval of the United States Forest Service to create year-round recreational services and facilities at Mineral King, California. Located almost halfway between the population centers of Los Angeles and San Francisco, in the Sequoia National Forest, the approximately twenty square miles known as Mineral King had enormous potential to provide recreational opportunities for Californians. But it was accessible during summer months only by a dangerous and substandard access road. More than six years after the company was selected by the U.S. Forest Service, lawsuits and political manipulating continued to stall, and eventually kill, the Mineral King project.

Frustrated by the political infighting and delays and seeking public support, Disney decided to let the public know that we were ready to move ahead. I wrote the following explanation, which appeared as a paid ad in the *Los Angeles Times* and other newspapers with Card Walker's signature:

I remember... because I was there with Walt Disney at Mineral King

The Disney plan at Mineral King

At a press conference in Visalia, California on May 3, 1972, E. Cardon Walker, President of Walt Disney Productions, announced several major revisions in the company's plan for recreational facilities and services at Mineral King. These revisions were developed over the past three years under the guidance and with the approval of the Walt Disney Productions Conservation Advisory Committee, composed of some of the most distinguished conservationists in America.

The members of this voluntary committee are:

Mr. Horace M. Albright
Former Director of the National Park Service

Dr. Ira Gabrielson
President, Wildlife Management Institute

Mr. Thomas L. Kimball
Executive Director, National Wildlife Federation

Mr. Bestor Robinson
Former President and Director of the Sierra Club

Mr. Eivind T. Scoyen
Former Superintendent of Sequoia National Park and Associate Director of the National Park Service

Mr. William E. Towell
Executive Vice President, American Forestry Association

The major features of Walt Disney Productions' revised plan include:

• *Elimination of the need for construction of a new access road across Sequoia National Park to Mineral King, as previously required by the United States Forest Service.* The elimination of this access road represents a potential savings to California's taxpayers of as much as $30 million.

• In place of the road, *we propose an electrically powered, cog-assisted railway to carry visitors* into the Mineral King area. This publicly owned, narrow-gauge railway would be operated on a non-profit basis and paid for by those using it. Built along the roadbed of the existing substandard access road, *this picturesque railway will eliminate the automobile from the Mineral King area.*

• The plan will provide a positive means of controlling, at all times, the number of visitors allowed into the Mineral King area.

• The electric-powered railway will also allow removal of many "gateway" and service facilities from the Mineral King area. *It will also eliminate the need for construction in the Mineral King area of a multi-level parking structure and all facilities previously necessary to accommodate the visitor automobile.*

• The electrical requirements for the Mineral King valley area can now be supplied by a power line buried underground in the roadbed of the railroad, eliminating the need for an overhead transmission line across the National Park.

The original Forest Service prospectus, which stipulated that access to Mineral King must be by automobile, made it necessary for Walt Disney Productions to plan enough recreational facilities to serve the largest number of visitors who could traverse the public road on any given day. In contrast, *the revisions outlined above allow Walt Disney Productions to scale down the number of recreational facilities, such as restaurants and ski lifts, which will be necessary to serve the public.*

Walt Disney Productions will provide quality base facilities and overnight accommodations for the general public which will make possible a wide variety of ski and family-oriented snow play activities in the winter, as well as camping, hiking, fishing, sightseeing, and equestrian activities in the summer.

What is Mineral King?

An area of approximately 20 square miles in the northern portion of Sequoia National Forest, almost halfway between Los Angeles and San Francisco, Mineral King is situated along the headwaters of the East Fork of the Kaweah River. Its valley floor is at an altitude of over 7,800 feet and the surrounding mountain peaks reach as high as 12,405 feet. There are over 20 fishing lakes accessible in summer by horse and hiking trails. *Eight major basins offer winter snow play and skiing conditions among the finest and most dependable in North America. Mineral King's outstanding alpine terrain is probably more similar to the European Alps than any other area in the Sierra.*

Mineral King is not a wilderness, since for many years it has been accessible via a dangerous and substandard access road and is the site of over 60 summer homes.

Early in 1965, the United States Forest Service sought proposals from private enterprise for the development of facilities to serve both winter and summer recreational visitors at Mineral King. After extensive public bidding, during which six competitive proposals were considered, the proposal of Walt Disney Productions was chosen as best serving the public need. In December, 1965, the Forest Service named the Disney organization to create these recreational services and facilities.

The right of the United States Government and its officials to permit recreational facilities at Mineral King has been challenged in the courts by the Sierra Club. Walt Disney Productions has never been a party to these lawsuits.

The public need for recreational areas clearly exists. We have now presented a plan which provides maximum protection for the National Park and Forest Lands involved. For the people of California, Mineral King indeed represents an opportunity which should not be lost.

For the past six years, there have been so many distortions, so much misinformation, so many lawsuits and press releases that no one seems to remember
what Walt Disney *really* had in mind at Mineral King.

What Walt Disney said was simply this: The creation of recreational services at Mineral King is *a challenge and an obligation*—a challenge to serve the growing public need; an obligation to preserve the beauty of the land.

I remember. Because I was there with Walt Disney when the picture on this page was taken in 1966. And I'm tired of hearing and reading the distortions, the misinformation, the lawsuits and all the press releases vilifying the concepts proposed by Walt Disney and Walt Disney Productions.

For example: The charge has been made that Walt Disney's concept was to build "a Disneyland in the mountains." That charge is absolutely false. No "Disneyland" or "amusement center" was ever contemplated.

What Walt Disney did propose was "to create, design and operate facilities at Mineral King that serve the public need and the interests of participants" who venture into this unique alpine environment.

Mineral King can become the finest year-round recreation area in North America. Why? Because of its unmatched winter recreational potentials, and because of its proximity to California's major population centers.

Over the years since Walt Disney's death, our company has remained strongly committed to his high goals. And we have found *even better ways* to accomplish what Walt Disney set out to do for the people of California. *We now have a plan, which has been approved by the U.S. Forest Service, to eliminate the highway across Sequoia National Park into Mineral King and replace it with an electrically powered narrow-gauge railway.* This plan will not only eliminate the automobile from Mineral King, but will enable the Forest Service to control the number of people allowed into the area at any given time.

With this plan, Walt Disney Productions has met all the objections to the creation of recreational services and facilities at Mineral King, save one: Shall this area remain totally inaccessible in winter and available only to a select few in summer, or shall it be made available for the pleasure, benefit and enjoyment of everyone?

That is the remaining question. That is where we stand today.

Now, where do we go from here?

Walt Disney Productions responded in good faith to the public need, as determined by the Forest Service. Our demonstrated concern for America's natural heritage is a matter of record. We will stand by, prepared to fulfill our commitments, should the public exert its right to the year-round recreational use of Mineral King.

However, we will no longer allow the good name and worldwide reputation of the Walt Disney organization to be attacked due to circumstances over which we have had no control. No longer will we allow our plans for this project to be misrepresented, as they often have been in the past.

If the concepts we have proposed are as important to you and your friends and family as we believe they are, then Walt Disney Productions is ready to move ahead. If you believe California needs recreational opportunities and facilities of the highest caliber, then the time has come to take a stand.

Who really speaks for Mineral King? And who really speaks for you?

E. Cardon Walker

President
Walt Disney Productions

6. "A Tribute to Harriet Burns" (2008)

As much as I enjoyed being "the kid" and having the opportunity to learn from so many Imagineering Legends in the fifties and sixties, there turned out to be an emotional payback. As my mentors passed away, their families asked me to organize and be the key speaker at the memorial services that celebrated the passion and the career of some of the great Disney talents: Richard Irvine, John Hench, Herb Ryman, Sam McKim, Claude Coats, Don Edgren, and Fred Joerger—and Harriet Burns, that special lady who was the queen bee of the Imagineering Model Shop. Even before the celebration of Harriet's life, I wrote this tribute for all the Imagineers, to a wonderful talent, the true spirit of so much that Imagineers represent:

Sklar, Martin

From: WDI Communications
Sent: Tuesday, July 29, 2008 9:06 AM
To: #WDI-CA All; #WDI-DL-Paris; #WDI-FL ALL; #WDIJ/TDR Design Office; #WDI HK Team HK; #WDI-Glendale Additions
Subject: A Tribute to Harriet Burns

As you all know, Harriet Burns passed away on Friday morning, July 25, after a brief illness. Marty Sklar collaborated with Harriet for decades and shares his thoughts and memories about this amazing Imagineer and Disney Legend.

A TRIBUTE TO HARRIET BURNS
By Marty Sklar

In the hospital they were calling her "Sleeping Beauty," but I likened her more to "Snow White," waiting for the kiss that would awaken her. Alas, the princes and kings who could do it were already gone, awaiting her arrival in a safer place.

As the first non-clerical woman Imagineer, Harriet Burns had to earn the respect of a male-dominated world. Beginning when WED Enterprises was still located at the Studio, she had to be as good as the men were with a table saw, lathes, drill presses and, as she put it, "other stuff." And she was, even holding her own when the off-color jokes came her way. With her soft Texas twang, she could sling it right back at them.

But what really earned respect for Harriet Burns was her creative skill. She became a design star on *The Mickey Mouse Club*, helping to establish its modern, graphic style. With Fred Joerger and Wathel Rogers, she became the WED Model Shop, heartbeat of Walt's design engine for Disneyland and beyond.

For 31 years until her retirement in 1986, Harriet was at the center of every Imagineering venture: "figure finishing" presidents and pirates, creating enchanted color schemes and frillery for singing birds, putting the glitter, flitter and jewels on the children and toys of *it's a small world*. For her achievements, she was named a Disney Legend in 2000.

Harriet never dressed the part of the jeans and tee shirt set. Her eclectic taste and sense of design fashion carried over to her working attire. She was always the best dressed member of the Model Shop, perhaps all of Imagineering.

Maybe that's one reason she caught Walt Disney's eye and appeared so often in those un-scripted strolls through the Model Shop that Walt loved to use in the TV show lead-ins, showcasing the newest concepts for Disneyland or the New York World's Fair. But we all knew better. It was really because, from the Studio days when Disneyland was just getting started, Walt loved to get his hands dirty in the Model Shop. And to "kick back" from the pressures of running his growing empire by sharing stories and one-liners with the Imagineer with that sweet Texas drawl.

That's why, when her favorite princes – fellow Disney & Imagineering Legends John Hench, Bill Cottrell and Fred Joerger – lined up last week to greet Harriet Burns, I'm sure it was the King who was first in line. Because Harriet Burns was Walt Disney's favorite Imagineer.

7. "Think Diversity" (2000)

As designers of projects that travel the world, Imagineers have an obligation to understand the impact not only of what they create, but of how their future attractions are communicated. When he was Disney's chairman in the early

1980s, Donn Tatum asked me to take a hard look at the illustrations we drew to communicate the stories, the themes, and the fun of our attractions. He wanted to be sure that our artists were being inclusive; that we depicted people of color and a variety of cultures. Simply put, were we making sure our audience of diverse backgrounds and colors knew that *they* were welcome in our parks and resorts.

More than a decade later, after learning that Frank Wells had funded a Disney Studio program to find and develop minority writers, I was able to secure funding for an Imagineering program to diversify our staff.

Called ImagiNations, it's a competition for internships, now in its twentieth year, seeking a diverse population of artists, designers, engineers—the whole mix of talent found in Imagineering's 140 different disciplines. We look for a variety of cultures, ethnic backgrounds, colors, and of course a mix of genders to become interns and, hopefully, Imagineers. More than twenty-five full-time Imagineers have been recruited through this competition, which has attracted as many as 140 different entries in one year from around the world.

But it all began with Donn Tatum's request that I write this memo that we distributed to all the Imagineers who reported to me in the Creative Development division. This is the second of the communications I sent out.

Creative Development   May 11, 2000

Marty Sklar   8223-7251

Think Diversity

Diversity is very important to The Walt Disney Company. We reflect it in our staffing and hiring practices. We try to reflect diversity in our attractions, so that the public knows that <u>we know</u> our society is a multi-cultural one. The sun never sets on the operation of our Disney parks around the world, and our guests come to us from all over the globe.

From time-to-time I find it appropriate to remind all of you that in the artwork you develop, it is important that our guests are ethnically and culturally diverse, too. This is especially important with artwork that is developed for marketing and publicity usage, but it should also become a habit for all of you to "think diversity" in all of your illustrations.

I recently attended .a presentation in the IRC and watched a series of slides illustrating new concepts. As excited as I was about the ideas, something disturbed me. I finally realized that in the guests depicted in the illustrations, there was a noticeable sameness. Only the ages of the guests differed.

I learned long ago from Donn Tatum, a former chairman of The Walt Disney Company, that diversity was especially important for Imagineering to reflect in our product. Showing ethnic and cultural diversity in the cast members in our shows and especially in the guests we depict visiting our attractions, is a clear reflection of The Walt Disney Company's intent that our theme parks and other attractions welcome people of all races, creeds and beliefs. (Not that we try to reflect "beliefs" in our artworks, but you understand the point!) When we see ourselves in situations we recognize, we know that we are welcome.

Thank you in advance for remembering the importance of diversity in our shows and attractions, and in our communications about them.

8. The Disney Difference: Rides Versus Attractions/
Adventures/Experiences (2006)

Over the years, there were two issues related to termin-ology that particularly irritated me. One was the word "escapism" to describe the "Disney Park" experience. John Hench was the passionate spokesman of antiescapism. "The parks are about *reassurance*," John argued. "Disneyland is a public place where you can talk to a stranger and let your children play without fear. We are proof that a public place can be clean and things can work. We *reassure* people that the world can be okay!"

The second issue was the use of the word "ride" to describe almost anything when vehicles and movement are involved. When the subject actually came up in a Disney shareholder meeting, I sent the attached memo to Jay Rasulo:

Sklar, Martin

From:	Sklar, Martin
Sent:	Tuesday, March 21, 2006 6:15 PM
To:	Rasulo, Jay
Cc:	Anthony, Matt; Fitzgerald, Tom; Lundgren, Teresa; Mendenhall, Michael; Muller, Marty; Warren, Linda; Weiss, Al
Subject:	Rides Versus Attractions/Adventures/Experiences

One of the audience speakers at Disney Annual Shareholders Meeting raised an issue which has been a concern to me again recently. He asked why we were using the word "ride" again in relation to our Disney attractions and shows.

I think this is an important issue in terms of communicating the Disney Difference. I still remember, in the first year Disneyland was open, going out to the ticket windows and listening to what guests were asking. Frequently it was, "I want to go on the *Flight to the Moon*, the *Jungle River Cruise* and the *Mark Twain* ... but I don't want to go on any of the rides!"

That's when we decided that we had to invent a new language to distinguish "what Disney does" from Knott's and the amusement parks of the time. So we developed the words "attractions," "adventures" and "experiences" to describe what guests would find at Disneyland compared to any competitor. Walt Disney had done such a great job of selling the Disney Difference through the television shows about Disneyland that preceded the opening and continued after, that visitors came *expecting* what they would find in Disneyland to be different than the "rides" they experienced in typical amusement parks.

What we do is so much different and better than "just a ride" that we should not lower ourselves to the competition's level by falling back on the word "ride." That word is so inadequate to describe the *adventure* and *experience* of *Expedition Everest*, for example, that if we refer to it as a ride or "thrill ride" we are diminishing an incredible attraction and, in my view, giving it a reference point in the Six Flags world. (Not saying that we are using this term regarding *Expedition Everest*, but simply making the point that we need to emphasize that "our game" is very different than "their game.")

Maybe a picture is worth a thousand words ... but one word can often paint a picture that lowers expectations and diminishes the uniqueness of the *attractions, adventures and experiences* we create.

MARTY

9. Note Cards and Red Pen Notes

Early in my years as creative leader of the Imagineers, I wrote a few thank-you notes to people whose work, or work ethic, had made a difference on a project. I began to notice these notes—written on three-and-a-half-by-seven-inch cards that Disney supplied with my name printed at the bottom and IMAGINEERING printed at the top—pinned on the walls of the offices of those who received them. So I made those note cards a metaphorical and actual signature of my leadership. I wrote literally thousands of them, thanking Imagineers not just for the success of their project, but for special effort, leadership, teamwork—almost any way I could personalize the message.

I have borrowed a few from the walls of offices at Imagineering as examples. I truly believe these personalized notes were as important as any other element of leadership I utilized in my thirty years as Imagineering's top creative executive.

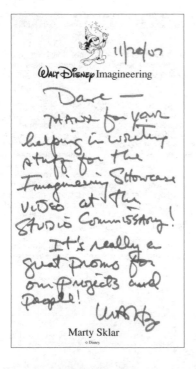
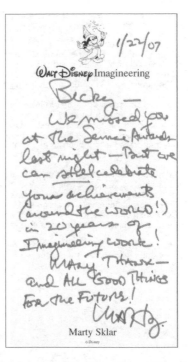

WALT DISNEP Imagineering

6/01/09

Joe —
I can't think
of anything more
pleasant than
congratulating you
on "30 BIG ONES"!
at Disney.
   YOUR GROWTH
AND TALENT AND
LEADERSHIP HAS
BEEN WONDERFUL
TO WATCH — AND FUN,
TOO!
   All Good Things
for the FUTURE!
Marty Sklar
YOUR FRIEND —

WALT DISNEP Imagineering

4/15/96

To: Becky B. —
The landscaping
in Toontown is
spectacular! your
creative touches with
color, form and
texture was a joy for
me to behold!
   Everyone was raving
about your work — and
everyone was well
aware of the obstacles
you faced in Japan — a
woman in winter trying
to find spring for a Toon
garden! Congrats — and
many THANX! —
Marty Sklar

Marty Sklar
creative
7/07/10

Kevin —
You were great
on the CAP
panel — again!
(The headline I wrote
is — "MR. POTATO Head
FRIES AGAIN!") —
   THANX so much
for "being you" — I
know the Educators
were "wowed" by
your creative talk —
as I was!
   MANY THANK Yous!

WALT DISNEP Imagineering

7/01/04

SUSAN —
MANY THANX
for all your
grand help on
the "Legends of
Imagineering
Presentation"!;
Well done!

Marty Sklar
© Disney

10. There Are Two Ways to Look at a Blank Sheet of Paper (1974-2004)

It became something of a cliché of my years at Imagineering. "There are two ways to look at a blank sheet of paper," I said. "You can see it as the most frightening thing in the world—because *you have to make the first mark* on it. Or you can see a blank page as the greatest opportunity—*you get to make the first mark* on it. You can let your imagination fly in any direction. You can create whole new worlds."

I didn't care that it became a cliché. I remembered that comment George Lucas made in a meeting about the Star Tours attraction: "Don't avoid the clichés," George said. "They are clichés because they work!"

We finally commemorated the importance of this approach in a nine-inch-by-twelve-inch sketchbook printed with the text and image on the facing page. My friend, artist John Horny, provided the official story sketch. Beyond the initial copy, all the pages were blank.

The Most Frightening Thing in the World

Go ahead—turn the page and do something exciting with this blank sheet of paper. Here's your chance to be an Imagineer!

19

THE BLACK SHEEP

The untimely death in July 2011 of my younger brother, Robert Sklar, in a bicycle accident in Barcelona, Spain, came as a shock to all of us. The tributes we read and heard afterward from the academic community and the publishing world made everyone in our family realize how much Bob, as professor of Cinema Studies at New York University (NYU), had affected so many lives so positively. His *Movie-Made America: A Cultural History of American Movies*, originally published in 1975 by Vintage Books, is still used as a textbook in university cinema courses.

Cineaste, AMERICA'S LEADING MAGAZINE ON THE ART AND POLITICS OF THE CINEMA (Bob was a contributing editor), wrote: "Several *Cineaste* editorial board members who were his former students and advisees have noted how Bob was a life-changing influence through his mentorship that went far beyond the confines of the classroom." William Simon, Bob's colleague as professor of Cinema Studies at NYU, told the *Los Angeles Times*: "He's among the most important and innovative historians of American film, especially in terms of his approach to understanding film history."

One of the most significant tributes came from Martin Scorsese, the great movie director, who served with Bob on film festival boards in New York City:

> *He has had a profound impact on film culture through his writings, scholarship, and film preservation efforts. As a beloved teacher, he has inspired generations of students.*
>
> *Bob will be sorely missed by those of us all over the world who admired him for his rare intelligence, passion, and spirit.*

I had often thought of myself as the "black sheep" of my family—the "outsider" as a teacher. After all, my father had taught students in Los Angeles for over thirty years, Bob served as a professor at the university level for over forty years, and our sons—my Howard and Bob's Leonard—are now respected teachers and researchers. Both have earned their PhD degrees.

When I retired from Disney in July 2009, I received many wonderful personal notes. They made me realize how much the Imagineers and others in our industry had learned from me. I have included a few of them here, and at the end of this chapter I have printed a special note from Craig Russell, chief design and project delivery executive for Imagineering.

* * * * * * * * * *

In many ways, whatever I've been able to accomplish in the last ten years, stems from my years with you. You taught me never to accept less than the best, to believe in the mission and a core set of values; to recognize the power of story; and to empower the people around me—to see their success as my own.

Kurt Haunfelner—Vice President, Exhibits and Collections, Museum of Science + Industry, Chicago

Congratulations on a fantastic career and being "the driving force" of the theme park industry for so many years. From your early days with Walt to all the CEOs to follow, they put and kept the right guy in charge of Walt's legacy and the right person to guide and teach thousands of professionals over the decades about "quality, show, and passion for excellence!!"

Mike Davis—Senior Vice President/Executive Producer, Entertainment Department, Universal Studios Japan

Congratulations on completing what is perhaps the most extraordinary ride in the Disney kingdom. Throughout this journey your insights, creativity, and leadership talents have contributed to a new entertainment lexicon that has touched the lives of millions of families around the world. Moreover, you generously provided encouragement, guidance, and direction to thousands of colleagues who have built a global industry that, undoubtedly, would have amazed Walt.

Peter Chernack—President, Metavision

You may retire, but you will always be a lighthouse for those of us who always sought out the true Disney Magic. Invariably, our search always seemed to end with you. You

*have so much wonderful Disney knowledge, experience,
and, especially, honor for the man we all looked to for
guidance, Walt Disney. Thank you for being that light in
my Disney life.*

Tony Altobelli—International Public Relations Director,
Disney Destinations

*I am a true believer that people can make a difference.
Some by their personality, some by their knowledge,
and some by their actions. Rare are the ones that can
make a difference because of those three things together,
but I am proud to say you did and you do! Your kindness,
the heritage you're always so generous to share, and
your humble way of presenting and making it easy and
fun to understand and follow. More importantly than only
affecting a company for business, design, or financial
decisions, you inspired people who then created magic
for guests, and it all started with a spark of your
imagination . . . or a Sklar of your imagination, if you
allow me.*

Laurent Cayela—French Language Show Writer, WDI
Disneyland Paris

*You always made us all feel part of the magic. No one
since has ever touched us guys on line in such a way. Thank
you for inspiring me that I "can do" anything I can imagine.
I tell my daughters that constantly.*

Ken Horii—Digital Media Production, Supervising Director,
WDI

You have led Disney and the Imagineers through

many, many successful projects over the years, but more importantly, you supported and nurtured the creative spirit in those that worked for you. I know this both from personal experience and from countless others telling me how great it is to work for you. You have created an amazing legacy and should be very, very proud.

Monty Lunde—President, Techniflex, Inc.

Today is Thank your Mentor Day, so, Thanks!
Not only for providing a shining example of leadership, but for taking the time to show that leadership can take time to invest in the smallest contributors, and groom them into big ones!

MK Haley—Associate Executive Producer, Entertainment Technology Center, Carnegie Mellon University (former Imagineer)

I wanted to thank you again for that conversation we had some fifteen years ago, when I was planning to leave WDI. Your input that day and your many notes to me over the years (I have saved every one of them) helped me feel that I was a key part of the WDI delivery process and this was my new home.

Frank Addeman—Vice-President, Planning/Scheduling and Management Controls, WDI (former Imagineer)

A window on Main Street beats a tombstone at the Haunted Mansion.

John Horny—Creative Artist/Illustrator (former Imagineer)

* * * * * * * * * *

As a leader, you don't often stop and think, "That was a great lesson I taught the Imagineers today." It was only much later, when I developed "Mickey's Ten Commandments," that I stopped long enough to reflect on the topic. When your leadership spans so many years, it's hard to know what was most effective in teaching and leading the Imagineers.

Since my wife, Leah, and I believe strongly in the value of education, we fund a scholarship at the California Institute of the Arts for graduates of the Ryman Arts program we helped to create in Southern California. Both the institution, and the program, are strongly related to my career, and my passions.

CalArts was Walt Disney's vision of a school where all the arts are integrated and interact—just as they do in developing motion pictures, television shows, and attractions for the Disney parks. CalArts brought together, in 1969, three years after Walt's passing, the Chouinard Art Institute and the Los Angeles Conservatory of Music as the foundation for a "school of all the arts." Among the many notable graduates of this institution created through Walt Disney's vision and personal funding are Pixar's John Lasseter, Brad Bird, and Andrew Stanton, plus Tim Burton, Ed Harris, Katey Segal, Bill Irwin, David Salle, Mike Kelly, Bob Rogers, Joe Lanzisero, and Don Cheadle.

Ryman Arts was created as a way to honor the dedication of Herb Ryman to passing on his knowledge and techniques to young artists. Herb's sister, Lucille Ryman Carroll, joined

Walt Disney's daughter Sharon Disney Lund, Buzz and Anne Price, and Leah and me as founders. We began with one class and twelve students in 1990. Today, every weekend at the Otis College of Art and Design in Los Angeles, we have ten classes for 150 talented young artists chosen competitively from ninety different high schools across Southern California. The program is entirely free of charge to talented students; it has been so successful that Ryman graduates are frequent recipients of scholarships and attend schools from east to west, including such leading art programs as the Rhode Island School of Design, CalArts, Otis, and Art Center College of Design in Pasadena. Ninety-eight percent of our graduates continue their education after high school, and our alumni surveys indicate that 40 percent of our graduates work professionally in art and design fields.

We are very appreciative of the great corporate and family foundations that have supported Ryman Arts, including the National Endowment for the Arts, The Walt Disney Company, and the Jack Kent Cooke Foundation, which provided funds for a traveling art program that Executive Director Diane Brigham and her staff brought to inner-city schools in Los Angeles. It allowed us to expand our teaching program emphasizing foundation drawing and painting skills to more than 4,500 young artists since 1990. Leah and I serve on the board of directors, which I have been honored to lead as president since the earliest years.

In 2012, the President's Committee on the Arts and Humanities and its partner agencies recognized Ryman Arts as a National Arts and Humanities Youth Program Award finalist. Fifty finalists were specially selected out of 373 nominations from forty-eight states. The announcement stated:

"Ryman Arts will be honored as one of the country's top arts programs—one that is transforming and enriching the lives of young artists by providing outstanding, high-quality arts instruction and opportunities in the arts."

It was a big surprise, and significant recognition, when Disney honored me and our dedication to talented young artists on the occasion of my retirement in 2009 by establishing "The Marty Sklar Legacy Fund." In its announcement, Disney said:

> To celebrate the legacy of Marty Sklar, The Walt Disney Company has turned to Ryman Arts. Walt Disney Parks and Resorts and the Walt Disney Studios will each host a Ryman Sklar intern every year and will help endow an important new fund.
>
> Disney has pledged $250,000 for the Marty Sklar Legacy Fund, provided it is matched by $100,000 in contributions from others. $350,000 will permanently endow an entire class of Disney Sklar Art Student scholars at Ryman Arts every year.

Within a few months, we had raised more than the $100,000 matching funds, enabling the program to begin in 2010 with a new Ryman Arts class, and the first interns—both graduates of Ryman Arts continuing their education at major universities—to participate in summer programs at Walt Disney Feature Animation and Walt Disney Imagineering. I am very proud of this Legacy Fund, directed in Disney's words to the, "Youth of today, artists of tomorrow."

Meanwhile, many of the Imagineers I played a role in hiring and mentoring have become today's leaders and mentors themselves: Tony Baxter, Patrick Brennan, Tom Fitzgerald,

Joe Garlington, Eric Jacobson, Joe Lanzisero, Kathy Mangum, Peter McGrath, Kevin Rafferty, Joe Rohde, Bob Weis, and many more. This tradition is one of Disney's greatest assets; I learned so much from Imagineering Legends John Hench, Claude Coats, Blaine Gibson, Herb Ryman, Harper Goff, Marc Davis, Fred Joerger, Harriet Burns, Dick Irvine, Bob Jolley, Bob Moore, and so many others. They taught us by example, by doing, never with a textbook, until John Hench's definitive *Designing Disney: Imagineering and the Art of the Show* with Peggy Van Pelt (a talented artist who became a key advisor to other artists—and to me) was published in 2003.

I would be remiss if I did not pay my respects to the first article that truly made an impact on me when I began to study the "how-to" of writing personal material for Walt Disney. It was a simple message in a book called *Words to Live By*, originally published in 1947, containing advice from a variety of well-known people. Walt's quote was so exactly "Walt" that I knew this was the kind of approach I would take when I ghostwrote for him in the years to come. It was called "Take a Chance."

TAKE A CHANCE
BY
WALT DISNEY
MOTION PICTURE PRODUCER

"In the lexicon of youth . . . there is no such word as fail!"

—EDWARD BULWER-LYTTON

I wonder how many times these sturdy old words have been used in graduation speeches each year. They take me back to my own high school days, when I had my first pair of white flannel trousers and the world ahead held no heartbreak or fear.

Certainly we have all had this confidence at one time in our lives, though most of us lose it as we grow older. Perhaps, because of my work, I've been lucky enough to retain a shred of this youthful quality. But sometimes, as I look back on how tough things were, I wonder if I'd go through it again. I hope I would.

When I was about twenty-one, I went broke for the first time. I slept on chair cushions in my "studio" in Kansas City and ate cold beans out of a can. But I took another look at my dream and set out for Hollywood.

Foolish? Not to a youngster. An older person might have had too much "common sense" to do it. Sometimes I wonder if "common sense" isn't another way of saying "fear." And "fear" too often spells failure.

In the lexicon of youth there is no such word as "fail." Remember the story about the boy who wanted to march in the circus parade? When the show came to town, the bandmaster needed a trombonist, so the boy signed up. He hadn't marched a block before the fearful noises from his horn caused two old ladies to faint and a horse to run away. The bandmaster demanded, "Why didn't you tell me you couldn't play the trombone?" And the boy said, "How did I know? I never tried before!"

Many years ago, I might have done just what that boy did. Now I'm a grandfather and have a good many gray hairs and what a lot of people would call common sense.

*But if I'm no longer young in age, I hope I stay young
enough in spirit never to fear failure—young enough still
to take a chance and march in the parade.*

* * * * * * * * * *

I hope I never forget Walt's advice. It was instrumental
in building and nurturing my career. It led me to develop
"Mickey's Ten Commandments" as an adjunct and expansion of Walt's own teachings. It inspired me to communicate the opportunity we were given over and over again at
Imagineering, to fill blank page after blank page with new
and exciting concepts for our Disney fans around the world.
It helped make us dreamers *and* doers.

As Ray Bradbury told us when we were developing Epcot
Center for Walt Disney World, it made us contemporary
Renaissance people. Bradbury said we were acting out what
Albert Schweitzer often spoke of in his philosophies years
ago. Schweitzer said, ". . . set a good example for the world.
If you are excellent, if you are of high quality, the world will
imitate you."

Bradbury told us, "It's a big project. But of all the groups
in the world, while everyone else is busy talking, you're
doing the stuff that's really going to count."

Among all those "retirement e-mails," the supreme com-
pliment came in a familiar "top ten" format from Craig
Russell, chief design and project delivery executive for
Imagineering:

*Pretty amazing couple of days a week ago, celebrating
the fulfillment of a truly amazing career. I found myself
talking with countless Imagineers past and present, about*

what you have meant to our company and have taught us over the years about being a disciple of Walt's. It was at the same time humbling and melancholy to be celebrating the end of the most fruitful career in the history of our company. As I reflect upon those celebrations and the first week of the "Post-Marty" era, I feel it's important to thank you for the many things you have helped teach me about being a great Imagineer. Stealing your idea of Mickey's Ten Commandments, here's a shot at the ten most valuable lessons you helped to teach me about leadership, our company, and the product we create:

1. The most valuable implements in our trade are trust, collaboration, and partnership. With these tools, you can do truly amazing things.
2. It's all about creating and delivering great stories and immersive environments for our guests. No schedule, budget, or strategy measures up in importance to the value of a product that WOWs our audience.
3. We must trust our instincts as design professionals about projects which inspire us. When we inspire ourselves, we will certainly WOW our guests.
4. Imagineering is a true team sport—there indeed is only one name on the door. We either make it great or mediocre together.
5. We are blessed as a company with *great* people. It's our responsibility as leaders to inspire and empower them to do great things.
6. One of our most important contributions as leaders is the acknowledgement and celebration of outstanding contribution and great achievement.

7. We must balance our tremendous success with an uncompromising will to improve.
8. We must every day remind ourselves to have fun in this business of fun.
9. Our heritage is important—so is the health of our culture and community.
10. As a group of professionals, we are set apart from most by our strength of passion for the guests we entertain and product we build. Our role as leaders is to allow that passion to flourish.

Thank you, Marty, for everything you've done to help build this amazing company and to teach those of us who are now privileged to carry on the legacy. Please stay in touch and feel free to stop by anytime you can. We're all anxiously awaiting the book—it will most certainly be required reading for all Imagineers!

"Thanx!"

20

"I'M WAITING FOR A MESSAGE."

When our children, Howard and Leslie, were very young, Leah and I read many stories to them, hopefully accounting for their love of good stories and good writing today. One evening, the story I read mentioned something about the brain; Howard quickly asked, "What does your brain do?" Not being an expert in neuroscience, I answered simply: "Your brain sends messages—orders to act—to different parts of your body."

I continued reading the story, but suddenly I realized that Howard was exceptionally still and quiet, so I asked if anything was wrong. Howard responded: "I'm waiting for a message."

At the time, I struggled not to laugh. But as I reflected on his answer, I realized that "out of the mouths of babes" was not a cliché. Whatever message Howard received, there was also a lesson for my approach to leadership . . . and it found its way into my "Mickey's Ten Commandments" in several important ways.

You will find it in *Take time to teach—mentors are mensches.* But there are few leadership skills more important to those you lead than this advice: *Be responsive and make decisions—that's what leaders do!*

We've all been there: everyone does his or her assignment; the time comes for the decisive meeting, and—nothing. How deflating is that? Granted, not everything is always black and white. But leadership is about making directions clear—and moving on. If you're not willing to make a decision and move on—to be *responsive*—then leadership isn't for you.

Shortly before I retired, a colleague at Disneyland reminded me of a note I had sent her. "We always have plenty of executives," I wrote, "but we never have enough leaders." Her note made me reflect on a few simple ideas I often pondered.

In leading a discussion, and especially in speechmaking, I tried always to recall this warning: "He has a way of saying nothing, in a way that leaves nothing unsaid." In other words, remember that famous KISS: keep it simple, stupid.

Behind the Concierge desk at a hotel I stayed in, I saw this sign about service:

THE ANSWER IS YES. WHAT WAS THE QUESTION?

It reminded me of the "creative service" we all learned: that we could never say "no" to Walt Disney. It was retired Admiral Joe Fowler, who headed the construction of Disneyland and Walt Disney World, who always practiced this philosophy. When Bob Gurr handed his design for the Disneyland submarines to Joe Fowler, with no idea about how they could be built and with Walt questioning their *doability*, the admiral gave this response: "Can do, Walt!" After the meeting, Bob Gurr asked Joe Fowler how he could be so positive about building the submarines, based on Bob's simple sketch. "I don't have a clue," Joe Fowler responded. "But we'll figure it out." And "we" did.

I could easily write a new "Leader's Bible" around these concepts. The answer is Yes—what was the question? Can do! Be optimistic—if you are not, who will be?

In our creation of enchanting and fantastic three-dimensional worlds, I often recalled that Disneyland actually grew out of Walt Disney's *disenchantment* with the amusements he visited with daughters Diane and Sharon.

The luckiest and smartest leaders I watched as role models as I grew up at Disney always surrounded themselves with people who were smarter, and more talented and productive than they were. I wanted to be sure that my direct reports, the creative leaders of Imagineering, knew how much I valued their knowledge, insights, ideas, and experiences, so I established a weekly Creative Leaders Lunch meeting, held every Wednesday, with those project leaders. These were especially important as we grew and spread out around the world.

These lunches were both "formal" and "informal": I wanted each leader to share something important happening on their projects; perhaps a challenge about which their colleagues could offer a new perspective. But I also provided time for anyone to talk about personal experiences: a movie or theatrical play they enjoyed, an artist whose exhibit they admired.

One key principle we practiced in those lunch meetings—in fact, in all Imagineering meetings: no idea is a bad idea! Okay, we all know that's not true. But what happens when you put someone down in a "Blue Sky" brainstorming meeting? As soon as you tell someone, "That's a stupid idea," you will probably never get a fresh, excited thought from that person again. You have just said, "You have a very short leash—we don't need your off-the-wall ideas."

So many times, after one of these "stupid" comments, someone else in the same meeting would come to my office the next day and begin the conversation with, "You know that dumb idea Jim suggested in the meeting yesterday? Well, suppose instead of 'xyz' we tried 'xyz plus zyx'—I think there's a potential in that." And we were off and running to test something new that "stupid idea" had sparked.

Staying in touch with the "outside world" of entertainment, museum exhibits, fashion—all the arts—was, and is, extremely relevant. I often recalled that prescient IBM advertisement I had pinned on my office wall during the development of Epcot Center: THE FUTURE IS A MOVING TARGET! How true! And it's moving faster and faster. Remember: the last three letters of trend are E-N-D!

Children learn early in school about the concept of sharing experiences. Walt was right again: "Adults," he said, "are only kids grown up." Sharing ideas and experiences—wherever we find them—is a leader's responsibility.

"At the end of the day" (thank you, Frank Wells) that one thought—sharing ideas and experiences—may be the most important advice I can pass on from my half century creating Disney's Magic Kingdoms, and before that, the wonderful educational opportunities I enjoyed at UCLA.

How can I possibly top the advice of Coach John Wooden in his "Preseason Letter to the Team" of July 23, 1971, reprinted in the McGraw-Hill 2007 book *The Essential Wooden* by John Wooden and Steve Jamison. Coach Wooden wrote:

> If each of you makes every effort to develop to the
> best of your ability, follow the proper rules of conduct
> and activity most conducive to good physical condition,
> subordinate individual acclaim for the welfare of the team,
> and permit no personality clashes or difference of opinion
> with teammates or coaches to interfere with your
> teammates' efforts, it will be a very rewarding year.

At the end of that season, the UCLA basketball team captured the eighth of ten national championships they won under Coach Wooden's leadership.

I keep a framed copy of Walt Disney's "Four C's" on my home-office wall, and I read it every day. I had discovered a poorly written version of this and rewrote it—then got Walt to record it this way for that "Disney Image" presentation in Florida. Now I believe this is the accepted quote. It pretty much says it all:

> Somehow I can't believe there are many heights that
> can't be scaled by a man who knows the secret of making
> dreams come true. This special secret can be summarized
> in four C's. They are Curiosity, Confidence, Courage,
> and Constancy, and the greatest of these is Confidence.
> When you believe a thing, believe in it all the way. Have
> Confidence in your ability to do it right. And work hard to
> do the best possible job.

Life is like a blank sheet of paper. You never know what it can be until you put something on it. So Dream It! Do It! And work hard to do the best possible job.

What are you waiting for?